The Hellenistic World

F. W. Walbank

THE HELLENISTIC WORLD

Harvard University Press
Cambridge, Massachusetts

This Harvard University Press paperback is
published by arrangement with Fontana.

Library of Congress Cataloging in Publication Data
Walbank, F. W. (Frank William), 1909–
   The Hellenistic world.
   Reprint. Originally published: [London] :
Fontana, 1981. (Fontana history of the ancient
world)
   Bibliography: p.
   Includes index.
   1. Greece—History—Macedonian hegemony,
323–281 B.C. 2. Greece—History—281–146 B.C.
3. Hellenism. I. Title. II. Series: Fontana
history of the ancient world.
DF235.W3 1982   938'.08   81–20050
ISBN 0–674–38725–2 (pbk.)   AACR2

For
Dorothy
Mitzi
Christopher
Robin

Preface

When writing about the hellenistic world it is not easy to strike a balance between a chronological treatment of the political events, and the discussion of special problems — whether those peculiar to particular regions or those relevant to all areas. In this respect the present book is not alone in being something of a compromise. Furthermore its emphasis is largely on the third and early-second centuries, since the main lines were laid down then and the greatest achievements of the hellenistic world belong to that period.

The manuscript and proofs have been read by Dorothy Crawford, to whose vigilance I owe many corrections; I have also profited from many valuable suggestions which she made, especially in the parts concerned with Ptolemaic Egypt. Oswyn Murray also read the manuscript and suggested several improvements, for which I am grateful. I should also like to express my debt to the published works of Anthony Long and Geoffrey Lloyd, which have been reliable guides in areas where I was less at home. Other debts are to the Coin Department of the Fitzwilliam Museum, Cambridge, for the photographs of coins and to the Museum of Classical Archaeology, Cambridge, for the rest of the photographs; in particular I wish to thank Professor Snodgrass, Mr T. Volk and Mr E. E. Jones. The photograph of the inscription from Ai Khanum is reproduced by permission of Professor A. Dupont-Sommer, given on behalf of the Académie des Inscriptions et Belles Lettres, Paris; I should like to thank him warmly too. Finally I am grateful to Miss Helen Fraser and the staff of Fontana Paperbacks and in particular to Miss Lynn Blowers for their help in getting the book out.

For any readers who wish to look at the original evidence quoted in the text I have provided a list at the end of the book indicating where the various items are to be found, together with further reading arranged under chapters and concentrating on books and articles in English. I have ventured to include a few titles in other languages, mainly French, where there was no satisfactory English equivalent. Unless otherwise indicated all dates are BC.

Cambridge
January 1980

Contents

List of Maps and Illustrations

The cover shows a mosaic from Thmuis in Egypt representing Alexandria personified as mistress of the seas. Thanks are due to the Forschungszentrum Griechisch-Römisches Aegypten in the University of Trier and to D. Johannes and the German Archaeological Institute in Cairo for a transparency of this and for permission to reproduce it.

1 *Introduction: The Sources*

I

For rather more than a century – from 480 to 360 BC – the city-states of Greece pursued their rivalries and feuds without serious challenge from outside. But from 359 onwards the growing power of Philip II of Macedonia threw a shadow over the Greek peninsula. In 338, at Chaeronea in Boeotia, Philip decisively defeated the armies of Thebes and Athens and through a newly constituted Council at Corinth imposed peace and his own policy on most of the cities. Already Philip had his eyes on Persia, the great continental power beyond the Aegean, whose weakness had been dramatically revealed sixty years earlier, when a body of Greek mercenaries in the pay of an unsuccessful rebel prince and led by the Athenian Xenophon had marched all the way from Mesopotamia to the sea at Trebizond (400/399). Polybius writes later:

> It is easy for anyone to see the real causes and origin of the war against Persia. The first was the retreat of the Greeks under Xenophon from the upper satrapies in which, though they traversed the whole of Asia, a hostile country, none of the barbarians ventured to face them (iii, 6, 10).

Encouraged by this and by the campaign of the Spartan king Agesilaus in Asia Minor shortly afterwards, Philip planned to invade the ramshackle Persian dominions of Asia Minor in search of money and new lands – though as a pretext he alleged the wrongs done to Greece during the Persian invasions of the early-fifth century. Philip did not live to carry out his plan. In 336 he was assassinated and the projected invasion of Persia was left as part of the inheritance of his son Alexander.

Alexander reigned for only thirteen years, but during that time he completely changed the face of the Greek world. In the great colonizing age from the eighth to the sixth centuries the shores of Spain, the Adriatic lands, southern Italy and Sicily, northern Africa and the Black Sea shores had been settled with Greek maritime colonies. The new expansion was of a different order. Advancing overland with his army – a mere 50,000 at the outset – Alexander marched through Asia Minor and Palestine to Egypt, from there to Mesopotamia and eastward through Persia and central Asia to where Samarkand, Balkh and Kabul now lie; thence he penetrated the Punjab and after defeating the Indian king Porus brought his forces partly by land and partly by sea back to Babylon, where he died.

The vast land empire which he left to his successors was without parallel in Greek history. It was in fact the old Persian empire under Greek and Macedonian management and it formed the theatre within which the events of Greek history were to be enacted during the next 300 years. The Greeks who during the seventy or so years following Alexander's death flocked southwards and eastwards to join new settlements or enlist in mercenary armies, hoping to make their fortunes, found themselves no longer insulated within the traditions of a city-state but living in any one of a variety of environments alongside native peoples of every race and nationality. The term 'hellenistic' – derived from a Greek word meaning 'to speak Greek' – is commonly used to describe this new world in which Greek was in fact the *lingua franca*. It carries a connotation, not so much of a diluted hellenism, but rather of a hellenism extended to non-Greeks, with the clash of cultures which that inevitably implies. There were of course still city-states in Greece and the Aegean – often powerful like Rhodes – and the relations between the cities of Greece proper and Macedonia, though often strained, were not seriously complicated by cultural differences. But within the kingdoms established by Alexander's successors in Egypt and Asia, whether we look at the armies or at the bureaucracies, Greeks and Macedonians occupied positions of dominance over Egyptians, Persians, Babylonians and the diverse peoples of Anatolia. The relationships thus established were uneasy and far from static. From the outset there were tensions, and as the flow of Greeks dried up the relative position of Greeks and barbarians changed gradually in many ways. The pattern of this development varied from kingdom to kingdom. Greeks influenced barbarians, and barbarians Greeks. It is indeed in this clash and coming together of cultures that one of the main interests of the period lies.

From the late-third century onwards a new power appears in the hellenistic world, the Roman republic. The taking-over of one after another of the hellenistic kingdoms by Rome will not be recounted here, though the cumulative effect of the first half-century of the process is discussed below in Chapter 13. The main emphasis in this book will be rather on the hellenistic kingdoms themselves and on their relations with each other and with the Greek cities in Europe and Asia. We shall be concerned with economic and social trends, with the cultural developments in the new centres set up at Alexandria and Pergamum, with the expanding (and contracting) frontiers of this new world, with its scientific achievements and with the religious experience of its peoples.

II

The evidence for the period is uneven. The career of Alexander himself presents a particular source problem. The most important surviving account of his expedition is that of Arrian, a Greek-speaking Roman senator from Bithynia in Asia Minor, who was active in the second century AD. Arrian opens his *Anabasis of Alexander* – the title echoes that of Xenophon's *Anabasis* – with these words:

Wherever Ptolemy son of Lagus and Aristobulus son of

Aristobulus are in agreement in their accounts of Alexander son of Philip, I record their statements as entirely true; where they disagree I have selected the version that seems to me more likely and at the same time more worth relating (Arrian, *Anabasis*, i, *praef.* 1).

(We may note that 'more likely' and 'more worth relating' are concepts that do not necessarily coincide.) Ptolemy, one of Alexander's generals, was later king of Egypt; his *History*, probably written many years later in Egypt, drew on Alexander's official *Journal*, and Arrian was right to regard it as generally reliable. Aristobulus also accompanied the expedition, probably as a military engineer. Unlike Ptolemy he was a Greek, not a Macedonian, and wrote at least two decades after Alexander's death. There were others who gave eyewitness accounts of the expedition. One was the official historian, Callisthenes, the nephew of Alexander's tutor, the famous philosopher Aristotle, but his account broke off early for the sufficient reason that he was executed for treason in 327. Another was the Cretan Nearchus, who sailed the royal fleet back to Susa from the Indus, and composed a description of India and a record (which Arrian uses) of his voyage; he later fought in the wars of Alexander's successors. Nearchus' lieutenant Onesicritus, who was the helmsman of Alexander's own ship on the voyage down the Jhelum (Arrian, *Indica*, 18, 1), also left an account but the surviving fragments do not make it easy to assess its character and it was not very influential. Finally mention should be made of the Alexandrian Cleitarchus, who though probably not a member of the expedition wrote a history of Alexander in at least twelve books. There is a vast literature on these lost sources. It is likely, but not certain, that Aristobulus, Ptolemy and Cleitarchus published their works in that order. Of the three Cleitarchus became the most popular, especially under the early Roman empire, though a discriminating writer like Arrian criticizes him (without actually naming him) for his many inaccuracies (Arrian, *Anabasis*, vi, 11, 8). Indirectly Cleitarchus' history provided one element in the *Romance of Alexander*, which was developed in successive versions from the second century AD until the middle ages, eventually in more than thirty languages – a striking testimony to the impression made on both his immediate successors and subsequent generations by Alexander's career and personality.

All these primary accounts are lost and our knowledge of them depends on later writers who used them and so indirectly caused them to be superseded. Apart from Arrian, the more important of these are Diodorus Siculus, a Greek who wrote a world history in the late-first century BC which, for Alexander, followed Aristobulus and Cleitarchus, Quintus Curtius (whose date and sources are both uncertain), Justinus, whose work epitomizes that of a lost Augustan historian from Gaul called Trogus Pompeius and in the second century AD Plutarch of Chaeronea, the popular philosopher and biographer, whose *Life of Alexander* (twinned with that of Caesar) mentions no less than twenty-four authorities – though how many of these he knew at first hand we cannot be sure. By Plutarch's time a vast amount of material concerning Alexander was available in the writings of rhetoricians, antiquaries and gossip writers, many of whom are but names today. The value of much of this is slight.

Thus for Alexander's career there is no lack of literary sources. The problem is to determine where they got their information from and to assess their merits and allow for their prejudices for or against the hero. For the period after Alexander's death – the hellenistic age proper – the historian faces a very different situation. Until we can begin to use Polybius from 264 onwards, we are still, to be sure, dependent on secondary sources but they differ from those concerned with Alexander in that after Alexander's death his empire was divided among his generals, and writers now attached themselves to one court or another. For the history of the first fifty years of the new regimes our best tradition goes back to a great historian, Hieronymus of Cardia, who served first his fellow-citizen Eumenes, Alexander's secretary, who fought loyally for the king's legitimate heirs, and then, after Eumenes' death in 316, Antigonus I, his son Demetrius I and his grandson Antigonus Gonatas (see pp.

50–9). Hieronymus' lost account of the Wars of the Successors went at least as far as the death of Pyrrhus of Epirus in 272, and was used by Arrian for his work on *Events after Alexander* and, indirectly by Diodorus (books 18–20), as well as by Plutarch in several *Lives* (those of *Eumenes*, *Pyrrhus* and *Demetrius*). Unfortunately, from book 21 onwards Diodorus' work survives only in fragments, of which the most important are from a collection of excerpts made on the orders of the Byzantine emperor Constantine VII in the tenth century.

Other lost writers were Phylarchus, who covered the years 272–219 in twenty-eight books and, according to Polybius (who was prejudiced against him for his support of Cleomenes of Sparta, the enemy of Achaea,) wrote in a sensational and emotional manner. Polybius has a virulent attack on his account of the Achaean sack of Mantinea in 223:

> In his eagerness to arouse the pity and attention of his readers, Phylarchus treats us to a picture of women clinging with their hair dishevelled and their breasts bare, or again of crowds of both sexes together with their children and aged parents weeping and lamenting as they are led away to slavery (ii, 56, 7).

Phylarchus' methods were not peculiar to him, but represent a type of writing well represented in hellenistic historiography. One noted forerunner was Duris of Samos, a pupil of Theophrastus, who wrote a *History* in the early part of the third century dealing with Macedonian and Greek events down to 280 (as well as a history of Agathocles of Syracuse). Other third-century writers were Megasthenes, who visited Pataliputra as the ambassador of Antiochus I, and wrote a book about his journey which later writers used, and the Sicilian historian Timaeus from Tauromenium (mod. Taormina), who spent some fifty years in exile in Athens and is savagely criticized by Polybius as an armchair historian who never took the trouble to visit the places he was writing about or to acquire essential political experience. It is probably to Timaeus that we owe an innovation which brought an immeasurable gain to the historian's craft, the adoption of 'Olympiad years', numbered from the institution of the Olympic festival in 776 to provide an era into which events all over the Greek world (and the Roman world later) could be fitted. Thus Polybius himself announces (i, 3, 1) that 'the date from which I propose to begin is the 140th Olympiad' (220–216) and after telling his readers (i, 5, 6) that he will begin his introductory books from 'the first occasion on which the Romans crossed the sea from Italy' (264) he goes on to explain that this follows on immediately from the close of Timaeus' history and took place in the 129th Olympiad (264–260). It was a popular practice among Greek historians to begin their history where a predecessor left off.

Polybius himself is the most important source for the years 264 to 146. His special concern was with Rome and his object was to explain 'by what means and under what kind of constitution the Romans in less than fifty-three years succeeded in subjecting the whole inhabited world to their sole government' (i, 1, 5). But Polybius was himself an Arcadian from Megalopolis, which was a member of the Achaean Confederation (see pp. 154 ff.) and he describes the growth of that confederation and also many other Greek events not directly relevant to Rome, such as the war between Antiochus III of Syria and Ptolemy IV of Egypt, which ended in the former's defeat at Raphia in 217. Unfortunately only the first five books survive intact; of the remaining thirty-five we have only fragments. Polybius is a sane and balanced writer (though not entirely free from prejudice). Without his work we should be infinitely poorer. 'His books', wrote the German historian Mommsen, 'are like the sun shining on the field of Roman history; where they open, the mists . . . are lifted and where they end a perhaps even more vexatious twilight descends.' They are no less valuable to the student of the hellenistic world generally. Poseidonius of Apamea, who lived for many years at Rhodes (whence he visited Rome), and was a philosopher as well as a historian, began his *Histories* (of which only fragments remain) at the point where Polybius left off. His work covered the Greek east and the western Mediterranean from 146 to the time of Sulla (d. 78) and was later drawn on by the Roman historians Sallust, Caesar and Tacitus and by Plutarch. Poseidonius gave a wealth of information especially about the west, and in some ways he became a spokesman for Roman imperialism.

For a consecutive account of events – something not available for all areas nor all periods of the hellenistic age – the historian must, however, turn to secondary authors, who include (as for Alexander) Diodorus, Arrian and Plutarch, and also Appian, an Alexandrian Greek, who in the second century AD composed a history of Rome tracing separately the histories of various peoples during the time when they were being absorbed into the Roman empire. Like Diodorus, Appian made great use of Polybius, though by no means exclusively nor always at first hand. Among Latin authors we have Justinus' epitome of the so-called *Philippic Histories* of the Gaul Trogus Pompeius (the title of this 'universal' history indicates his approach, independent of the Roman patriotic tradition) and, more importantly, Livy, who fortunately used Polybius as his primary source for eastern affairs. But Livy's history, written under Augustus, is itself fragmentary, for only books 1 to 10 and 21 to 45 survive, taking us to 168 and the end of the Third Macedonian War (172–168). Both the geographer Strabo, also writing under Augustus, and Pausanias, who composed his periegesis of Greece in the middle of the second century AD, furnish valuable historical and topographical information, while for Jewish history several books of the Old Testament and the Apocrypha (especially the Maccabees) are of relevance, as is Josephus, who wrote his *Jewish Antiquities* under the Flavian emperors (AD 69–96) at Rome (see further pp. 222 ff.). Later Eusebius, the bishop of Caesarea (c. AD 260–340), composed a chronicle of universal history which is important for chronology. It was translated into Latin and expanded by St Jerome.

This rapid review of fragmentary sources, all of which present many problems of accuracy and reliability, must also include Memnon of Heraclea Pontica, who wrote an important history of his native city, probably in the first century AD, and Polyaenus, whose book on military stratagems was composed a century later. With the help of these, along with other, minor sources, uneven in scope and often quoting incidents out of context, it is possible to write some kind of history of some parts of the three hundred years which constitute the hellenistic age. Fortunately this can be supplemented from other sorts of historical evidence which, it is true, generate problems of their own, but allow us to check the statements of literary historians against more immediate and normally non-literary documents. It is thanks to the regular growth in the amount of such evidence that the history of this period (and of others in antiquity) is constantly being reshaped in detail as the availability of new information leads to the revision of current hypotheses.

III

This new material falls mainly into three categories. The first consists of inscriptions on stone or marble. The classical world was addicted to inscribing information on durable material of this kind. For the period with which we are concerned, including the reign of Alexander, the majority of these inscriptions are in Greek but from Egypt we have also Egyptian inscriptions in both the hieroglyphic and the demotic forms. The famous Rosetta Stone, now in the British Museum, is a piece of black basalt containing a decree passed by the Council of Priests at Memphis on 27 March 196 and enumerating the good deeds of Ptolemy V Epiphanes and the honours which they proposed to pay to him (*OGIS*, 90). The Greek version was followed by a translation into Egyptian, which was recorded in hieroglyphic and demotic, and it was this that enabled the French scholar Champollion, from 1820 onwards, to begin the long process of unravelling the Egyptian hieroglyphics. There are also a few Latin inscriptions but most of the documents which concern Roman relations with Greece come from Greece and are in Greek. They have been conveniently assembled in R. S. Sherk, *Roman Documents from the Greek East*. There are also several cuneiform inscriptions from Babylonia of relevance to the history of the Seleucids.

Inscriptions were set up for a variety of reasons. A few are directly concerned with recording historical facts, such as the so-called Parian marble, of which two fragments survive and which gave an account by an unknown author of

the dates from the beginning, derived from all kinds of records and general histories, starting from Cecrops, the first king of Athens, down to the archonship of [Ast]yanax at Paros and Diognetus at Athens (264/3) (*Fragmente der griechischen Historiker*, 239).

But the majority are preserved for other reasons. Many register official matters such as a treaty or law or agreement to exchange citizenship (*sympoliteia*) or the findings of an arbitration; here the purpose is to set up a public record, available to all and sundry, of decisions taken publicly by sovereign and other bodies. For the hellenistic period a special group of inscriptions records relations between Greek cities and the kings; often a letter from a king is inscribed in full followed by decisions taken in accordance with its instructions. Some examples of these will be considered below in Chapter 8. Others record decrees passed by city assemblies honouring eminent citizens of the same or some other city for services rendered – financial, political and, especially, for serving on important embassies. There are also building inscriptions recording expenditure, details of loans incurred by cities, requests for grants of immunity from reprisals (see pp. 145 ff.) by temples, cities and other bodies, and records of their concession by kings and cities, details of embassies sent to solicit collaboration in the setting-up of new religious festivals or the up-grading of established ones, or of the manumission of slaves (in which temples like that of Apollo at Delphi were regularly concerned), and a score of other categories, all having one thing in common, someone's need to keep a permanent record.

The historian requires a special technique and experience to extract the fullest information from this epigraphic material. The exact provenance of many inscriptions is uncertain and they are usually fragmentary or partially illegible. Happily they tend to be couched in somewhat stereotyped language and the study of the vocabulary and phraseology used in various contexts at various dates enables the skilled epigraphist to suggest plausible restorations to fill lacunae on the stone. It is however vitally important to distinguish clearly between what actually stands on the stone and what is someone's more or less convincing restoration. To make such restorations it is of course essential to be able to date an inscription at least approximately and this can be done by taking note of the letter forms and the context and character of the inscription, including in some cases the names of the persons mentioned in it. But letter forms can persist over several decades and it is by no means always possible to identify an individual mentioned in an inscription with certainty, since many Greek names are quite common and boys were often named after their grandfather. For example, a series of eighteen Megarian decrees which mention a king Demetrius were for a long time habitually referred to Demetrius I Poliorcetes, who captured Megara towards the end of the fourth century, until in 1942 a French scholar argued that the Demetrius in question was Demetrius II, who ruled in Macedonia from 239 to 229. This hypothesis substantially modified our picture of the reign of Demetrius II and his activity in Greece. Quite recently, however, it has again been argued that the attribution to Demetrius I is correct and the history of the two reigns has thus once more been thrown into the melting-pot.

If inscriptions require special care and knowledge for their effective use, they are nevertheless among the most important sources of new information. Moreover, because of their stereotyped form it is not only possible to use one to restore gaps in another, but inscriptions falling into certain categories – building inscriptions, manumissions, decrees in honour of doctors, funerary inscriptions, records of private associations, etc. – can be used together to furnish information on such diverse subjects as price levels, the status of occupations, the incidence of slavery or the structure of royal bureaucracies and, as we have just seen, the publication of new inscriptions (or the more accurate republication of old ones) often leads to the revision or abandoning of established theories and assumptions.

IV

A second category of document important for the study of this period consists of papyri, mainly from middle Egypt and especially the Fayum, where the dry soil and climate have preserved through the centuries scraps of paper consigned to rubbish tips or reused, for example in stuffing the mummy-cases of sacred ibises, cats or crocodiles. The information contained in these papyri is in many ways different from that furnished by inscriptions. The latter have survived because they were intended to be preserved, the former because they were discarded. Papyri, too, furnish information which is usually more local in its relevance. If we ignore the fragments containing extracts from literary works, which range from the discovery nearly a century ago of Aristotle's lost *Constitution of Athens* to that, more recently, of long sections of lost plays by Menander, we are dealing in the main with the waste-paper baskets of minor civil servants – correspondence, petitions and drafts of replies, summonses, depositions, records of judgements, administrative details concerning the billeting of troops, the passing on of edicts and orders, the auctioning of leases, the making of contracts and submission of tenders, the uneasy relations with the temples and public announcements like that offering a reward for information on the whereabouts of a runaway slave. The papyri already discovered include several major finds, such as the archive of Zenon of Caunus, the agent of Apollonius, the *dioiketes* or head of the civil administration under Ptolemy II, which gives a detailed picture of the working of a great estate, a gift from the king, on which much took place that was not perhaps typical of life generally among the Greeks in Egypt (on this see further p. 106), or the so-called *Revenue Laws of Ptolemy II* (cf. *Select Papyri*, 203) introduced by Apollonius, which contain regulations for the control of the royal oil monopoly. We have also several royal ordinances and indulgences (concessions to the populace in the form of amnesties, tax remissions and the like). An example is that of 118, in which

> King Ptolemy (Euergetes II) and Queen Cleopatra (II) the sister and Queen Cleopatra (III) the wife proclaim an amnesty to all their subjects for errors, crimes, accusations, condemnations and offences of all kinds up to the 9 Pharmouthi of year 52 except to persons guilty of wilful murder or sacrilege (*Select Papyri*, 210).

These concessions are then elaborated for another 260 lines. Another papyrus from Tebtunis (*P. Tebt.*, 703) contains instructions sent by the *dioiketes* to a newly appointed subordinate in the Egyptian countryside (see pp. 106–7).

The papyri thus throw light on everyday life as well as on official policy and activity. But they have to be used with circumspection. Since there are some 30,000 Greek papyri available compared with only 2000 demotic, it is clear that the conclusions they lead to are likely to be heavily weighted towards the Greek minority, a situation which can be rectified only as more work is done on the still unpublished documents in Egyptian. Furthermore, the papyrological evidence concerns administration at the local end rather than the centre of government in Alexandria, where soil conditions have prevented the survival of papyri. What we have can only be used safely for the place and time to which it belongs, since we have reason to believe that conditions changed considerably from place to place and from decade to decade. Nevertheless, here, as on the stones, there is a growing mass of evidence invaluable for the study of Ptolemaic Egypt. Elsewhere this sort of material is not usually available, though in the Dead Sea scrolls and other similar documents the caves of the Jordan valley have supplemented the written authorities, usually for a period rather later than that with which we are concerned.

Coins also provide valuable evidence for the historian. In the classical world coins were more often minted to satisfy the needs of government than to facilitate trade (though of course they incidentally did this too). Hoards of coins hidden in a crisis and never recovered afford useful means of dating, and, where dates can be attached to particular issues, it is sometimes possible to correlate minting with general policy. The location of coin finds furmshes information on currents of trade, and the relative absence of Ptolemaic coins abroad illustrates the strict monopoly enforced by the Ptolemies upon those trading with Egypt (see p. 105). The coin-types minted also throw light on policy and attitudes. Thus Alexander's decision to strike Persian-type *darics* after Darius' death clearly indicates his claim to the Persian throne whereas the opening of mints at Sicyon and Corinth had the more practical aim of financing the recruitment of mercenaries. For some time after Alexander's death his successors issued coins on the same standard in the name of the kings, that is Philip Arrhidaeus and later Alexander IV. But towards the end of the third century they began one by one to issue coins with their own heads on' the obverse, thereby signifying their rejection of a united empire and claim to independent kingship. Thus coins provide evidence for political pretensions, military ambitions and of course economic policy but they require a certain expertise on the part of the historian to master the technical problems surrounding dies and mints, weight standards and, especially, dating.

Of less importance, but by no means negligible, are the documents that have turned up in other materials or tongues. As examples I will mention two. In 1954 A. J. Sachs and D. J. Wiseman published a cuneiform tablet from Babylon containing a list of kings reigning in the Seleucid dominions from Alexander the Great to the accession of Arsacid (Parthian) rule in Mesopotamia and providing new or confirming old dates for Seleucid reigns down to about 179 (*Iraq* (1954), pp. 202–12). Secondly, in 1976 J. D. Ray published an archive of documents on potsherds (ostraca) consisting of drafts of letters written by a certain Hor, an Egyptian from Sebennytus, who in support of his claims in a feud quoted his own prophecy that Antiochus IV, who was invading Egypt, would leave that country by sea before

'Year 2, Payni, final day' (30 July 168) and, on a separate ostracon, asserted that Antiochus had fulfilled his prophecy by leaving before that date. Thus from an obscure document in a curious context we obtain a firm date for an important event not only in Seleucid and Ptolemaic relations but in Mediterranean history generally.

The use of this non-literary evidence, which is essential to our growing knowledge of the period, depends upon its availability to the historian. Some of the main publications in which inscriptions, coins and papyri are assembled can be found listed in the bibliography but these quickly become out of date and have to be supplemented from articles in journals and such annual surveys of recent publications as the learned and comprehensive *Bulletin épigraphique* published annually by J. and L. Robert in the French quarterly *Revue des Études Grecques*.

Evidence of this kind supplements, but does not replace, the work of the ancient writers, even when these are mediocre, for only they can give us a narrative of events and they are usually essential for a chronological framework. But inscriptions and papyri provide a new perspective and often information which prompts the historian to ask a new type of question. They give a glimpse into the working of governments and sometimes enable us to attach names to the bureaucrats themselves. Occasionally they allow families to be traced from generation to generation; they provide evidence for social mobility in a particular community and by their help we can sometimes discover details of land tenure, social hierarchies, and the economic conditions of different groups and classes. Provided we exercise caution and remain aware of the vast gaps in our knowledge, it is still possible to attempt an answer, with far more nuances than in the past, to such questions as where, in this or the other monarchy, power really lay. But, as has already been indicated, answers to these questions are valid only for the time and place to which the evidence refers. The hellenistic world was a dynamic society, one which in some ways never achieved stability but carried on in a state of tension created on the one hand by the fact that the existing balance of power was only accepted *faute de mieux* and not as a recognized way of organizing international relations, and on the other by a shifting and uneasy relationship between the Greco-Macedonian ruling class and the native populations. Starting from the original impact of Alexander's career the hellenistic world gradually ran down until eventually, shorn of everything east of the Euphrates, it was incorporated into the Roman empire. When in the fourth century AD the Roman empire itself split into two halves, the hellenistic world still enjoyed a ghostly existence in Byzantium.

I

When Alexander succeeded his father Philip II as king of Macedonia in 336, he found it a country radically changed from what it had been when Philip assumed the crown twenty-three years earlier. Hitherto a backward frontier kingdom on the fringe of Greece proper, Philip had transformed Macedonia into a powerful military state with a tried army and well-chosen frontiers, dominating Greece through the League of Corinth (see p. 13) and all set for the invasion of Persia. The cultural level of the population had also risen. In a speech which Arrian (*Anabasis*, vii, 9, 2) puts into his mouth, Alexander described Philip's transformation of the Macedonian people in these terms:

> Philip found you vagabonds and poor, most of you clothed in sheepskins, pasturing a few sheep on the mountains and putting up a poor fight in defence of these against the Illyrians, Triballians and Thracians on your borders. He gave you cloaks to wear instead of sheepskins and brought you down out of the mountains into the plains, making you a match in battle for the barbarians who were your neighbours, so that now you trusted in your own courage rather than in strongholds. He turned you into city-dwellers and civilized you by the gift of good laws and customs.

When one has disallowed the rhetoric, this passage fairly describes the conversion of a pastoral people into settled farmers and town-dwellers, wearing woven clothing and enjoying the benefits of an ordered life. The population had also expanded. It has been calculated by G. T. Griffith on the basis of recorded troop figures that Philip's economic policy brought about an increase of over 25 per cent in the numbers of men available for the army between 334, when Alexander mobilized 27,000 Macedonians for his Persian expedition and for service in Greece (with some 3000 men already in Asia and perhaps 20,000 old and young for home defence), and 323, when the figures reached about 50,000 (including a margin for casualties meanwhile sustained in Asia).

Philip's army had won him control over Greece, but he could not afford to leave it idle. No sooner had he established peace there than he planned to invade Persia. The idea was not new. Ten years earlier the Athenian publicist Isocrates had addressed a speech to Philip urging this very course.

> I am going to advise you to become the leader both of Greek unity and of the expedition against the barbarians; it is advantageous to employ persuasion with Greeks and a useful thing to use force against barbarians. That is more or less the essence of the whole matter (Isocrates, *Philip*, 10).

Isocrates continues a little later in the same speech:

> What opinion do you imagine everyone will form of you if you try to destroy the whole Persian kingdom or, failing that, to annex as much territory as you can, and to seize Asia, as some are urging you, from Cilicia to Sinope, and if as well you found cities in this region and settle in them there those men who are now wandering around through lack of their everyday needs, and doing outrage to whomsoever they fall in with? (Isocrates, *ibid.*, 120).

It is likely that Philip saw Asia as a source of wealth and new lands in which to settle the many exiles and dispossessed people who were at this time a general threat to both Greece and Macedonia, given that there were states with sufficient wealth to hire them as mercenaries. Whether the territorial limits suggested by Isocrates formed part of Philip's original plan we cannot tell. Isocrates later admitted that his advice merely chimed in with Philip's own inclinations, and perhaps what matters most is that such ideas were in the air. Philip, however, saw his enterprise in a much more obviously Macedonian context than Isocrates had envisaged. When in 336 Philip was assassinated, an advance force of 10,000 men was already across the Hellespont. Thus on his accession Alexander found the Persian War half-begun but it had his wholehearted approval, for by it he hoped to win personal glory – and also to strengthen his position *vis-à-vis* the senior advisers whom Philip had left him (for he was only twenty). His first two years (336–4) were spent securing his northern frontiers in Thrace and Illyria and suppressing a revolt in Greece. Then in spring 334 he crossed over into Ásia with a modest force of about 37,000 men, of whom 5000 were cavalry. There were 12,600 Greeks (7600 sent by the League and 5000 mercenaries), about 7000 tribal levies from the Balkans, nearly 2000 light-armed and cavalry scouts from Thrace and Paeonia and the remaining 15–16,000 were Macedonians and Thessalians. Europe he left in the charge of his general Antipater with an army of 12,000 infantry and 1500 cavalry – about as many Macedonians as he took with him (Diodorus, xviii, 17, 3 and 5). His finances were shaky and on arriving in Asia he planned to live off the country.

Alexander's army was to prove especially effective because of its balanced combination of arms. A great burden lay on the light-armed Cretan and Macedonian archers, Thracians and Agrianian javelin-men. But the striking force was the cavalry and, should the cavalry-charge leave the issue still undecided, the infantry phalanx, 9000 strong, armed with 15–18 foot spears and shields, and the 3000 hypaspists of the royal battalions would deal the final blow. The army was accompanied by surveyors, engineers, architects, scientists, court officials and historians. From the start Alexander seems to have envisaged an operation with no clear limits.

After a romantic visit to Troy he won his first battle at the river Granicus near the Sea of Marmara, and as a gesture sent 300 suits of armour from the spoils as a dedication to Athena at Athens by 'Alexander, son of Philip, and the Greeks (except the Spartans) from the barbarians who inhabit Asia' (Arrian, *Anabasis*, i, 16, 7). His intention, underlined by the omission of all reference to the Macedonians, was clearly to emphasize the 'panhellenic' aspect of the campaign. At Dium in Macedonia on the other hand he set up brazen statues of twenty-five Macedonians who fell in the first encounter (Arrian, *Anabasis*, i, 16, 4). The victory gave access to western Asia Minor and by the spring of 333 Alexander was master of the western seaboard, most of Caria, Lycia and Pisidia, and could press ahead through Gordium (where tradition told of his loosing – or cutting – the famous Gordian knot, a feat which could only by performed by the man who was to rule Asia) to Ancyra and thence into Cilicia. In autumn 333 he encountered Darius himself at Issus (near Iskenderun) and by a second great victory laid open the route into Syria. There Tyre held out for seven months, but Alexander did not relax the siege, and meanwhile received peace proposals from Darius, whose family had fallen into his hands at Issus. Darius offered him a ransom of 10,000 talents for his family, the cession of all lands west of the Euphrates and a marriage alliance (Arrian, *Anabasis*, ii, 25, 1) but Alexander's ambitions had now clearly expanded and he rejected the offer. By the winter of 332 all Syria and Palestine was in his hands and he was in Egypt, where he founded a new city, Alexandria, before making a journey through the desert to consult the famous oracle of Amon at Siwah. His strategic object at this time seems to have been to seize the whole sea-coast and so protect his base in Greece and Macedonia from any possible naval attack. For he had already taken a bold step: he had 'decided to disband his navy both from lack of money at the time and also seeing that his fleet was not capable of an action against the Persian navy' (Arrian, *Anabasis*, i, 20, 1). Perhaps too he mistrusted the Greeks who manned it. In fact, the death of Darius' admiral Memnon in 333 had deprived the Persian fleet of most of its bite, and on land a Persian counter-attack in Asia Minor in winter 333/2 had been defeated.

In the summer of 331 Alexander once again met Darius' army, this time at Gaugamela beyond the Tigris, not far from Nineveh. It was the decisive battle of the war and again Alexander was victorious, pursuing the retreating forces for thirty-five miles and then quickly advancing to occupy Babylon. Seizing the royal treasures, which amounted to 50,000 gold talents, he advanced further into Persia proper, where he took Persepolis and Pasargadae. The burning of Xerxes' palace at Persepolis was perhaps intended as a symbolic end to the war of revenge, the panhellenic war; such at least is Arrian's view (*Anabasis*, iii, 18, 11), though other writers explain the incident, less probably, as arising out of a drunken escapade, inspired by a courtesan. At any rate, 'on reaching Ecbatana Alexander sent back to the sea the Thessalian cavalry and the rest of the allies, paying each the agreed pay in full and himself making a largess of 2000 talents' (Arrian, *Anabasis*, iii, 19, 5). Henceforth Alexander was to be waging a personal war. Placing the treasure under the control of Harpalus and leaving Parmenion, one of Philip's generals, to control communications, he now pressed on at high speed after Darius. But Darius had been deposed by a usurper, Bessus, and Alexander found him stabbed and dying near Shahrud. Nothing now stood in the way of his claim to be the Great King, and a dedication of arms and bulls' skulls at Lindus, probably in 330, was accompanied by the record:

> King Alexander having defeated Darius in battle and become lord of Asia sacrificed to Lindian Athena in accordance with a prophecy in the priesthood of Theogenes, son of Pistocrates (Timachidas, *Fragmente der griechischen Historiker*, 532, c. 38).

The wording shows that Alexander's new pretensions were now conveyed to the Greeks at home.

Crossing the Elburz mountains the king now advanced into Hyrcania, which lay to the south of the Caspian Sea, and after a short westward diversion towards the region of Amol, he accepted the surrender of Darius' Greek mercenaries. He then marched east through Aria and Drangiana where at Phradah he found an excuse to eliminate the now irksome. Parmenion. Parmenion's son, Philotas, the commander of the élite

Companion cavalry, was here accused of plotting against Alexander's life and having been found guilty by the Macedonians was executed. At once a secret messenger was dispatched to Media to ensure the assassination of his father:

> possibly because ... Parmenion was already a grave danger, if he survived when his own son had been put to death, being so highly thought of both by Alexander himself and throughout all the army (Arrian, *Anabasis*, iii, 26, 4).

In the winter of 330/29 Alexander continued from Phradah along the Helmand into the Paropamisadae, where he founded Alexandria-by-the-Caucasus before crossing the Hindu Kush northwards into Bactria in pursuit of Bessus, who fled beyond the Oxus. There Bessus was deposed by the Sogdian leader Spitamenes and was taken prisoner by the Macedonian general Ptolemy; he was flogged, mutilated and in due course executed at Ecbatana. As Great King, Alexander thus in true Persian fashion avenged Darius, his predecessor.

Meanwhile he had crossed the Jaxartes to attack and defeat the Scythians with the aid of catapults and had founded Alexandria Eschate, 'the farthest', on the site of modern Leninabad in Tadzhikistan but it took him till autumn 328 to crush the national rising led by Spitamenes. A marriage with Roxane, the daughter of a Sogdian baron, Oxyartes, helped to reconcile his opponents in those outlying areas. His stay thereabouts was marked by incidents within his own camp which indicated a growth in royal absolutism and will be considered below (pp. 38–9).

In summer 327 Alexander recrossed the Hindu Kush and took his forces in two divisions over separate passes into India, and the following spring after some remarkable feats of warfare, including the capture of the almost impregnable pinnacle of Aornus (Pir-Sar), he crossed the Indus at Attock. The ruler of this area near the Jhelum and Chenab, the powerful prince Taxiles, now offered him elephants and troops in return for help against his rival Porus and on the left bank of the Hydaspes (modern Jhelum) Alexander won his last great victory against

Porus, who now became his nominal ally. How much of India beyond the Punjab was known to Alexander is uncertain but he would have marched yet further east had not his troops mutinied. Reluctantly he agreed to return. On the Jhelum he built a fleet of 800 to 1000 ships and proceeded downstream to the Indus and so to the Indian Ocean, fighting and massacring as he went. At Patala, at the head of the delta, he built docks and a harbour and explored the two arms of the river. Then at last in October 325 he set off with part of his forces through Gedrosia (mod. Baluchistan) while the fleet under Nearchus sailed along the coast. An officer, Craterus, had already been sent with the baggage and siege train, the elephants and the sick and wounded, via Kandahar and the Helmand valley, whence he was to join Alexander on the river Minab in Carmania. Here eventually Alexander's forces were reunited after he had suffered appalling losses in Gedrosia.

Both while he was in India and after his return to Mesopotamia Alexander carried out a drastic policy of dismissing and even executing many of his satraps.

> Alexander is said to have grown at this time more ready to listen to any accusations, as if they were wholly reliable and to punish severely those who were convicted of slight errors because he felt they might, in the same frame of mind, commit heavier crimes (Arrian, *Anabasis*, vii, 4, 3).

Whether in fact this campaign is to be regarded as a somewhat severe but justifiable disciplining of errant governors or a reign of terror inflicted by a despot is a matter on which historians disagree but Arrian's comments are the more telling in that he usually judges the king favourably. The Persian satraps in Paropamisadae, Carmania, Susiana and Persis are all known to have perished and at least three generals had already been brought from Media to Carmania, there convicted of extortion and executed. It was in this context that on his arrival at Susa, Alexander discovered that Harpalus, his treasurer, had fled with 6000 mercenaries and 5000 talents to Athens. He was later arrested, but escaped to Crete, where he was murdered.

Alexander's stay in Susa was marked by a great feast held to celebrate the conquest of the Persian empire and also to encourage a new policy – that of fusing Macedonians and Persians into a master race. Alexander, his friend Hephaestion, and 80 officers all took Persian wives and dowries were given to 10,000 soldiers who had acquired native partners. This policy led to several acts which aroused bitter resentment among the Macedonians, for instance the arrival of 30,000 Asian youths who had been given a Macedonian military training, and the incorporation of orientals from Bactria, Sogdiana and Arachosia into the Companion cavalry. These and other steps designed to iron out the distinctions between conquerors and conquered came to a head at Opis in 324, when all but the royal bodyguard mutinied. Whereupon Alexander – for, says Arrian (*Anabasis*, vii, 8, 3) 'he had grown worse-tempered at that time and oriental subservience had made him less disposed than before to the Macedonians' – had the thirteen ringleaders executed and dismissed the rest. The opposition collapsed, and a vast banquet was held to celebrate the reconciliation. At this 'Alexander prayed for all sorts of blessings and especially for harmony and fellowship in the empire between Macedonians and Persians' (Arrian, *Anabasis* vii, 11, 9), indicating very clearly his concept of a joint condominium of the two peoples (though not of others too, as some scholars have thought). The same year Alexander sent two requests to Greece. First a decree was brought by Nicanor of Stagira to Europe and proclaimed at Olympia, requiring the Greek cities to receive back all exiles and their families (except for the Thebans). The second, a sequel to Hephaestion's death at Ecbatana, was a request that he be honoured as a hero and (perhaps at the same time) that Alexander himself should be accorded divine honours. What these demands implied will be discussed below.

The following spring (323) Alexander received embassies from various parts of the Mediterranean world at Babylon, and busied himself with plans for exploration (which included the Caspian) but in June he suddenly fell ill after a prolonged banquet and drinking bout and on 13 June he died at Babylon, in his thirty-third year, after a reign of twelve years and eight months.

II

Alexander's career has necessarily been sketched only in outline; it gives rise to many problems which cannot be considered here. It is however of special interest to consider to what extent his actions foreshadow and point forward to institutions and attitudes characteristic of the hellenistic world of which he was in some sense the initiator. The rest of this chapter will be devoted to some such aspects of Alexander's life.

(a) First, the change in Alexander's attitude towards Persia and his attempt to transform his army from a primarily Macedonian force, which still exercised the residual powers of the Macedonian people, into a cosmopolitan international force owing loyalty only to himself, in many ways anticipates the military foundation on which the personal monarchies of the hellenistic age rested. By 323 'King Alexander' was the personal ruler of a vast spear-won empire which had little to do with Macedonia. His successors likewise were to carve out kingdoms for themselves with the help of armies bound to them only by personal bonds.

(b) Similarly, there was an increase in Alexander's autocracy foreshadowing that of the hellenistic kings. In distancing himself from Macedonia and its national traditions Alexander had moreover necessarily assumed an autocratic power. The growth of this can be traced in a series of events which aroused the army's hostility and often involved the elimination of his opponents. The first such incident occurred in 330 at Phradah, when Philotas' execution was used as a pretext to have Parmenion assassinated. The next was at Maracanda (Samarkand) in 328, when Alexander murdered Black Cleitus, one of the Companions – the group constituting the king's intimate advisers – and a leading cavalry officer, after provocation in a drunken brawl. Alexander subsequently reacted with a theatrical display of remorse but was persuaded by the philosopher Anaxarchus that the king stood above the law (Plutarch, *Alexander*, 52, 4).

> In order that he might feel less shame for the murder, the Macedonians decreed that Cleitus had been justly put to death (Curtius, viii, 2, 12).

In the hellenistic monarchies (except Macedonia) the king's decrees normally had the force of law and the king could do no wrong.

The third incident took place the next year at Bactra (mod. Balkh) and was the result of Alexander's policy of surrounding himself with Persians as well as Macedonians. The presence of both at court led inevitably to difficulties, since the two peoples had very different traditions concerning the relationship between king and subject. To Macedonians the king was the first among his peers, to Persians he was the master and they were his slaves and the outward sign of this was an act of obeisance (*proskynesis*), which a Macedonian or Greek was prepared to perform only to a god. Its exact character is controversial: some believe it to have involved physical prostration, others argue that it consisted merely in the blowing of a kiss from the upright, bowed or prostrate position. Whatever its precise form it was repulsive to Greeks and Macedonians when performed before a man, and when at Bactra in 327 Alexander tried to persuade the Macedonians to follow the Persians in according him this gesture, the Greek Callisthenes opposed him. There are two versions of what happened. According to the first, there was a debate between Anaxarchus and Callisthenes on Alexander's proposal, in which the latter 'while irritating Alexander exceedingly, found favour with the Macedonians' (Arrian, *Anabasis*, iv, 12, 1), and the whole plan was dropped. According to the second, Alexander sent round a loving-cup, which each was to take, offer *proskynesis*, and finally receive a kiss from the king; Callisthenes omitted the *proskynesis* and was denied the kiss

(Arrian, *Anabasis*, iv, 12, 3–5). Whatever the truth of the details – both versions could be true – the incident led to Callisthenes' destruction, for he was soon afterwards accused of being privy to a murder-conspiracy by some of the royal pages.

> Aristobulus declares that they [sc. the conspirators] said that it was Callisthenes who had urged them to the plot; and Ptolemy agrees. But most authorities do not say so, but rather that through his dislike for Callisthenes . . . Alexander easily believed the worst about him (Arrian, *Anabasis*, iv, 14, 1).

Callisthenes was tortured and executed; the sources disagree only on the details. The whole incident smacks of the tyrant's court.

(c) Alexander's authoritarianism revealed itself, as that of his successors was also to do, in his relations with the Greeks. The expedition, as planned by Philip, had as its excuse the avenging of the wrongs suffered by the Greeks at the hands of the Persians. At the outset Alexander had been at pains to emphasize the panhellenic aspects of the war (see p. 31 for the panoplies sent to Athens after Granicus) but unfortunately our evidence is not sufficiently clear to allow us to say what status was accorded by Alexander to the 'liberated' Greek cities of Asia Minor. According to Arrian

> he ordered the oligarchies everywhere to be dissolved, democracies to be set up, each city to receive back its own laws and to cease paying the taxes they had paid to the Persians (*Anabasis*, i, 18, 2).

But an inscription from Priene (Tod, 185) shows Alexander interfering extensively in the city's affairs and although the Prieneans are declared 'free and autonomous' and released from the payment of 'contributions' – the word used, *syntaxeis*, suggests that these were payments made hitherto to Alexander for the prosecution of the war rather than tribute paid to Persia – it is not clear just what 'free and autonomous' meant to the king.

Some scholars have argued that the Greek cities of Asia Minor became members of the League of Corinth. This seems to have been true of the cities of the Aegean islands for an inscription from Chios, dealing with Alexander's restoration of exiles there (probably in 332), declares that 'of those who betrayed the city to the barbarians . . . all still remaining there shall be deported and tried before the Council of the Greeks' (Tod, 192), which suggests Chian membership of the League of Corinth. But there is no firm evidence to determine whether the same was also true of the cities of Asia Minor. In practice they certainly had to do what Alexander ordered, like Ephesus where he restored the democracy but 'gave orders to contribute to the temple of Artemis such taxes as they had paid to the Persians' (Arrian, *Anabasis*, i, 17, 10).

This, however, also applied to the cities of the League, as the events of 324 clearly show. Faced with a problem of rootless men in Asia – unemployed mercenaries, political exiles, and settlers who (like 3000 from Bactria) had abandoned their new colonies and were on their way back to Greece – Alexander published an edict authorizing their return. According to Diodorus (xviii, 8, 4) he stated in this that 'we have written to Antipater (who was in charge in Europe) about this, that he shall use compulsion against any cities that are unwilling to take back their exiles'. To ensure the maximum publicity for this decree, which, as an inscription from Mytilene (Tod, 201) shows, applied to Asia and Europe alike, Nicanor, Aristotle's adopted son, was sent to Olympia to have read out to the Greeks assembled for the games a statement that 'all exiles were to return to their countries, excepting those guilty of sacrilege and murder' (Diodorus, xviii, 109, 1). A Samian inscription (*Syll.*, 312) shows that Alexander had already previously made a similar announcement to the army. Though Diodorus says that the decree was welcomed, it certainly caused complications and even chaos over property, confiscated and sold, in every city (as inscriptions make clear) and it can hardly have pleased Antipater. It is a measure of Alexander's disregard for the rights of the cities that he could take such a step without consulting them. In this, as in so much else, his actions were arbitrary and authoritarian. Traditional Greek rights were disregarded.

(d) Both Alexander and, later on, the hellenistic kings reinforced their autocratic power with claims to divinity. About the same time as he ordered the return of the exiles Alexander published a further demand in Greece, which met with a mixed reception. According to Aelian (*Varia historia*, ii, 19), 'Alexander sent instructions to the Greeks to vote him a god' and this is borne out by other sources, none of which, however, mentions the exact context in which this request was sent. However, according to the Athenian orator Hypereides (*Funeral Speech*, 6, 21, delivered 323), the Athenians had been forced

> to see sacrifices accorded to men, the statues, altars and temples of the gods disregarded, while those of men were sedulously cared for, and the servants of these men honoured as heroes.

The reference must be to the worship of Alexander and to the heroic honours which he had accorded to his dead friend Hephaestion. In the spring of 323 Alexander was visited at Babylon by embassies from Greece 'wreathed in the manner of sacred envoys arriving to honour some god' (Arrian, *Anabasis*, vii, 23, 2). In view of this evidence and a number of other passages, often ironical like the report of Damis' motion at Sparta – 'if Alexander wishes to be a god, let him be a god' (Plutarch, *Moralia*, 219E) – it seems likely that the request was sent about the same time as the demand for the restoration of exiles, though there is little to be said for Tarn's view in *Alexander the Great*, Vol. II, pp. 370–3, that 'his divinity was intended by Alexander to give a political sanction to the latter request, which no existing powers authorized him to make'.

The request for divine honours seems more likely to have been a final step in the direction in which Alexander's thoughts had been moving for some time. His father Philip had been honoured at Eresus on Lesbos by the erection of altars to Zeus Philippios (Tod, 191, ll. 5–6), a statue to him stood in the temple of Artemis at Ephesus (Arrian, *Anabasis*, i, 17, 11) – though this need not necessarily imply a cult – and at Aegae in Macedonia for 'because of the greatness of his rule he had counted himself alongside the twelve gods' (Diodorus, xvi, 95, 1). Recently an inscription has been found which attests the existence of a cult to him at Thasos. As for Alexander himself, he had been recognized as a Pharaoh, and so as a divine being (see p. 217), and early in 331 he had visited the oracle of Amon at Siwah in the Libyan desert, where, Callisthenes reported, 'the priest told the king that he, Alexander, was the son of Zeus' (Strabo, xvii, 1, 43), a statement generally interpreted to mean that the priest greeted Alexander as 'son of Amon'. Shortly afterwards, and quite independently, the oracles at Didyma and Erythrae put out the same story 'concerning Alexander's descent from Zeus' (Strabo, *ibid.*). To Greeks and Macedonians it was common practice to identify foreign gods with their own and Callisthenes called Amon Zeus, just as Pindar had done in his hymn to Amon, where he addressed him as 'Amon, lord of Olympus', and in a Pythian ode (4, 16) where he speaks of Zeus Amon. That Alexander encouraged the connection with Zeus, as his son or (like Philip) identified with him, can be seen from a silver decadrachm issued later to celebrate his victory over Porus, which depicts Alexander on horseback charging Porus on an elephant and on the reverse shows a figure of Zeus, wearing a strange amalgam of dress and wielding a thunderbolt in his right hand, which has also been identified with Alexander.

A further stage in the advance towards deification can be traced in the scheme, already discussed above (pp. 38–9), to introduce *proskynesis* at Bactra. In order to raise the topic, Anaxarchus, the amenable philosopher from Abdera, asserted that

it would be far more just to consider Alexander as a god than Dionysus and Heracles; . . . there could be no doubt that when Alexander had passed away men would honour him as a god; how much more just was it then that they should so honour him in his lifetime rather than when he was dead, and the honours would be no use to him (Arrian, *Anabasis*, iv, 10, 6–7).

But however attractive to Alexander, this argument went down badly with the Macedonians, as we have seen, and the plan to introduce *proskynesis* had to be·shelved, largely in the light of Callisthenes' speech in opposition. The final stage came with the request of 323, as a result of which several Greek cults of Alexander appeared – at Athens, probably at Sparta, and perhaps elsewhere. But Alexander's death followed soon afterwards and any cults established seem to have been shortlived, at any rate on the Greek mainland. Cults established in Asia Minor, for example the festival of the *Alexandreia* attested in an inscription found in Thasos, seem often to date from his original campaigns there in 334/3 and not to be a response to the message of 323. In their case the cult was often accompanied by the setting-up of a new dating era (as in Priene and Miletus), both being a spontaneous expression of gratitude for 'liberation'. But the Greeks of the mainland needed no liberator and there cults were instituted only in response to pressure and soon disappeared. The difference is noteworthy. It is the Asian tradition which serves to throw light on the character of hellenistic ruler-cult during the next two centuries (see pp. 212 ff.).

(e) Finally we must consider Alexander's cities. Throughout the lands covered by his march he founded Alexandrias, not seventy, as Plutarch (*On Alexander's Fortune*, 1) alleged, but a substantial number, perhaps about a score in all, mainly east of the Tigris, where hitherto urban centres were rare. Most of these foundations are merely names in lists, official names moreover, which were not always those by which they were later known. They were intended to serve a variety of purposes, some to guard strategic points, passes or fords, others to supervise wider areas; they presupposed an adequate territory to maintain the colonists and, preferably, a local population who could be pressed into agricultural work. Some were later to develop into centres of commerce, while others withered and perished. It seems certain that the bulk of the settlers were Greek mercenaries.. This can be deduced from calculations based on recorded troop movements and is confirmed by remarks in our sources. To take the latter first, Diodorus reports that the Greeks whom Alexander had settled in the upper satrapies (especially Bactria)

> were sick for Greek training and the Greek way of life and having been relegated to the frontiers of the kingdom they put up with this from fear so long as Alexander was alive, but when he died they revolted (xviii, 7, 1).

They were in fact 23,000 in number and had come out East to make their fortunes – their fate was to be disarmed by the Macedonians and massacred for plunder. The picture of reluctant settlers is confirmed from a speech which Arrian put into the mouth of the Macedonian Coenus when the troops in the Punjab mutinied rather than march further east. After mentioning the sending home of the Thessalians from Bactria, he continues:

> Of the rest of the Greeks some have been settled in the cities which you have founded, and they do not all remain there willingly; others including Macedonians, sharing in your toils and dangers, have in part perished in battle, while some have become invalids from wounds and have been left scattered here and there throughout Asia (Arrian, *Anabasis*, v, 27, 5).

Firm numbers elude us but Griffith has calculated (*The Mercenaries of the Hellenistic World*, pp. 20 ff.) that in the course of his expedition Alexander received at least 60,000 (and more probably 65,000) fresh mercenaries, and that he left behind him as garrisons or settlers a minimum of 36,000, which together with the numbers not recorded and casualties from battle or sickness must have reached a total equal to that of the new recruits. Eventually, at Babylon,

> having sent home the older of his soldiers to their native land (Diodorus (xvii, 109, 1) puts their numbers at 10,000) he

ordered 13,000 infantry and 2000 horse to be selected for retention in Asia, thinking that Asia could be held by an army of moderate size, because he had distributed garrisons in many places and had filled the newly founded cities with colonists eager to maintain things as they were (Curtius, x, 2, 8).

The Bactrian revolt shows how far Alexander had miscalculated the temper of these settlers.

Not all, however, broke loose. And though many of the cities (like Bactra) must have incorporated a strong native element, they maintained their Greek organization and later under the Seleucids they were reinforced by the establishment of new settlements. The character of these will be considered below (pp. 130 ff.). Here we may conclude this brief consideration of Alexander's programme, which foreshadowed the many later foundations of his hellenistic successors, by noting that his first Alexandria, that founded on the Nile in spring 331, and his only settlement west of the Tigris, survived to become one of the most famous centres of the Roman empire and indeed of later times.

3 The Formation of the Kingdoms (323–301)

On his death Alexander left an empire stretching from the Adriatic to the Punjab and from Tadzhikistan to Libya. But much of it was loosely held and parts of northern Asia Minor had never come under Macedonian control at all. Whether, had he lived longer, Alexander could have organized and co-ordinated this inchoate area effectively is a moot question. Without him even the survival as a whole seemed unlikely. The history of the next twenty years – from 323 until 301 – is of a struggle between Alexander's generals to take what they could for themselves. For a time that could have meant the whole. But the assumption of the royal title by several of the contestants from 306 onwards and the defeat and death of Antigonus at Ipsus in 301 marked two decisive steps in the process of dissolution. This process can be traced in detail since the period down to 301 is well documented, with Hieronymus' solid account standing behind our extant sources, especially Diodorus, whose narrative is intact down to that date.

I

Of those who were at Babylon when Alexander died the most important were Perdiccas, the senior cavalry officer and probably, since the death of Alexander's favourite, Hephaestion, 'chiliarch' (in effect vizier), Meleager, the senior phalanx-leader, Ptolemy and Leonnatus (both related to the royal house), Lysimachus, Aristonous and Peucestas (who was satrap of Persis and Susiana). Others who were to play a major part later on were Seleucus, the commander of the hypaspists (a crack guards' regiment), Eumenes of Cardia, Alexander's secretary and the only Greek among the leading Macedonians, and Cassander, the son of Antipater. Antipater had been left by Alexander as regent in Macedonia, and Craterus, who had been sent to replace him, had already reached Cilicia. Finally there was Antigonus Monophthalmus, the One-eyed, a man (like Antipater) of the older generation, satrap of Phrygia. The struggle broke out at once and was to last in various forms until *c.* 270. Because the contestants, apart from Eumenes, were Macedonians, Macedonia was to play a special role in the conflict. It is perhaps not mere chance that it was the last major division of the empire to acquire a stable dynasty.

The twenty years we are now considering fall into two periods. The first, from 323 to 320, represents Perdiccas' attempt to devise a compromise settlement which could claim legitimacy while leaving power in his hands. It ended in his violent death. The second period is longer; it covers the years from 320 to 301 and is dominated by Antigonus' efforts to bring the whole empire, or as much of it as possible, under his control. Details are complicated. The scene shifts from Asia to Europe and back again to Asia where at Ipsus in 301 a coalition of his enemies brought about Antigonus' defeat and death. After 301 the struggle continued with Demetrius Poliorcetes, Antigonus' son, attempting to revive his father's empire from a base in Greece and Macedonia but a coalition between Lysimachus and a new contestant, Pyrrhus of Epirus, brought about his fall and he died in captivity. In effect Ipsus had confirmed the existence of separate dynasties in Egypt (Ptolemy), Babylonia and northern Syria (Seleucus) and northern Anatolia and Thrace (Lysimachus). Only the fate of the homeland, Macedonia, remained undecided. Between 288 and 282 Lysimachus made a determined attempt to annex it, first in alliance with Pyrrhus and then alone but in 282 he was defeated by Seleucus at Corupedium, where he fell fighting, and after a period of near anarchy, with Gaulish invasions and rapid dynastic changes, Macedonia too at last obtained a permanent ruler in Demetrius' son, Antigonus Gonatas.

The main territorial divisions of Alexander's former empire were now established and were to survive with only minor changes for the next two centuries. In the present chapter we shall look briefly at the course of events which ended in this division of territories and power, and the dissolution of Alexander's world-empire into a group of rival kingdoms and a *de facto* (though never properly recognized) balance of power.

Alexander's death nearly precipitated civil war over the succession between the cavalry and the infantry sections of his army. Perdiccas proposed waiting for the birth of the unborn child of Alexander and Roxane and (if it was a boy) making it king but the phalanx led by Meleager put forward Philip II's feeble-minded bastard Arrhidaeus and thanks to Eumenes a compromise was made, appointing the two jointly. They were in due course recognized as Philip III and Alexander IV, but from the outset both were pawns in a struggle for power. Perdiccas now summoned a council of friends to assign commands. The army agreed

> that Antipater should be general in Europe, Craterus 'protector' (*prostates*) of Arrhidaeus's *basileia*, Perdiccas chiliarch over the chiliarchy which Hephaestion had commanded (which meant charge over the whole *basileia*) and Meleager Perdiccas' subordinate (Arrian, *Events after Alexander*, *Fragmente der griechischen Historiker*, 156, F 1, 3).

Craterus' position in this settlement is far from clear, since *basileia* can mean either 'kingdom' or 'kingship' (it has the former meaning in the parenthesis on Perdiccas' command), and the post of *prostates* can be interpreted in several ways. Other sources, moreover, have slightly different versions; for example, Q. Curtius (x, 7, 8–9) has Perdiccas and Leonnatus designated guardians of Roxane's child without any mention of Arrhidaeus. On the whole it seems likely that Perdiccas' position as 'chiliarch' put him above Craterus (who was absent from Babylon) but in any case Perdiccas very soon had Meleager murdered, after which Craterus' powers seem limited to sharing Macedonia with Antipater. So perhaps his post as *prostates* was a temporary concession to the phalanx and Meleager.

Perdiccas was now clearly on top – though, as Arrian remarks, 'everyone was suspicious of him and he of them' (*Events after Alexander, Fragmente der griechischen Historiker*, 156, F 1, 5). Of the rest Ptolemy received Egypt, and soon afterwards embellished his position there by cunningly sidetracking to that province the cortège containing Alexander's embalmed body. Antigonus was given all western Asia Minor (including Greater Phrygia, Lycia and Pamphylia), Lysimachus received Thrace (which was separated from Macedonia), Leonnatus Hellespontine Phrygia (but he soon died) and Eumenes was sent to expel a local dynast Ariarathes from Cappadocia and Paphlagonia. Of these men Ptolemy, Antigonus, Eumenes and Lysimachus were to prove the most tenacious over the next decades and to play the greatest part in the conflict. Perdiccas was soon eliminated. While Craterus and Antipater collaborated under the command of the latter to suppress a Greek revolt (the so-called Lamian War ended in a crushing blow to the Greeks and especially Athens), Perdiccas took control of the kings and alienated Antipater by jilting his daughter in order to marry Alexander's sister Cleopatra. A coalition of Antipater, Craterus, Antigonus, Lysimachus and Ptolemy was formed against him and only his murder in Egypt in 320 averted war. The first stage in the struggle was over and at a meeting of the coalition at Triparadeisus in north Syria (320) Antipater was made guardian of the kings (for Craterus had died operating against Eumenes) and removed the court to Macedonia. 'Antigonus', Diodorus tells us (xviii, 40, 1), 'was declared general of Asia and assembled his forces from winter quarters to defeat Eumenes.' The title suggests a division of the empire with Antipater, who was general in Europe and an old man; he had never had much interest in Asia. Already therefore the attempt to maintain the empire in one set of hands had suffered a serious setback. Macedonia, Asia and Egypt were under separate control. Though the dynasties controlling the first two were later to change, the pattern of the hellenistic world was already beginning to emerge.

II

The next twenty years (320–301) are dominated by Antigonus. It was widely believed – Polybius (v, 102, 1) quotes the fact, not very appropriately, in connection with Philip V of whom it was not true – that the house of Antigonus had always aimed at universal dominion. We cannot be quite sure what was in Antigonus' mind, but the sources certainly insist that he was never prepared to settle for less than the whole empire. The years down to 316 were devoted to hounding down and eliminating Eumenes. In 319 this was within Antigonus' grasp but when he heard that Antipater had died having appointed one of Philip II's officers, Polyperchon, as regent, he came to terms with Eumenes and joined Lysimachus, Ptolemy and Antipater's son Cassander in a new alliance against Polyperchon. The latter, despite a proclamation 'liberating the cities of Greece and dissolving the oligarchies set up by Antipater' (Diodorus, xviii, 55, 2), failed to win support in Greece, where his move was seen as a propaganda exercise, and very soon Cassander's forces were in the Piraeus and Athens under the control of his protégé, the Aristotelian philosopher, Demetrius of Phalerum. Meanwhile in Macedonia Philip III's wife Eurydice declared for Cassander. When Polyperchon replied by inviting Alexander's mother Olympias back from Epirus, she engineered the death of Philip III and Eurydice but was in turn tried and executed by the forces of Cassander, who invaded Macedonia. The legitimate house was now represented only by Alexander IV. Over in Asia Antigonus soon resumed the war against Eumenes, who scored some successes in Asia Minor, Phoenicia and Babylonia until in 316/15 he was betrayed by his troops to Antigonus, who had him tried and executed. This victory enabled Antigonus to extend his power into Iran and this made him the avowed enemy of the rest.

In the settlement of Triparadeisus Babylonia had been assigned to Seleucus. In 315 Antigonus, now back from a visit to the east and master of all the lands from Asia Minor to Iran, expelled him and he took refuge with Ptolemy. Largely at his instigation Ptolemy, Cassander and Lysimachus now served an ultimatum on Antigonus, demanding that he surrender most of his gains, restore Babylonia to Seleucus and share Eumenes' treasure with them (Diodorus, xix, 57, 1). Antigonus can hardly have been expected to comply, nor did he. Instead he continued with his conquests, seizing southern Syria, Bithynia and Caria and he made a prudent alliance with Polyperchon. Moreover at Tyre in 314 he issued a proclamation that precipitated a thirteen years war with Cassander.

> Calling together an assembly of his soldiers and those living there, he issued a decree declaring Cassander an enemy unless he destroyed the recently founded cities of Thessalonica and Cassandreia and, releasing from his custody the king (i.e. Alexander IV) and his mother Roxane, handed them over to the Macedonians and in short showed himself obedient to Antigonus, who had been constituted general and had taken over the control of the kingdom. All the Greeks too were to be free, without garrisons and self-governing (*eleutherous, aphrourologētous, autonomous*) (Diodorus, xix, 61, 1–3).

Largely intended as propaganda this proclamation was to have far-reaching repercussions, for its last clause raised an issue which had already been put forward by Polyperchon in 319 as a weapon against Cassander (see p. 50) and was later to re-echo through the politics of the hellenistic age, until eventually the Romans took it up and adapted it to their own ends. We shall be considering it further in Chapter 7. Here we need note only that the significance was immediately evident to Ptolemy who

> hearing of the resolution passed by the Macedonians with Antigonus concerning the freedom of the Greeks, himself wrote a similar declaration, being anxious that the Greeks should know that he was no less solicitous for their autonomy than was Antigonus (Diodorus, xix, 62, 1).

For Antigonus, however, it remained a cardinal principle of his

Greek policy for the rest of his life and it was probably at this time and in accordance with this programme that he promoted the foundation of the League of Island Cities –the Nesiotes –in the Aegean, our knowledge of which is derived solely from inscriptions. Some scholars have attributed the foundation of this league to the Ptolemies, in 308 or even as late as 287. But a League inscription (*IG*, xi, 4, 1034=Durrbach, *Choix*, 13) records the celebration in Delos in alternate years of festivals entitled *Antigoneia* and *Demetrieia*, and it seems likely (a) that these are federal festivals and (b) that the Demetrius and Antigonus whom they commemorate are Antigonus I and Demetrius I. If that is so, though it later fell under the Ptolemies, the League will have originated now as an instrument of Antigonid policy. The separation of Delos from Athens struck a blow at a city now under Cassander's control.

Reacting to an invasion of Caria by Cassander (313), Antigonus now crossed the Taurus, sent various officers to intrigue in the Peloponnese and himself took action against Lysimachus in Thrace, where he intervened to assist Callatis and other Pontic cities which were in revolt (312). The same year he had an abortive meeting with Cassander on the Hellespont (Diodorus, xix, 75, 6). But meanwhile Demetrius, who had been left in charge of Palestine, was attacked by Ptolemy, who routed him at Gaza. Seleucus thereupon seized the chance to recover Babylon with forces provided by Ptolemy and Antigonus had to abandon fighting in the north in order to restore the situation in Syria. Both Antigonus and Ptolemy were by now ready for peace and this was agreed in 311 on the basis of the *status quo*. According to Diodorus (xix, 105, 1),

Cassander, Ptolemy and Lysimachus made peace with Antigonus and subscribed to a treaty, the terms of which were that Cassander should be general of Europe until Alexander, Roxane's son, should come of age, Lysimachus should be lord of Thrace, and Ptolemy of Egypt and the cities bordering Egypt in Africa and Arabia; Antigonus should be in charge of all Asia and the Greeks should live according to their own laws. But they did not abide by this contract for long, but each one of them put forward plausible excuses for trying to acquire more territory.

The treaty of 311 was a setback to Antigonus' ambitions but in a letter to the Greek cities, a copy of which was found at Scepsis (mod. Kurşunla Tepe), he represents it as a success and refers to the freedom of the Greeks as his main concern.

> What zeal we have shown in these matters will, I think, be evident to you and to all others from the settlement itself. After the arrangements with Cassander and Lysimachus had been completed . . . Ptolemy sent envoys to us asking that a truce be made with him also and that he be included in the same treaty. We saw that it was no small thing to give up part of an ambition for which we had taken no little trouble and incurred much expense, and that too when an agreement had been reached with Cassander and Lysimachus and when the remaining task was easier. Nevertheless, because we thought that after a settlement had been reached with him the matter of Polyperchon might be arranged more quickly as no one would then be in alliance with him, because of our relationship to him [what this was is uncertain] and still more because we saw that you and our other allies were burdened by the war and its expenses, we thought it was well to yield and make the truce with him also . . . Know then that peace is made. We have provided in the treaty that all the Greeks are to swear to aid each other in preserving their freedom and autonomy, thinking that while we lived on all human calculations these would be protected, but that afterwards freedom would remain more certainly secure for all the Greeks if both they and the men in power are bound by oaths (Welles, *R.C.*, no. 1, ll. 24–61 = *SVA*, 428).

In this letter Antigonus not surprisingly makes no reference to Demetrius' defeat at Gaza. It is of interest in that it provides evidence that Polyperchon was still active in the Peloponnese and also shows that Antigonus, now 71, is beginning to consider what is to happen after his death. More immediately, however, the swearing of oaths would enable him to call on Greek help if in the future he could plausibly allege a breach of the treaty.

By that treaty the unity of the empire had suffered a perhaps fatal blow, for by implication it recognized the existence of four independent powers – not to mention Seleucus and Polyperchon, who were both excluded from it. Shortly afterwards Cassander took the callous but logical step of assassinating Alexander IV and Roxane.

> Cassander, Lysimachus and likewise Antigonus were now freed from their fears in regard to the king. For since no one now survived to inherit the kingdom, each one who was exercising rule over peoples or cities began to cherish hopes of sovereignty and to hold the territory under him as if it were a spear-won kingdom (Diodorus, xix, 105, 3–4).

Antigonus regarded the peace as a breathing-space before his next move. The events of the ten years which followed are complicated because, despite the general alignment against Antigonus, his rivals intrigued against each other and even made temporary arrangements with the common enemy. There is some evidence that the period opened with an unsuccessful attempt by Antigonus to recover the eastern satrapies, but that after being defeated by Seleucus he made a treaty with him giving him Iran and leaving him free to fight Candragupta in India. That struggle ended about 303 with the secession by Seleucus of at least Gandhara and eastern Arachosia and Gedrosia. 'Seleucus gave them to Sandracottus (Candragupta) on terms of intermarriage and receiving in exchange five hundred elephants' (Strabo, xv, 2, 9). These elephants were to prove a notable addition to hellenistic warfare. Meanwhile Ptolemy seized Cyprus and it was probably now that he contracted an alliance with the powerful, independent maritime city of Rhodes. Control of the Aegean was a bone of contention between Ptolemy and Antigonus, each of whom posed as the guardian of Greek liberty but when Cassander patched up a peace with Polyperchon (the price was the murder of Heracles, an alleged bastard of Alexander whom

Polyperchon was using to rally support), Ptolemy and Antigonus drew together in circumstances which remain obscure. The agreement did not last. Faced with the alliance of Cassander and Polyperchon the Greek cities appealed to Ptolemy, who invaded the Peloponnese in 308 but then, having obtained little solid support, soon made peace with Cassander (though his garrisons remained installed at Corinth and other Greek cities). In 307, while Cassander was in Epirus, Demetrius sailed to Athens, expelled Demetrius of Phalerum, and set up a democracy and in 306 Antigonus sent him against Cyprus, where he won a resounding victory over the Ptolemaic governor and then over Ptolemy himself. Cyprus passed into Antigonid hands but a further sequel to this victory was even more significant.

For the first time the multitude saluted Antigonus and Demetrius as kings. Antigonus accordingly was immediately crowned by his friends, and Demetrius received a diadem from his father with a letter in which he was addressed as king. The followers of Ptolemy in Egypt on their part also, when this was reported, gave him the title of king so that they might not appear to be downcast because of their defeat. And in this way their emulation carried the practice among the other successors. For Lysimachus began to wear a diadem, and Seleucus also in his encounters with Greeks; for already before this he had dealt with the barbarians as a king. Cassander, however, although the others addressed him as a king in their letters and addresses, wrote his own letters in the same form as he had done previously (Plutarch, *Demetrius*, 18, 1–2).

Antigonus' assumption of kingship was in 306, that of Ptolemy shortly afterwards in 305/4, and that of Seleucus, as we know from cuneiform texts, likewise in 305/4. A cuneiform tablet containing a Babylonian king list of the hellenistic period (see p. 26) adds to our information about this. Lines 6–7 (obv.) read:

Year 7 (Seleucid era), which is [his] first year, Seleucus [ruled

as] king. He reigned 25 years. Year 31 (Seleucid era), month 6,
Se[leucus] the king was killed in the land [of the] Khani.

This text, besides giving the date of Seleucus' death (between 25
August and 24 September 281) also makes clear that his first
regnal year (305/4) was the seventh year of the Seleucid era,
which therefore began in 312/11 (in fact in October 312 in the
Greek reckoning and in April 311 in the Babylonian). The
document proves that Plutarch's statement that Seleucus had
already previously dealt with barbarians as a king is not literally
true nor should his statement about Cassander be taken to imply
that he refrained from using the royal title generally, since he is
called 'King Cassander' on coins, and an inscription from
Cassandreia recording what is probably the confirmation of a
grant of land begins:

> The king of the Macedonians Cassander gives to Perdiccas
> son of Coenus the land in Sinaia and that at Trapezus which
> was occupied by his grandfather Polemocrates and his father
> in the reign of Philip (II) etc. (*Syll.*, 332).

This sudden spate of royal titles marked yet a further step in
the break-up of the empire – though just what each king took his
title to mean we can only speculate. It is unlikely that each
general was staking out a claim to the whole empire – unless this
was perhaps Antigonus' idea. More likely, as the passage from
Diodorus quoted on p. 54 suggests, they were exploiting the
death of Alexander IV to claim kingship within their own
particular territories – though not kingship *of* those territories.
Ptolemy was already king of Egypt to the native population but
he never calls himself king of Egypt in any Greek document. And
of what kingdom – if any – was Antigonus king? The later career
of Demetrius, who was for several years a king without a
kingdom, is some indication that these monarchies were felt to be
personal, and not closely linked with the lands where the king
ruled. They constituted recognition of a claim based on high
military achievement by men who through their efforts

controlled 'peoples or cities'. The exception was Macedonia and in the inscription quoted above in which Cassander calls himself 'king of the Macedonians', his purpose in doing so is perhaps to assert a unique position not open to any of his rivals (rather than simply to affirm his authority to validate a land-grant within the kingdom of Macedonia, as has been suggested).

Demetrius followed up his victory in Cyprus with the famous attack on Rhodes which brought him his title of Poliorcetes, the Besieger (305). This attack was a further provocation to Ptolemy, the close friend of Rhodes. The siege lasted a year and was celebrated for the siege-engines which Demetrius deployed, though unsuccessfully, in order to reduce the city. It ended in a compromise peace (304), in which the Rhodians gave 100 hostages and agreed to be 'allies of Antigonus and Demetrius, except in a war against Ptolemy' (Plutarch, *Demetrius*, 22, 4). In 304/3 Demetrius seized the Isthmus of Corinth and in 302, in preparation for war on Cassander, he resurrected the Hellenic League of Philip and Alexander 'thinking that autonomy for the Greeks would bring him great renown' (Diodorus, xx, 102, 1). An inscription found at Epidaurus (*SVA*, 446) contains the constitutive act setting up the League. In it provision was made for regular meetings of the Council and for Antigonus and Demetrius as leaders to exercise an even closer control than Philip and Alexander had done over their League of Corinth. The Epidaurus inscription is extremely fragmentary, but the information it contains can be supplemented from a Delphic inscription containing a letter written by Adeimantus of Lampsacus to Demetrius and an Athenian decree honouring Adeimantus (Moretti, i, 9; ii, 72). These inscriptions show that so long as the war with Cassander lasted, Demetrius appointed the presidium of the League personally and also that Adeimantus, known hitherto mainly as a flatterer of the king and friend of philosophers, played an important role as Demetrius' representative at the council of the League and perhaps in proposing the institution of a festival in honour of the two kings.

The League however was not destined to last long, for in 301 a coalition consisting of Cassander, Lysimachus and Seleucus (who brought with him his 500 elephants) forced the combined armies of Antigonus and Demetrius (whom his father had summoned from Europe) to battle at Ipsus in Phrygia, and there inflicted a decisive defeat; Antigonus perished and Demetrius fled. In the sharing of spoils Lysimachus took most of Asia Minor as far as Taurus and Ptolemy, who had been campaigning separately in Palestine, took all the area south of Aradus and Damascus, as well as Cilicia and parts of Lycia and Pisidia. Ipsus marked the end of any pretence that there was still ¹a single empire and despite the fact that Lysimachus' kingdom straddled the straits, Asia and Europe now went different ways.

III

Between 301 and 286 Demetrius tried to restore his fortunes in Greece and for a time held Macedonia (after Cassander's death) in spite of pressure from Pyrrhus. But from 289 onwards his position deteriorated. He lost his Aegean possessions and Athens to Ptolemy and was expelled from Macedonia by the combined forces of Lysimachus and Pyrrhus. In 285 Seleucus took him prisoner and he died of drink two years later. This episode left the possession of Macedonia still undecided. After the expulsion of Demetrius Lysimachus had first divided it with Pyrrhus and then, in 285, had contrived to annex the whole. But nemesis now overtook him. He was persuaded by his third wife, Arsinoe, to put his son Agathocles to death (to the advantage of Arsinoe's children). Agathocles' widow Lysandra and her brother Ptolemy Ceraunus – they were half-brother and half-sister to Arsinoe, all three being children of Ptolemy – therefore incited Seleucus to challenge Lysimachus. In 282 Seleucus invaded Asia Minor and early in 281 at Corupedium Lysimachus was defeated and killed. But on crossing into Europe Seleucus, now redundant, was assassinated by his ally Ceraunus, who seized the throne of Macedonia.

Two years later (279), weakened by Lysimachus' defeat, the country was overrun by an army of Gaulish marauders, part of a large-scale migration. Another group established a kingdom in Thrace, others reached Delphi but were destroyed by the Aetolians, and yet further bands crossed over into Asia Minor and settled in what was henceforth to be known as Galatia. What happened subsequently in Macedonia is obscure. A series of weak reigns with anarchic conditions gave Antigonus Gonatas, Demetrius' son, who had managed to hold on to the strongpoints at Corinth, Chalcis and Demetrias (his father's foundation in the Pagasean Gulf), the opportunity for which he was looking. In 276, after winning a much publicized victory over the Gauls at Lysimacheia, he established himself as king in Macedonia and Thessaly. Thus the dynasty founded by Antigonus the One-eyed gained possession of the last unpre-empted territory, the homeland of Macedonia.

Lysimacheia confirmed the result of Ipsus. The hellenistic world of territorial states was now in being, with the Antigonids in Macedonia, the Ptolemies in Egypt and the Seleucids in the area covered by Syria, Mesopotamia and Iran. In each monarchy the sons or (in the case of Macedonia) the grandson of Alexander's successors were on the throne – Antiochus I, Ptolemy II and Antigonus II – and the dynastic principle was firmly established. Politically Alexander's empire had fragmented but in many ways the new kingdoms had much in common. Before looking at the separate kingdoms, therefore, we shall in the next chapter consider to what extent the hellenistic world constituted a homogeneous whole, and how far the co-existence of Greeks and Macedonians alongside the indigenous populations created problems for both peoples.

4 The Hellenistic World: A Homogeneous Culture?

I

Towards the middle of the third century the inhabitants of a Greek city lying at the site of Ai Khanum on the northern frontier of Afghanistan (its ancient name is unknown) erected in the gymnasium beside the river Oxus (mod. Amu Darya) a pillar inscribed with a list of some 140 moral maxims copied from a similar pillar which stood near the shrine of Apollo at Delphi, over 3000 miles away. An adjoining verse inscription reads:

> These wise words of famous men of old are consecrated in holy Pytho. Thence Clearchus took them, copying them with care, to set them shining from afar in the sacred enclosure of Cineas (Robert, *CRAI* (1968), 422).

Cineas – his name suggests that he was probably a Thessalian – will have been the city's founder, whose shrine stood within the gymnasium, and Clearchus has been identified by Robert as the Aristotelian philosopher, Clearchus of Soli, a man with an interest both in Delphi and in the religion and philosophy of the Indian gymnosophists, the Persian magi and the Jewish priests. If this Clearchus was indeed he, we have here our first indication that he made a journey to the far east and there found distant Greek communities ready to hear him lecture and, at his prompting, to inscribe an authenticated copy of Delphic wisdom in that very Greek institution of culture and training, the gymnasium. To set up Delphic maxims in gymnasia was quite a normal practice. Examples are known from Thera (*IG*, xii, 3, 1020) and Miletopolis in Mysia (*Syll.*, 1268). The list at Ai

Khanum is fragmentary and in fact only five maxims now survive but comparable lists elsewhere enabled the French epigraphist, Louis Robert, to reconstitute the whole collection – a striking illustration of how an inscription, of which the greater part is lost, can occasionally be restored with virtual certainty. An interesting feature of the Ai Khanum inscription is that despite the remoteness of this city the lettering is not at all crude or provincial. It is of the highest quality and in the best tradition of the Greek lapicide's craft, worthy of the kingdom of Bactria, which also produced some of the finest Greek coins of the hellenistic period.

Along with this inscription, when it was first discovered in 1966, was another, containing a dedication by two brothers, 'Triballus and Strato, sons of Strato, to Hermes and Heracles' (Robert, *CRAI* (1968), 422), who were the patron gods of the gymnasium, and subsequent excavation has revealed the full plan of the gymnasium itself, which incidentally contained a sundial of a type known, but not hitherto found. There was also a theatre holding 5000 spectators and, dating from about 150, a large administrative centre of palatial proportions, in which were found storing vessels labelled in Greek, a mosaic 5.7 metres square and, most remarkable of all, from what was evidently its library, imprinted on fine earth formed from decomposed wall-bricks, the traces of a still partially legible text from a now perished piece of papyrus, which was evidently a page in a philosophical work which appears to have been written by a member of the Aristotelian school (of which Clearchus himself was a member). These finds confirm the picture of a city in which, despite its later isolation, Greek traditions continued strong right down to the time of its destruction by the nomads of the steppes in the second half of the second century.

But Ai Khanum was not the first site to furnish epigraphical evidence for a strong hellenic presence in Bactria, for only a few years earlier two Greek inscriptions, one with an Aramaic counterpart, had been found at Kandahar (see Schlumberger, *CRAI* (1964), 126–40). These contained fragments of the moralizing edicts of the Mauryan king Aśoka and they too were elegantly carved and in an excellent Greek, which betrayed an intimate knowledge of the vocabulary of Greek philosophy and considerable skill in adapting it to render the thoughts of a Buddhist convert. Anxious to convey his lessons to those living in what now formed part of his dominions, Aśoka used Aramaic, the official language of the Persian empire, and of course Greek. More recently a further Greek inscription has been found in Kabul and more can be expected.

This use of Greek, in the popular cosmopolitan form called the *koine*, the 'common tongue', is characteristic of the whole vast area covered by Alexander's conquests. It pays no heed to the later frontiers and serves to bind the whole into a single cultural continuum. Its prevalence is the result not merely of political domination, but also of a great movement of colonization which began under Alexander and continued in full spate until about 250, after which it slackened off. Ai Khanum has provided clear evidence of this, for a study of the traces of habitation in a wide area around this city has shown it to be virtually unpopulated under the Achaemenid kings, but with a dense population in hellenistic times.

II

Under Alexander the agents of colonization were largely mercenaries whom he left behind to hold strategic points. Conditions were rough and lacking in civilized amenity and so (as we saw, p. 44) provoked revolt. But the finds on the Oxus and at Kandahar and Kabul are not the only evidence that by the mid-third century or even earlier conditions had improved. The growth in the number of colonists had brought with it a deepening of Greek civilization, not least in Bactria, and we can occasionally trace the process. A decree passed by the assembly of Antioch-in-Persis, recognizing the international character of the festival of Artemis Leucophryene at Magnesia-on-the-Maeander, recalls the kinship existing between the two peoples, for when Antiochus I (281–261) was anxious to reinforce the population of Antioch, the Magnesians had responded to his invitation by sending 'men sufficient in number and outstanding in merit for the purpose' (*OGIS*, 233, l. 18). A generation later the bond was still remembered. As in the great European emigration to the United States in the nineteenth and early-twentieth centuries many went out in groups but others would have gone individually to try their fortune in new lands. The new cities of the east contained a mixture of Greeks from all parts, a motley throng from every sort of environment and social class, from the main centres of civilization and from the fringe areas.

Once in their new homes these Greeks and Macedonians sank their many differences to become the new master race – for Alexander's notion of a joint Greco-Persian ruling class never took hold. From the outset these newcomers formed the governing minority in the areas where they settled. One of the great problems of the period is to define and analyse the shifting relations between this minority and the peoples whose lands they shared. It was not always a hostile relationship. Strabo (xi, 14, 12) describes how Cyrsilus of Pharsalus and Medius of Larissa, officers in Alexander's army, set out to trace a cultural relationship between Armenia and Media and their native Thessaly. Their attitude was clearly open and friendly but what they were hoping to do was not to understand these people in their own environment but to prove that they were really some sort of Greeks. This, as we shall see (p. 228), is precisely what some Greeks tried to do when brought up against the phenomenon of Rome. Occasionally, especially in the early days, osmosis occurs between the different cultures. A dedication by 'Diodotus, son of Achaeus, to King Ptolemy Soter' (*OGIS*, 19) is bilingual, in Greek and demotic Egyptian, and we shall look at further similar evidence later (p. 117). It suggests some cultural interchange, but this is scanty and its importance must not be exaggerated nor is it safe to use material from one area to make generalizations applying to others. It is noteworthy that the inscription from Antioch-in-Persis mentions the sending of men from Magnesia, but not of women, presumably because they would find women on arrival, Greek or more likely barbarian. Ai

Khanum too will certainly have contained a substantial proportion of non-Greeks, and probably their numbers increased
with the passing of time. But it seems fairly clear, given the
attitudes which led to the setting-up of the Delphic precepts by
Clearchus, that in the early-third century at any rate native
Bactrians will not have been admitted to the gymnasium and
that, faced with a large non-Greek group around them, the usual
reaction of Greeks and Macedonians was to close ranks and
emphasize the Greek institutions of government, religion and
education, in short their Greekness.

III

Greekness expressed itself primarily through the gymnasium,
but there were also other institutions which catered for the
private and social life of the citizens of hellenistic cities, both new
and old. These were especially important in the new cities with
their mixed populations and absence of traditions but they were
also an integral part of life in the older cities. These associations
are known as *eranoi*, *thiasoi*, and also by special names, such as
Poseidoniastai, linking them with some particular deity worshipped as the patron of the association and the strong feeling of
devotion to such bodies by their members comes out clearly from
the inscriptional evidence. Here is an example from second-
century Rhodes:

> In the priesthood of Theophanes, the chief *eranistes* being
> Menecrates son of Cibyratas, on the 26th day of Hyacinthius,
> the following *eranistai* promised contributions for the
> rebuilding of the wall and the monuments which fell down in
> the earthquake: Menecrates son of Cibyratas [undertook] to
> rebuild the wall and monuments at his own expense. The
> money coming from the [other] sums promised will be at the
> society's disposal . . . [Dion]ydus 5 . . . (here the inscription
> breaks off) (*Syll.*, 1116).

The 'walls' are those of the clubhouse, the 'monuments' the graves of past members, for such guilds frequently combined the functions of a friendly society, dining club and burial club. In a city like Rhodes they were an important element in private life and in the new centres of the far east they were a means of building new loyalties in what was at first a rather drab and alien world. What is more, they were far less exclusive and purely 'hellenic' than the gymnasia. Though their structure and procedures often seem to imitate those of the city, they were catholic in their membership, and frequently included both Greeks and barbarians, free men and slaves, men and women. They gave opportunities for mixing which were less easy within the framework of the city institutions.

In public life the Greeks and Macedonians formed the ruling class. They were a closed circle to which natives gained access only gradually and in very small numbers – and then usually only by the difficult method of turning themselves culturally into Greeks. The creation of this ruling class was the direct outcome of the decisions taken by the armies and generals of Alexander, who after his death decisively rejected his policy of racial fusion and very soon expelled all Medes and Persians from positions of authority. The setting-up of the monarchies did not alter this attitude. It has been calculated that even in the Seleucid kingdom, which faced the greatest problems of cultural conflict, after two generations there were never more than 2.5 per cent of natives in positions of authority (out of a sample of several hundred names) and most of this 2.5 per cent were officers commanding local units (see p. 125). This was not due to incompetence or reluctance to serve on the part of the easterners, as some have argued, but to the firm determination of the Greeks and Macedonians to enjoy the spoils of victory.

When therefore we speak of the unity and homogeneity of hellenistic culture, it is of this Greco–Macedonian class we are speaking, a minority in every state made up of men from many parts of the Greek world, springing from various social origins which could be conveniently forgotten in the new environment. These immigrants, like Americans today, maintained lively memories of where they or their parents had come from but these origins had little significance, other than in sentiment, compared with the reality of their new homes and new status. The old frictions between city and city, class and class, were ironed out in the solidarity of life as a Greek minority in this new milieu. Their importance sprang from the fact that the hellenistic kings depended upon this Greco-Macedonian minority to provide them with their administration at the higher levels. Their role in Ptolemaic Egypt and Seleucid Asia will be our concern later, when we consider these states in greater detail. But first it is convenient to glance at those features and institutions of the hellenistic world which held the Greeks together in the alien environment of Egypt and across the vast spaces of Asia, and made them more and more indistinguishable from each other as time passed.

IV

Two points should perhaps be noted at the outset. First, the special problems presented by a Greek minority in an alien environment did not arise in continental Greece and Macedonia, in the cities of the Aegean or (any more than they always had) in the cities of western Asia Minor. These areas continued to serve as a reservoir of Greek culture as well as of manpower (so long as the wave of emigration lasted). The Greeks living in the monarchies were still in contact with the world of city-states which had hitherto furnished the background for all Greek civilization. Secondly, though Alexander's conquests had resulted in a vast extension of hellenism over central Asia, by 303 Seleucus had ceded Gandhara, eastern Arachosia and Gedrosia to Candragupta (above, p. 54) and subsequently Bactria became independent of the Seleucids. Hence, although Greek culture continued to survive in the eastern provinces and re-established itself in India in the second century, politically the Seleucid empire became relatively more Mediterranean-based and Antioch began to take precedence over Seleuceia-on-the-Tigris as the main Seleucid centre. The Báctrian Greeks and that branch of them who set up a kingdom in India after the fall of the Mauryan empire were increasingly cut off from the mainstream of hellenistic life, especially after the rise of the Parthians in the later second century. It seems likely that in these circumstances and in response to the threats from the marauders of the steppes there was a closer collaboration between Greeks and natives there than elsewhere. By the second century the great centres of Greek culture were located on or close to the Mediterranean – Pergamum, Alexandria, Athens, Antioch. Thus the Mediterranean Sea was itself a factor making for homogeneity in hellenistic culture, since it facilitated movement and intercommunication.

Ease of travel between the various parts of the hellenistic world was both a cause and a result of the common civilization which Greeks now shared; far more than in the past travellers of all kinds were constantly on the move. Perhaps the most obvious group were the mercenaries. They formed an appreciable part of every hellenistic army and as the prosopography drawn up by Launey (*Récherches sur les armées hellénistiques*, pp. 1111–271) makes clear, they came from all parts of Greece, from Macedonia and the Balkan peninsula generally, from Asia Minor, from Syria, Palestine and Arabia, from central Asia and India, from north Africa and from Italy and the west. Of the Greeks the Cretans were perhaps the most prominent. In an account of the career of his great-grandfather, whom he describes as a military expert, Strabo relates how

> because of his experience in military affairs, he was appointed (sc. by Mithridates Euergetes, the king of Pontus) to enlist mercenaries and often visited not only Greece and Thrace, but also the mercenaries of Crete, that is before the Romans were yet in possession of the island and while the number of mercenary soldiers in the island, from whom the piratical bands were also wont to be recruited, was large (Strabo, x, 4, 10).

It is noteworthy that for many men piracy and mercenary service were alternative means of livelihood; we shall look at the conditions which encouraged both of these below (p. 163). But for the moment our concern is with the effects of mercenary service, which kept large numbers of more or less rootless people constantly on the move wherever wars called for their assistance. Sometimes they settled down if they could find a city ready to replenish its reduced numbers with men whom its citizens had got to know. An inscription set up probably in 219 at Dyme in western Achaea introduces a list of fifty-two names with this statement:

> The following were created citizens by the city having shared in the fighting during the war and having helped to save the city; each man was selected individually (*Syll.*, 529).

Dyme stood in an exposed position near the border with Elis and the war was evidently that against Aetolia (220–217). It is probable that the names are those of mercenaries, though they could be part of a Macedonian garrison, for one of the names, Drakas, is Macedonian. In either case the enrolment of citizens – which can be paralleled two years later from Larissa in Thessaly (*Syll.*, 543) and may likewise have been instigated by Philip V of Macedonia, who was in close alliance with Achaea at the time – illustrates the greater possibilities now available, not only in new areas, for resettlement. As we shall see, citizenship was more flexible.

Mercenaries were the most noteworthy but by no means the only travellers. In the spring of 169 Antiochus IV of Syria invaded Egypt and the authorities in Alexandria decided

> to send the Greek envoys then present at Alexandria to Antiochus to negotiate for peace. There were then present two missions from the Achaeans, one consisting of Alcithus of Aegium, son of Xenophon, and Pasiadas, which had come to renew friendly relations and another on the subject of the games held in honour of Antigonus Doson. There was also an

embassy from Athens headed by Demaratus about a present (i.e. to give one or to thank Ptolemy for one) and there were two sacred missions, one headed by Callias the pancratiast (i.e. a competitor in a sort of all-in wrestling) on the subject of the Panathenaean games, and another, the manager and spokesman of which was Cleostratus, about the mysteries. Eudemus and Hicesius had come from Miletus and Apollonides and Apollonius from Clazomenae (Polybius, xxviii, 19, 2–5).

Thus we learn, quite by chance, that at this particular moment seven separate embassies or sacred delegations were present in Alexandria. If we multiply this figure to take account of all the Greek states and the important centres of Greece and the hellenistic world generally, we can form some impression of what was involved in the constant diplomatic interchanges which went on without abatement both before and after the Romans arrived on the scene. From the early-second century onwards, however, it was increasingly to Rome or to Roman generals in the field that the major embassies were directed.

Two of the embassies mentioned by Polybius as present in Alexandria in 169 were concerned with festivals. And where these included the holding of theatrical performances, they involved the participation of professional actors, the so-called 'artistes (*technitai*) of Dionysus', who regularly moved on circuit. These *technitai* were organized in guilds centred in Athens, at the Isthmus of Corinth, and in Teos, a city for some time under the control of the Attalid dynasty of Pergamum, and their function was to provide the specialists needed for the holding of festivals. Officially the guild at Teos was a religious body. As an inscription puts it,

Craton (sc. the recipient of an honorary decree passed by the guild) did everything pertaining to the honour and repute of Dionysus and the Muses and Pythian Apollo and the other gods and the kings and the queens and the brothers of King Eumenes (Michel, *Recueil*, no. 1015, ll.11–13).

The power and influence of the guild were such that it operated almost like an independent state within the small city of Teos and after a stormy history of quarrels and despite an attempt at mediation by Eumenes II recorded on a long, but now fragmentary, inscription set up at Pergamum (Welles, *R.C.*; no. 53), the *technitai* were forced to flee to Ephesus and later were removed by Attalus III to Myonnesus. They had an evil reputation and a school exercise is recorded on the theme: 'Why are the *technitai* of Dionysus mostly scoundrels?' (Aristotle, *Problems*, 956b, 11). Stage people leading irregular lives were naturally viewed with suspicion by the steady citizens who only set eyes on them at festival times, for indeed they moved from one festival to another, to the Delphic *Pythia* and *Soteria*, to the *Museia* at Thespiae, the *Heracleia* at Thebes, the *Dionysia* at Teos, the festival of Artemis Leucophryene at Magnesia. Like a city they sent sacred delegates (*theoroi*) to the mysteries at Samothrace as well as holding their own festival. Whatever their morals, they were clearly a channel of cultural interchange between city and city.

So far we have been considering mainly organized groups, but many individuals also travelled in pursuit of their trade or profession. Traders and their importance will be looked at in more detail in Chapters 9 and 11 but travellers also included philosophers, like Clearchus of Soli, whose name we have seen recorded on the banks of the Oxus (p. 60), and doctors, many of whom were trained at Cos, with its associations with the great medical teacher Hippocrates and its famous temple of Asclepius, but might respond to requests for help from other friendly states. Thus an inscription dating to the late-third century found in the Asclepieum at Cos records the thanks conveyed by the people of Cnossus in Crete for the loan of a doctor to Gortyn. It provides an interesting picture of conditions in that turbulent island, where at that time, as a result of civil strife (Polybius, iv, 54, 7–9), Gortyn had come under the control of her old rival Cnossus.

The *kosmoi* and the city of the Cnossians greet the council and people of the Coans. Whereas the people of Gortyn sent an embassy to you about a doctor and you, with a generous show of haste, dispatched the doctor Hermias to them, and civil strife having then broken out in Gortyn and we, in accordance with our alliance having come to share in the battle which took place among the Gortynians in the city, it came about that some of our citizens and others who accompanied our side to the battle were wounded and many became exceedingly ill as a result of their wounds, whereupon Hermias, being a man of worth, on that occasion made every effort on our behalf and saved many of them from great peril and subsequently continued unhesitatingly to fulfil the needs of those who called upon him, and when a further battle took place near Phaestus and many suffered wounds and likewise many were critically ill, he made every effort in tending them and saved them from great peril, and subsequently showed himself zealous to those who called upon him (*Syll.*, 528).

Here the somewhat repetitive account breaks off but the context of the battles described can be filled out from the record of this war in Polybius, iv, 54–5. Another example of a city honouring a doctor is the grant by Ilium to Metrodorus of Amphipolis mentioned below (p. 149). The provision of doctors was a public responsibility in many cities. At Samos, for example, the assembly makes the appointment, and in several towns a special 'medical tax' (*iatrikon*) was levied to pay the doctor's salary (cf. *Syll.*, 437).

V

The central role of the gymnasium in Greek communities went with a long-standing passion for athletics and athletes of all ages also travelled around the Greek world bringing fame to their cities and themselves if they carried off prizes at international festivals. An example is provided by a late-second-century inscription found on the site of Cedreae, a small city lying under what is now Şehir Ada in the Ceramic Gulf in south-western

Turkey, which at that time belonged to Rhodes.

> The Confederation (or Guild) of the peoples of the
> Chersonese salutes Onasiteles the son of Onesistratus, victor
> in the furlong-race three times in the boys' category at the
> Isthmia, in the beardless category at the Nemea and at the
> Asclepieia in Cos, in the men's category at the Dorieia at
> Cnidus, at the Dioscureia and at the Heracleia, in the boys'
> and ephebes' category at the Tlapolemeia, victory in the
> furlong-race and the two-furlong-race in the boys' category at
> the Dorieia in Cnidus, in the ephebes' category at the
> Poseidania, in the furlong-race and the race in armour at the
> Heracleia and in the long race in the men's category twice, in
> the torch-race 'from the first point' (?) in the men's category at
> the great Halieia and twice in the small Halieia, twice at the
> Dioscureia, twice at the Poseidania, in the furlong-race and
> race in armour in the men's category (*Syll.*, 1067).

This record could be reproduced again and again, for victors in
athletics contests, especially in the festivals adjudged 'equal to
the Olympic games' (*isolympia*), were highly honoured for the
prestige which they brought to their native cities.

Among professional men whose careers took them to many
cities and even more to the royal courts, where the hope of
employment was higher, were engineers, architects and teachers
at all levels. Musicians and poets (and poetesses) too might
wander from place to place in the expectation of patronage,
adapting their verses to suit the place of performance. Thus a
Tean envoy, Menecles, seeking concessions for his city in Crete
is praised at Cnossus for giving frequent performances, during
his stay there, on the *cithara* (a stringed instrument), singing the
songs of Timotheus and Polyidus and other ancient poets 'in a
manner befitting an educated man' and at Priansus in addition he
performed a 'Cretan cycle' about the gods and heroes of the
island, collected from many poets and historians. The Priansians
accorded him special praise for his regard for culture (*SGDI*,
5186–7). Undoubtedly Menecles served his city well.

From Lamia, a city in the Aetolian confederacy, comes an inscription of 218/7, commemorating a successful venture:

> Good fortune. The people of Lamia decreed: Whereas Aristodama daughter of Amyntas of Smyrna in Ionia, an epic poetess, came to the city and gave several readings of her own poems in which she made appropriate mention of the Aetolian nation and the ancestors of the people (sc. of Lamia), showing zeal in her declamation, that she be a *proxenos* of the city and a benefactor, and that citizenship, the right to acquire land and property, grazing rights, exemption from reprisals (*asylia*), and safety by land and sea in peace or in war be granted to her and her children and her property for all time together with all the grants made to other *proxenoi* and benefactors. To O . . . neus her brother and his children there shall be rights of *proxenia*, citizenship and *asylia* (*Syll.*, 532).

A *proxenos* was originally the representative of a foreign state in another city, somewhat like a modern consul, but by hellenistic times the grant of *proxenia* had become a mainly titular honour, though it could have its practical uses in giving access to the courts in the city granting it. We shall be looking both at this institution and also at the granting of *asylia* in more detail in Chapter 8. O . . . neus (his name is partly illegible) had evidently accompanied Aristodama on her tour, for a respectable woman would not wander around alone. The absence of any reference to her husband suggests that the granting of honours to her children was the usual formula and referred to any children she might subsequently have.

Finally, to complete our picture of the world of travellers we must think of a host of others, including judges and arbitrators (see p. 145) and pilgrims on their way to consult oracles, going between the old cities of Greece and the new centres within the kingdoms, bringing news, gossip and fresh ideas. Wherever they went they found men like themselves, speaking the same kind of Greek, living under similar systems of private law in cities planned in the same familiar gridiron fashion and containing temples dedicated to the same Greek gods. In particular, throughout the hellenistic world life was given a certain homogeneity from the existence of the new monarchic states, successors to the world-kingdom of Alexander.

VI

For classical Greece monarchy was, with a few exceptions such as Sparta with its archaic institution of two kings, something belonging to the distant past or currently to be found only in regions on the fringe of Hellas, such as Cyprus, Epirus and Macedonia, or in frankly barbarian lands like Illyria, Dardania and Thrace. And of course the King *par excellence* was a barbarian – the king of Persia. The career of Philip II had once more brought monarchy into the heart of Greece. Philip was not an absolute ruler; he was the national king of the Macedonians, and they indeed possessed and exercised certain traditional, though limited, powers, including the right to appoint their king himself by acclamation and to act as judge in cases of high treason. In practice these rights did not amount to a great deal and indeed their very existence has been questioned by some scholars. We shall examine the evidence for these rights in the next chapter. Certainly under the conditions of Alexander's expedition they were rights not very easy to exercise and Alexander himself had grown increasingly authoritarian. His great multinational empire retained only the faintest links with the Macedonian monarchy. After his death, his successors tended at first to consult their armies, or such elements of them as were available, partly as a matter of public relations and partly because Alexander's own experience had shown that you had to carry the troops with you. When the kingdoms were set up (and probably even before the successors began to assume the royal title) there was a gap to fill in the administration. The use of Persian help had been rejected and the successors, unlike Alexander, could lay no claim to the loyalty of the Macedonian nobility – to which indeed they themselves belonged. Their rule was personal, not in any sense national (except in Macedonia), for though within their own realms the Ptolemies and Seleucids succeeded to the role of the Pharaohs and the kings of Persia and Babylon respectively, this was of no relevance to the Greeks on whom they relied. This dual role is of importance in the development of both these monarchies and it is the existence of a single indigenous population which differentiates the position of the Ptolemies from that of the Seleucids in Antioch or the Attalids in Pergamum. These differences are, however, better left until we examine their kingdoms in greater detail. Here it is the resemblances and common aspects of the hellenistic monarchy that interest us, the forms and structure which it developed and which can be identified, not only in the major monarchies, but also in the minor Anatolian states like Cappadocia, Bithynia and Pontus, and indeed as far west as Syracuse, where the rule of Hiero II, in a kingdom consisting virtually of Greeks alone and after a rise to power much resembling the typical career of a Greek tyrant, displays many of the characteristics of hellenistic monarchy.

We may neglect the superficial signs of kingship, the wearing of a diadem and the rituals which, though almost entirely absent in the early-third century, gradually grow more prominent in the second. But a more interesting and in some respects unique feature of hellenistic monarchy is the nature and composition of the king's helpers, his 'Friends'. Hellenistic kings were kings by virtue of conquest or inheritance; for a time at least there was no such thing as legitimacy. Nor, as we have seen, was there any group to whom by virtue of their position they could turn for help. And so they chose their Friends personally from wherever they thought fit with little regard for class, birth, wealth or state. The king's council, which operated constantly, though inform-ally, the army commands, offices of state, ambassadorships, were all entrusted to men of the king's choice, his Friends. They came from all parts of the Greek world, attracted by the hope of riches, advancement and the exercise of power. The kings cast a wide net. We find many refugees among their Friends, for these had the skills they required and would be likely to remain loyal. But there are also artists, writers, philosophers, doctors and scholars to be found in the hellenistic courts acting as councillors, envoys and generals – rather as in a large modern company scientific specialists of various disciplines are apt to end up in management.

Contemporary evidence illustrates the position of these men within the kingdoms; they were not mere servants, but sharers in power. Thus a decree in honour of Antiochus by the city of Ilium, which refers to the king's suppression of a sedition in Seleucis (in northern Syria), records how

> having conceived a fine and just plan, he took his Friends and forces into the struggle for his kingdom, and having a favourable fortune working with him, brought the cities and the kingdom back to their ancient state (*OGIS*, 219; cf. Holleaux, *Études d'épigraphie*, vol. iii, p. 118).

Later the same inscription records how ten envoys were sent to offer congratulations upon their health to 'the king, his queen and children, and his Friends and the armed forces'. The relationship between the Friends and the king was based on mutual advantage and depended on reciprocal good faith. When in 292 Lysimachus was under threat from a Thracian army and

> his Friends kept advising him to save himself as best he could ... he replied to them that it was not honourable to provide for himself by abandoning his army and his Friends (Diodorus, xxi, 12).

He was in fact taken prisoner (though later he was released).

By the second century the institution of the Friends had changed its character. As the various kingdoms acquired dynasties, notions of legitimacy crept in, and this had its effect on the Friends. The strength that a king could now exercise merely by being the king is to be seen, towards the end of the third century, in the reaction of the rebel Molon when faced with Antiochus III of Syria. 'Molon,' says Polybius (v, 52, 9), 'bearing in mind that for a rebel a direct attack by day on the king is a hazardous and difficult enterprise, decided to attack Antiochus by night.' Molon's fears were fully justified for, having been compelled after all to fight a regular battle by day, he found that 'the left wing, as soon as they closed and came in sight of the king, went over' (Polybius, v, 54, 1) and Molon committed suicide. Shortly afterwards another pretender, Achaeus, a member of the Seleucid royal house, had got as far as Lycaonia when his troops mutinied, 'the cause of their dissatisfaction being that, as it now appeared, the expedition was against their original and natural king' (Polybius, v, 57, 6). With this growth in the concept of legitimacy came also the subdivision of the Friends into a series of hierarchic positions, defining their status in relation to each other and binding each of them more closely to the king as the fount of honour.

This is a trend that can be observed in more than one monarchy, but only the rich evidence from Egypt has so far enabled it to be traced in detail. Thus in Alexandria in the early-second century we find a series of grades entitled Kinsmen, First Friends, Chief-Bodyguards, Friends, Followers and Bodyguards and a little later these were supplemented by 'Those of Equal Honour to Kinsmen' and 'Those of Equal Honour to First Friends'. Moreover what began as a genuine system recompensing individuals for their merits now became institutionalized, so that the titles were closely associated with the holding of a particular post in the bureaucracy. Whether the same development took place in the Seleucid monarchy the evidence is not yet adequate to reveal.

The structural similarity between the various monarchies made it easy for men of high calibre – men that is to say who could offer the qualities which the kings needed – to move around with ease and make their fortunes, just as men of lower social rank and more everyday talents could improve themselves and their fortunes by going out to a new colony or enlisting as mercenaries in one or other of the royal armies. A good example of such mobility is the Aetolian Scopas, who

having failed to obtain office . . . turned his hopes towards
Alexandria. When he reached Alexandria, in addition to the
profit which he drew from the force in the field; which had
been placed at his disposal, the king assigned him personally a
daily pay of ten minae, while those serving under him in any
command received one mina each (Polybius, xiii, 2, 1, 3).

Scopas was a mercenary captain but within three years we find
him in command of Ptolemy V's army in the campaign leading
up to the battle of Panium.

For Greeks then it was one world, easy to move in and one
which offered high status and wealth if one was prepared to take a
chance. But it was no longer one world once one moved outside
the Greco-Macedonian ruling class. The multitude of different
peoples in Asia and Egypt who found themselves subjects of
these Greek overlords had each their own cultural history and it
is their experience which creates the problems which emerge
when one looks more closely at the separate monarchies.
Different languages, different religions, different social traditions, different systems of land tenure, different attitudes
towards the king and the state separated the peoples of the
kingdoms one from another. In the next three chapters we shall
examine some of these differences and how the Macedonian
rulers in the separate states reacted to them.

5 *Macedonia and Greece*

I

One important part of the hellenistic world was free from the clash of cultures which characterizes the eastern monarchies. That was the homeland of Philip II and Alexander, the kingdom of Macedonia which from 276 until its dissolution at the hands of Rome in 168, was ruled by the Antigonid dynasty. As we have already seen in Chapter 3, Macedonia was the last of the three great areas to settle down to a regular dynastic succession. From 316 until his death in 297 it was controlled by Cassander, who used the title of king from about 305 onwards (p. 56) but during the next twenty years the country was torn apart by the rival attempts of Demetrius, Pyrrhus, Lysimachus, Seleucus and Ptolemy Ceraunus to seize and hold it, and stability returned only with the arrival of Antigonus Gonatas in 276 and Pyrrhus' death a few years later. As the son of Demetrius Poliorcetes, Antigonus II Gonatas belonged to a family which had continued longer than any other to assert a claim to the whole of Alexander's empire. When he became king of Macedonia such a claim was already meaningless but in another respect his position was very different from that of his rivals in Egypt and Syria.

In Macedonia, as we have already noted (p. 74), the monarchy was a national institution. By tradition Macedonian kings had to respect certain customary rights of the people. The experience of his father and grandfather (and himself hitherto) must have habituated Antigonus II to personal monarchy, as the hellenistic world had learnt to understand it. But in Macedonia he had to take national attitudes into account. How far these attitudes had their counterpart in any genuine share in state power is not easy to discern. An inscription recording the accounts of the Amphictyonic Council, responsible for administering Delphi, in autumn 325 (Bousquet, *Mélanges Daux*, pp. 21 ff.) states that the Macedonian delegates (*hieromnemones*) are appointed 'by Alexander', but the payment of 10,000 staters was made by 'the Macedonians', and Diodorus (xvi, 71, 2) reports that when Philip II defeated the Thracians in 343/2 'he compelled them to pay tithes to the Macedonians'. But it is hard to envisage a separate 'national' Macedonian treasury, distinct from that controlled by the king, out of which payments to the Amphictyony were to be met, and the Macedonians are perhaps mentioned here merely because the other members of the Amphictyony were peoples. Similarly, Diodorus' reference to the Macedonians may be a verbal variant without significance.

On the other hand there are undoubtedly occasions when 'the Macedonians' are distinguished from their king. Justinus (xxiv, 5, 14) informs us that after Cassander's son Antipater perished, in 279, a certain Sosthenes, 'one of the leaders of the Macedonians', successfully warded off hostile attacks but, 'when he had been hailed king by the army, obliged the soldiers to take the oath to him not as king, but as general'. This passage is evidence that the army (probably representing the people) normally swore an oath to the new king. What form that oath took is not recorded. We know, however, from Plutarch (*Pyrrhus*, 5, 2) – who is probably following Hieronymus – that in the neighbouring kingdom of the Molossians (in Epirus)

> it was customary for the kings, after sacrificing to Zeus Areius at Passaron . . . to exchange solemn oaths with the Epirotes, the kings swearing to rule according to the laws and the people to maintain the kingdom according to the laws.

It may well be that the Macedonian oath took a similar form but clearly we cannot be sure. Nor have we any idea how often the Macedonians were called together. At the outset of Philip's reign, when morale was low, 'he gathered the Macedonians together in a series of assemblies and by his remarkable oratory inspired them with courage' (Diodorus, xvi, 3, 1) but this may have been exceptional, and it is perhaps significant that no inscription containing any decree emanating from a national Macedonian assembly has yet been found.

There is some evidence suggesting that the Macedonian people, or army (for in a state like that of the Molossians or Macedonians the two are almost indistinguishable), possessed a traditional right on the death of a king to appoint (not merely to acclaim) his successor. Philip II, for example, 'took the throne under compulsion of the people' (Justinus, vii, 5, 10) and after the murder of Cassander's son Alexander in 294,

> the Macedonians . . . owing to their hatred of Antipater (another son of Cassander) who was a matricide, and for want of a better man, proclaimed Demetrius king of the Macedonians and at once led him back to Macedonia (i.e. from Larissa, where these events took place) (Plutarch, *Demetrius*, 37, 1–2).

In fact, evidence for this popular right is rather scanty. In the case of Demetrius 'the Macedonians' were simply that section of the Macedonian army that had accompanied Alexander into Thessaly, and we do not know what *legal* significance resided in this acclamation: of its practical value to Demetrius there was of course no doubt. Similarly, the active role of Macedonian forces at Babylon immediately after the death of Alexander the Great and elsewhere during the early years of his successors is not surprising, given the irregular conditions. The active part played by the armies at this time could be the result of unruliness on the part of the troops or of calculations of expediency by the various generals, who naturally wanted to maintain the goodwill of their forces; it need not necessarily imply that traditional Macedonian popular powers were being exercised.

The other right attributed to the Macedonian people is that of judging cases of high treason. The main evidence for this lies in a general statement of Quintus Curtius about the nature of treason

trials in Macedonia, introduced (vi, 8, 25) in the context of
Alexander's action against Philotas, who had been charged with
high treason.

> It was the ancient custom of the Macedonians for the army to
> investigate criminal cases (*inquirebat exercitus*) – in peace time
> this was the function of the people – and for the power
> (*potestas*) of the king to count for nothing unless his influence
> (*auctoritas*) had earlier had weight with them.

The value of this passage is rendered somewhat doubtful because
the words *potestas* and *auctoritas* both carry a flavour of the time
just before Q. Curtius was writing, for both figure in a central
passage in *The Deeds of the Divine Augustus* (*Res gestae divi
Augusti*), set up in an inscription shortly after Augustus' death in
AD 14, and are concepts which attained notoriety at the outset of
the Principate. They may therefore have been introduced
anachronistically into Curtius' account of the powers of
Macedonian kings three centuries earlier. However, the passage
seems to mean that the army held the trial – for *inquisitio* is a legal
investigation – and that the king did not determine the verdict by
reason of his royal power, but could influence it through his
prestige, perhaps by his intervention at the hearing. The problem
has been unnecessarily complicated by the widespread adoption
of a textual emendation in the passage so that the sense is 'the
king investigated criminal cases, and the army passed judgement
(*inquirebat <rex, iudicabat> exercitus*)'. This emendation rests
upon a later passage (Curtius, vi, 9, 34), in which Alexander says
to Philotas: 'The Macedonians are about to pass judgement upon
you', and on the fact that in his speech Philotas addresses the
army as his judges. But in fact it is Alexander and his
companions, not the army, who take the final decision after the
army has been dismissed. Since therefore the passage contains
these contradictions, it is preferable not to tamper with the text of
Curtius vi, 8, 25. As it stands, this passage affords good evidence
that the people (or army) traditionally exercised power in treason
trials and these popular judicial rights, together with the rather

less clear rights exercised at the end of a reign, appear to place the king of Macedonia on a different footing from his rivals elsewhere.

In practice, however, these rights were little heeded. According to Plutarch (*Aemilius Paulus*, 8, 2) upon the death of Demetrius II in 229,

> the leading Macedonians, fearing the anarchy that might result (sc. from the fact that his son Philip was only a boy), called in Antigonus, a cousin of the dead king, and married him to Philip's mother, making him first regent and general and then, finding his rule moderate and conducive to the general good, giving him the title of king.

This account, which makes no reference to any popular assembly, attributes the decision to 'the leading Macedonians', and it can be assumed that even on occasions when an assembly was called together, it was these leading Macedonians whose decision really counted.

Popular rights in Macedonia were thus somewhat vestigial. But the leading Macedonians represented an element in the state for which there was no counterpart in Syria or Egypt, where the king's Friends, as we have seen (pp. 75 ff.), were chosen by the king from all parts of the hellenistic world and bound to him only by personal ties (at any rate during the third century). This kind of courtier and administrator was not unknown at the Antigonid court, nor indeed at the court of Philip II earlier, but at all times kings of Macedonia had to take account of a native nobility whose loyalty might be crucial to the safety and prosperity of the kingdom.

The Macedonians, moreover, survive as an element in the state, however slight and neglected their powers. In a rather fragmentary treaty made by Antigonus III Doson with the Cretan city of Eleutherna (*SVA*, 501), its people apparently undertake not to make any alliance which runs counter to 'that made with Antigonus and the Macedonians' and a Delian dedication set up after Antigonus III's victory over Sparta in

222, reads: 'King Antigonus son of King Demetrius and [the Macedonians] and the allies from [the spoils of] the battle of Sellasia to Apollo' (*Syll.*, 518). In this inscription the allies are the members of the Hellenic Confederacy set up by Doson (see p. 97); and though the word 'Macedonian' is not visible on the stone, it is a certain restoration, which is confirmed by the text of a treaty sworn between the Carthaginian general Hannibal and Philip V and recorded by Polybius (vii, 9, 1), which refers to the plenipotentiaries sent to Hannibal by 'King Philip the son of Demetrius on behalf of himself and the Macedonians and the allies', and goes on to mention these three as parties in the treaty. The Macedonians are also referred to as a *koinon*, a Greek word with a wide connotation but meaning fundamentally 'common weal' or 'state' or 'public authority' or (very frequently at this period) 'confederacy'. A Delian dedication inscribed on a third-century portico set up by Philip early in his reign reads: 'The *koinon* of the Macedonians in honour of King Philip son of King Demetrius on account of his merit and goodwill towards them' (*Syll.*, 575). This *koinon* can be paralleled from the Molossian kingdom, where an inscription from Dodona, dated to 370–368, when Neoptolemus was king, records a grant of citizenship by 'the *koinon* of the Molossians' (Hammond, *Epirus*, pp. 530–1). But, judging from our evidence, the Macedonian *koinon* had far less power than that of the Molossians, and once on the throne the Antigonids reigned autocratically and with few limitations beyond the need to keep the goodwill of the people and the nobles.

The evidence for this is unequivocal. Macedonian treaties were usually made in the name of the king alone. The presence of the Macedonians in those with Eleutherna and with Hannibal is exceptional and may connect with a reference to Greek allies, which stands in the Punic treaty and has been plausibly restored in that with the Cretan city. There is no hint anywhere in the contemporary historian Polybius that the Antigonids had to take account of any joint authority. The Macedonians, to be sure, always employed a traditional frankness in addressing their king. Polybius (v, 27, 8) emphasizes this in his account of the outspoken manner in which a body of Macedonian troops demanded that their commander, who was under arrest, should not be tried by the king in their absence. Moreover, unlike the cities inside the country and many outside it, the Macedonians never made their king the object of ruler cult. But, despite all this, for practical purposes the Antigonids were the state.

II

In other respects too Macedonia grew increasingly like the other hellenistic states, notwithstanding the national basis of the monarchy and the fact that both king and people belonged to the same stock. The king's Friends, for instance, were chosen from outside as well as inside the kingdom. When the young Philip V wanted to assert his independence, one of his earliest actions was to rid himself of the group of Macedonians whom he had inherited as his Friends from Antigonus Doson – Apelles, Megaleas, Leontius, Crinon and Ptolemaeus. Subsequently outsiders occupy a prominent place in his counsels, men such as Aratus of Sicyon, Demetrius of Pharos, Heracleides of Tarentum, Cycliadas the Achaean and Brachylles the Boeotian, whom indeed Antigonus Doson had already enrolled in Macedonian service, when in 222 he put him in charge of Sparta (Polybius, xx, 5, 12). We also hear, mainly from the time of Philip V when Polybius becomes available as a source, of many of the typical posts characteristic of the hellenistic courts, such as the Secretary of State, the Captain of the Guard, the Treasurer and the Bodyguards (a group of officers employed by the king on confidential duties).

Antigonid Macedonia experienced a growth of urbanization, which brought it closer to the cultural level of southern Greece. Under Philip and Alexander the highlands had been divided into cantons governed by their own princes and if we disregard the Greek colonies on the coast, such as Amphipolis and Pydna, there were few cities in lower Macedonia, and most of these were

little more than market towns. Under Philip the Greek colonies
had been incorporated into the kingdom, and there is evidence
that some of the Greeks eminent in Alexander's counsels and
serving in his fleet had been allotted land within the territory of
Amphipolis and had in that way acquired Macedonian citizenship. Under the successors cities multiplied. In 316 Cassander
founded two important cities, Cassandreia on Pallene (Diodorus,
xix, 52, 2) and Thessalonica, a synoecism of several towns at the
head of the Thermaic Gulf (Strabo, vii, 330, fgs. 21, 24). Both
these towns had large Greek populations, and it is perhaps a
mark of the growing unity and national consciousness that during
this period men from all the cities of Macedonia, whatever their
origin, count themselves as Macedonians. Outwardly the cities
had the structure and the institutions of Greek democratic
states. Four inscriptions from Cos, recording decrees passed by
Philippi, Cassandreia, Pella and Amphipolis (*SEG*, xii (1955),
373–4), and according freedom from reprisals (*asylia*) to the
temple of Asclepios in 242, furnish information about their
organization. Cassandreia had a council (*boule*) and Thessalonica
both a council and an assembly (*ecclesia*). An assembly is also
attested for Philippi and Amphipolis, and it seems highly likely
that all the cities, including the older Macedonian cities such as
Pella and Aegae, possessed both institutions. Like cities elsewhere they were divided into tribes and demes, and generals, law-
guardians, treasurers, archons and priests are mentioned from
various cities. Other inscriptions also show the cities of Macedonia
actively cultivating an exchange of embassies and honorific grants
of *proxenia* (see p. 73) with cities throughout the Greek world, as if
they were independent city-states. But in reality they were clearly
under the entire control of the king. A letter written by Philip V to
Andronicus, his representative in Thessalonica, indicates that the
municipal authorities might not touch the revenues of the temple
of Sarapis without permission from the royal governor (*epistates*)
and judges (*IG*, x, 2, 1 no. 3). Such *epistatai* were stationed in the
main cities of Macedonia and other areas under the king's
control, and they had the assistance of financial officials like
Harpalus at Beroea, to whom Demetrius II wrote a letter in

248/7, while still crown prince:

> Demetrius sends greeting to Harpalus. The priests of
> Heracles tell me that certain of the revenues of the god have
> been incorporated in those of the city. See to it therefore that
> they are restored to the god. May you flourish (*Syll.*, 459).

These officials ensured that all decisions of importance had the
royal consent. But within these limitations the cities possessed
local autonomy and controlled their own funds and they were
able to confer their own local citizenship on Macedonians from
other cities.

It is not easy to make a definite estimate of Macedonian
economic prosperity in the third century. Phenomenal progress
had been made under Philip II, who, as we saw (p. 29),
transformed the highlanders from skin-clad shepherds into
civilized farmers and town-dwellers, and not only stimulated a
growth in the native population, but also reinforced its numbers
with Scythians, Thracians and Illyrians. He had also opened up
new agricultural land through flood-control, drainage and
deforestation. This programme had been financed by the
acquisition and development of the silver mines of Pangaeum
near Amphipolis, Philippi and Damastium near Lake Ochrid,
and the mineral wealth drawn from this source also went to pay
for the costly military developments essential to Philip's
expansionist plans and the Persian expedition. The expedition
itself was costly to Macedonia in men and money and though a
few returned wealthy, during the fifty years following
Alexander's death emigration to the new cities of the east must
have exerted a strain on Macedonian prosperity, as must the
constant wars. The issue of an abundant and reliable silver
coinage by Antigonus Gonatas has, however, been taken as
evidence that his reign was prosperous and his adoption of a
naval policy against Egypt must also indicate the possession of
some resources. But from the mid-third century evidence is
scanty.

On conditions under Philip V (221–179) and Perseus

(179–168) rather more is known, since in addition to Polybius' (fragmentary) narrative and that of Livy derived from it, several inscriptions throw light on Macedonian economic affairs. An active military programme and a policy of patronage towards both major and minor religious centres abroad were both methods of asserting parity of status with richer rivals in other kingdoms but both laid a heavy burden on Philip V's treasury. His defeat by the Romans in the Second Macedonian War (200–197) saddled him with an indemnity of 1000 talents and shortly afterwards he embarked on a policy designed to expand his revenues.

> He not only increased the revenues of the kingdom by taxes on agricultural produce and by import and export duties; he also restarted the working of old mines that had been abandoned and opened new workings in many places. Moreover, in order to restore the population to its ancient level after the losses sustained in the disaster of war, he not only sought to ensure an increase in the native stock by insisting that everyone must beget children and rear them, but he had also introduced a large number of Thracians into Macedonia. The considerable period of respite from warfare had enabled him to devote all his attention to increasing his kingdom's resources (Livy, xxxix, 24, 2–4).

The resemblance to Philip II's methods is striking and probably deliberate. Philip V also issued large quantities of coins and for the first time in the history of the dynasty coins were issued by regional mints and by several Macedonian cities. We have specimens of bronze coins in the name of the Macedonians, the Bottiaeans, and two Paeonian peoples on the northern frontiers, and also coins from Amphipolis, Thessalonica, Aphytus, Apollonia in Mygdonis, and Pella. There is no evidence that they were intended for the hiring of troops; the local designations would make them unsuitable for that purpose. A good coinage could assist commerce and the local districts and cities may have paid   for   the   privilege   of   minting.   Twenty   years later in 169/8 Antiochus IV of Syria similarly encouraged municipal coining within his kingdom. It has been plausibly suggested that his object was to make the cities 'active partners in the internal regeneration of his kingdom' (Mørkholm, *Antiochus IV*, p. 130). Perhaps Philip's object was similar – though indeed the local coinages were not accompanied in this case by any relaxation in the centralized power of the monarchy.

Philip's efforts to build up his resources were continued by his son Perseus, who continued to amass wealth. Livy, following Polybius, records accusations made by his enemy Eumenes of Pergamum to the Roman Senate about his resources on the eve of the Third Macedonian War: their source of course makes them a little suspect.

He had in store a ten years supply of grain for 30,000 infantry and 5000 cavalry, so that he could be independent of his own land and of the enemy countryside in the matter of provisions. He had by now so much money that there was in hand pay for 10,000 mercenaries for the same period of time, in addition to his Macedonian forces, apart from the annual revenue which he received from the royal mines. Weapons enough for armies even three times as large had been piled up in his arsenals. And he now had the youth of Thrace under his control . . . if ever Macedonia's supply should fail (Livy, xlii, 12, 8–10).

Perhaps more to the point, the size of the armies which Perseus fielded in his war with Rome (172–168) shows that since 197 the national levy had risen by 9000 men.

The development of urbanization in Macedonia under its kings from Philip II to Perseus progressed further than was once supposed and excavations have shown how Demetrias in Thessaly, which remained under Macedonian control for most of the period, developed into a large and flourishing cosmopolitan port between 200 and 150. Thessaly, so long as they held it, was always treated by the kings of Macedonia as part of their own realm and Demetrias, founded by Demetrius I in 293, was a favourite city of the Antigonids; recent excavations there have identified their palace. But many Macedonians still lived in the countryside as peasant farmers or as tenants farming the estates of the king or the nobles. We have no information on the political status of the labour imported from Scythia, Illyria and Dardania, and such evidence as we have suggests that apart from some domestic slaves in the cities, slavery was not widely developed in Macedonia.

The country never achieved the scale of wealth to be found in Egypt and some other hellenistic states. Plutarch (*Aemilius Paulus*, 28, 3), records that, after the Roman victory at Pydna in 168, the Macedonians 'were to pay the Romans 100 (silver) talents in tribute, a sum less than half of of what they used to pay the kings'. If, despite all the efforts of Philip and Perseus to increase the productivity of Macedonia, its land-tax was bringing in only a little over 200 silver talents per annum, we are talking about a country with very modest resources. In 196 the Romans, who had a good idea of what the market could stand, imposed an indemnity of 1000 talents. In 188 Antiochus was required to pay 15,000 talents (in addition to 3000 already handed over). The difference is some measure of the relative wealth of the two powers.

III

Its situation ensured that Macedonia had a more direct and intimate relationship with mainland Greece than had any other of the hellenistic states, and that for the very simple reason that Macedonia was essential to their safety.

Flamininus, at a conference held in 198 during the Second Macedonian War, stated that:

It was decidedly in the interest of the Greeks that the Macedonian dominion should be humbled, but not that it should be destroyed. For in that case they would very soon experience the lawless violence of the Thracians and Gauls, as they had on more than one occasion (Polybius, xviii, 37, 8–9).

In fighting a series of wars against the Illyrians, Dardanians and Thracians, the Macedonians were indirectly protecting the Greeks and when the Romans in 148 took over Macedonia as a province the same task fell to them. It is necessary, in any assessment of the role of Macedonia in the hellenistic world to bear in mind that although our sources naturally, being Greek or based on Greek writers, lay their emphasis on Macedonian policy towards Greece, Macedonia was in fact equally a Balkan power for which the northern, western and north-eastern frontiers were always vital and for which strong defences and periodic punitive expeditions over the border were fundamental policy. It has to be remembered that Lysimachus was on one occasion a prisoner in Thracian hands (cf. p. 76), that Ptolemy Ceraunus fell in battle against the Gauls, that the deaths of both Demetrius II and Antigonus Doson are associated with Dardanian wars, and that the Romans enlisted Dardanian support in their war with Philip.

If however the Macedonians were an essential bulwark to the north of Greece, the Antigonids regarded control of Greece itself as essential to their security and since they never attempted to translate that control into outright conquest (as they did effectively in Thessaly), one must conclude that their object was to deny Greece to any other power – Ptolemy, Pyrrhus, the Aetolians (see pp. 152 ff.), Pergamum – which might constitute a threat to Macedonia itself. In addition there was the weight of precedent. Philip II had imposed his hegemony on Greece and Demetrius had occupied many strong points. It was probably a point of honour for Antigonus Gonatas to do no less.

From the time of Philip II onwards Macedonia was the subject of strong ideological passions in Greece. In a speech delivered at Sparta in 210 the Aetolian Chlaeneas, appealing for Spartan collaboration in the Roman alliance against Macedonia, is said by Polybius (ix, 28, 1) to have opened with the truism: 'Men of Sparta, I am quite certain that nobody would venture to deny that the slavery of Greece owes its origin to the kings of Macedonia'. He goes on to describe in detail the outrages which Philip, Alexander and their third-century successors have inflicted on the Greek cities. This was in the grand tradition of Demosthenes, who had branded statesmen from Arcadia, Messenia, Argos, Thessaly and Boeotia as traitors for collaborating with Philip, an accusation which was to bring a sharp retort from Polybius (xviii, 14, 6), in whose opinion these men

> by inducing Philip to enter the Peloponnese and humbling the Lacedaemonians, in the first place allowed all the inhabitants of the Peloponnese to breathe freely and to entertain thoughts of liberty and next by recovering the territory and cities of which the Lacedaemonians in their prosperity had deprived the Messenians, Megalopolitans, Tegeans and Argives, unquestionably increased the power of their native towns.

These remarks show clearly that the relationship with Macedonia was as loaded a question in the third and second centuries as it had been in the fourth. The Macedonian policy of controlling Greece was up against the Greek passion for freedom and autonomy. Yet some states, like those of the Peloponnese, had profited from the Macedonian connection and were still ready to collaborate with the Macedonian king against their neighbours.

IV

A general pattern can be detected in the attempts made over a century and a half by kings of Macedonia to achieve and maintain a firm control over Greece. The most usual method was the garrisoning of strong points in Greece. But this was varied – or at times supplemented – by declarations of Greek independence and, under Antigonus III, by the setting up of an organization of Greek states along the lines of Philip II's League of Corinth (p.

13). Of these devices the first was generally no more than a hollow slogan. The second, as we shall see (p. 97), was designed to line up the Greeks behind Macedonian policy and eventually proved disastrous for Hellas.

On his death Antipater left Polyperchon as regent of Macedonia (see p. 50) and he in 319 called a council of his Friends at which it was decided, in order to meet the threat from Antipater's son Cassander,

> to liberate the cities of Greece and to dissolve the oligarchies set up there by Antipater. In that way they would most easily weaken Cassander and win themselves great renown and many noteworthy alliances (Diodorus, xviii, 55, 2).

Once raised, the slogan of 'Greek freedom' continued to be bandied about as a propaganda theme to win Greek support. Four years later, generalized to appeal to *all* Greeks, it was incorporated in the ultimatum sent to Cassander by Antigonus the One-eyed that (above, p. 51): 'all Greeks were to be free without garrisons and autonomous' (Diodorus, xix, 61, 3) and in fact this remained Antigonus' stated policy. A clause to that effect was included in the peace of 311 (Diodorus, xix, 105, 1).

Unfortunately, whether translated into reality or as mere words (which is what they usually remained), freedom and autonomy did not provide control over Greece, and in 304/3 Antigonus and his son Demetrius tried to revive Philip II's League of Corinth as a method of marshalling the Greeks against Cassander. This interesting venture did not however outlive Antigonus' death at Ipsus in 301 and for the next twenty-five years both Greece and Macedonia served as a battleground for various generals hoping to gain possession of Alexander's homeland. In 276 Antigonus Gonatas, Demetrius' son, ended the chaos by seizing the Macedonian throne but his rival Pyrrhus of Epirus made a final attempt to dislodge him in 272 by invading the Peloponnese, and on that occasion he told Spartan ambassadors 'that he had come to free the cities which were subject to Antigonus' (Plutarch, *Pyrrhus*, 26, 7).

Antigonus and Demetrius had not put all their cards on the League of Corinth. They also kept Acrocorinth itself firmly garrisoned and when Antigonus Gonatas became king of Macedonia he maintained this fortress as a vital link in his system of control over Greece. The Greeks themselves were under no illusions about the significance of this garrison. In winter 198/7 Greek envoys sent to Rome in the hope of securing Philip V's complete expulsion from Greece

> all took pains to impress on the Senate that so long as Chalcis, Corinth and Demetrias remained in Macedonian hands, it was impossible for the Greeks to have any thought of liberty. For Philip V's expression when he pronounced these places to be the 'fetters of Greece' was, they said, only too true, since neither could the Peloponnesians breathe freely with a royal garrison established at Corinth, nor could the Locrians, Boeotians and Phocians feel any confidence while Philip occupied Chalcis and the rest of Euboea, nor again could the Thessalians or Magnesians ever enjoy liberty while the Macedonians held Demetrias (Polybius, xviii, 11, 4–7).

With the aid of these garrisons, supplemented for many years by troops in Athens and Piraeus, Antigonus Gonatas aimed at securing southern Greece. There was a strong current of opposition and in 268/7 the intrigues of Ptolemy II bore fruit in the outbreak of a Greek revolt against Macedonia known as the Chremonidean War after the Athenian Chremonides, who organized an alliance between Athens and Sparta and the allies of Sparta in the Peloponnese and Crete. Ptolemy's motives are not clear but the most likely explanation of his initiative is that Antigonus' decision to build a fleet seemed to threaten his own maritime supremacy, thanks to which he was master of the Asia Minor coastline and the Aegean islands. Chremonides' success in organizing the anti-Macedonian alliance is recorded in an Athenian inscription of 268, part of which reads:

> In order that the Greeks, who enjoy a common unanimity

against those who have recently acted with injustice and
committed outrages against the cities (i.e. Antigonus), may be
enthusiastic in the struggle together with King Ptolemy and
each other and may for the future preserve the cities by their
unanimity, with good fortune, the people decrees that
friendship and alliance shall exist between the Athenians, the
Lacedaemonians and the kings of the Lacedaemonians, and
the Eleans and the Achaeans and the Tegeans and the
Mantineans and the Orchomenians and the Phigaleans and
the Caphyeis and the Cretans, who are in the alliance of the
Lacedaemonians and Areus [the king] and the rest of the
allies, valid for all time, as brought by the ambassadors (*Syll.*,
434/5, ll. 32 ff. = *SVA*, 476).

Of the war itself few details survive. Egyptian coins of Ptolemy
II found exceptionally (see above, p. 26) in Attica and several
contemporary forts on Attic soil probably indicate some
Ptolemaic help, but this proved insufficient. The war ended in
disaster for the Greeks, and in 261 Athens had to surrender.
Areus of Sparta was killed fighting near Corinth, and for about
ten years Antigonus' control of Greece was unchallenged. As
governor of Corinth his half-brother Craterus was virtually an
independent viceroy but upon his death Alexander his son, who
succeeded to the command, revolted against Antigonus. This
was a severe blow to Macedonian power and although in 245
Antigonus recovered Corinth, by a trick, from Alexander's
widow, he lost it again two years later to the Achaean leader
Aratus (243). Twenty years were to elapse before the Macedonian
position in southern Greece could be restored.

It is probably to the years immediately following Alexander's
revolt that we must attribute Antigonus' sponsorship of a system
of tyrannies in the Peloponnese – though not all these are datable
and some at least, like that exercised by the family of Aristippus
at Argos, probably belong earlier. But it was as a supporter of
tyrants that Antigonus was remembered. In his speech at Sparta
(see p. 91) Chlaeneas asked his Spartan audience:

Who is ignorant of the deeds of Cassander, Demetrius and Antigonus Gonatas, all so recent that reference to them is superfluous? Some of them by introducing garrisons to cities and others by implanting tyrannies left no city with the right to call itself free (Polybius, ix, 29, 5–6).

Elsewhere (ii, 41, 10) Polybius complains that Gonatas 'planted more tyrannies in Greece than any other king'.

Deprived of Corinth, Antigonus (and after him his son Demetrius II) was in no position to defend the tyrants against a concerted campaign by the Achaean Aratus. One by one they were expelled and their cities brought into the Achaean League, which from the beginning of the third century became as powerful in the Peloponnese as the Aetolian League was in central Greece. Both these institutions will be examined in Chapter 8 (see pp. 152–8). Allied from 239 onwards they offered a serious obstacle to Macedonian ambition under Demetrius II (239–229) and when he died in 229 leaving an eight-year-old son, Philip, as his heir, Macedonia was in serious trouble. The leading Macedonians chose a certain Antigonus (known as Doson), the cousin of Demetrius, as regent and very soon as king (see p. 83). His reign saw an unforeseen reversal of Macedonian fortunes. At first the situation was black. Dardanians had overrun the northern frontiers, the Aetolians had seized much of Thessaly, and further south Boeotia had wavered in its loyalty, Athens had bought its freedom from the Macedonian garrison commander, and the tyrants in Argos, Hermione and Phlius had all laid down their powers and joined Achaea. But these Achaean successes coincided with the rise to power in Sparta of a vigorous young king, Cleomenes III, who sought to harness a programme of social revolution to a policy of Spartan expansion. A few years' campaigning saw Achaea in utter disarray and Aratus was driven to make a sensational *volte-face,*

which would have been unsuitable for any Greek to make, but was most shameful for him and most unworthy of his career as soldier and statesman. For he invited Antigonus into Greece

1 This relief from the Temple of Amon-Re at Luxor in Upper Egypt shows Alexander the Great (on the left), wearing the double crown of Upper and Lower Egypt, and making offerings to the god (on the right). It illustrates the extent to which the priests imposed the native Egyptian style in representations of the foreign dynasty.

2 The inscription from Ai Khanum, containing the
verses translated on p. 60 and the five surviving
Delphic maxims. Reproduced by permission of the
Académie des Inscriptions et Belles Lettres, Paris.

3 Some early hellenistic rulers. These coins, from the collection of the Fitzwilliam Museum, Cambridge, are reproduced by permission of its Department of Coins and Medals.

(a) Alexander the Great on a silver tetradrachm of Ptolemy I.

(b) Ptolemy I Soter on a silver tetradrachm from Egypt.

(c) Arsinoe II, the wife and half-sister of Ptolemy II Philadelphus on a silver decadrachm of Ptolemy II or Ptolemy III.

(d) Demetrius I Poliorcetes on a silver tetradrachm from Sicyon.

(e) Antiochus I Soter on a silver tetradrachm from Seleuceia-on-the-Tigris.

(f) Antiochus III the Great on a silver tetradrachm from Antioch-on-the-Orontes.

4 The Winged Victory of Samothrace, a third-century piece of sculpture, now in the Louvre, Paris, which may perhaps celebrate the naval victory gained by Antigonus II Gonatas over Ptolemy Philadelphus off Cos.

and filled the Peloponnese with Macedonians, whom he himself had driven out of the Peloponnese when, as a young man, he delivered the Acrocorinth from their power (Plutarch, *Cleomenes*, 16, 3).

Aratus was in a quandary but his fear of social revolution – it was widely though quite unnecessarily feared in Achaea that if victorious Cleomenes would carry out land-redistribution and debt-cancellation (see pp. 172 ff.) – and his dread of being ousted by Cleomenes from the position of dominance which he had held for over twenty years, led him to prefer Macedonia to Sparta. By 224 Antigonus was in possession of Corinth.

This time Macedonian power was to rest on a new basis, an alliance consisting of federal organizations under the leadership of the king of Macedonia, who was very soon to be not Antigonus (who died in 221) but the young Philip, Demetrius' son, for whom he had kept the succession open. The new alliance signified a return to the policies of Philip II and Antigonus I, except that the new units were not city-states, but confederations, a change reflecting a new emphasis in the political shape of Greece, which we shall look at in Chapter 8. The original members of the new 'Symmachy' were the Achaeans, Macedonians, Thessalians, Epirotes, Acarnanians, Boeotians and Phocians. The Council of the Symmachy could be summoned by the president and was charged with the responsibility for peace and war and matters of supplies and membership. There was no treasury, however, and decisions had to be ratified by member states, hence the fundamental weakness, which prevented this body ever developing an independent strength of its own. The Symmachy was from the outset a compromise between the Greek ideal of liberty and the Macedonian aim at control; it was at least tantamount to a renunciation of Gonatas' system of tyrants.

The Symmachy encircled Aeotolia and it was used first to fight an inconclusive war against the Aetolian League (220–217). But subsequently it became the fatal means of drawing the Achaeans and the other Greek allies into a devastating war with Rome,

provoked by the ambitions of the young Philip. In that war
Aetolia took the Roman side and the outbreak of a second war
between Rome and Macedonia in 200 put too great a strain on an
alliance which had ceased to offer any advantages to the Greeks.
In 198 the Achaeans voted to join Rome, and Philip's defeat at
Cynoscephalae in 197 resulted in his confinement within the old
limits of Macedonia. It was followed, at the Isthmian games of
196, by a theatrical pronouncement, which showed the Romans
quick to learn how to exploit the ancient propaganda slogan of
Greek liberty.

> The Roman Senate and T. Quinctius the proconsul, having
> defeated King Philip and the Macedonians, leave the
> following peoples free, without garrison and subject to
> no tribute and governed by their countries' laws – the
> Corinthians, Phocians, Locrians, Euboeans, Phthiotic
> Achaeans, Magnesians, Thessalians and Perrhaebians
> (Polybius, xviii, 46, 5).

The peoples mentioned had all been under Macedonian control,
some, like the Thessalians, since the time of Philip II. In the
Roman war against Antiochus III of Syria (192–189) Philip
fought on the Roman side and recovered some territories on the
borders of Thessaly, including Demetrias, but in a series of
adverse judgements the Romans gradually whittled these away
and their hostility to his successor Perseus (179–168) culminated
in the Third Macedonian War and the end of the Antigonid
kingdom. From 168 to 150 Macedonia survived as four
independent tribute-paying republics, then after a revolt led by a
pretender called Andriscus, who claimed to be Perseus' son, it
was made into a Roman province.

For Greece too the declaration at the Isthmus led not to a
period of glorious independence, but to qualified freedom,
compromised by the need to refer all serious problems to Rome
(see pp. 233 ff.). The war with Antiochus and Aetolia brought
new decisions and more Roman commissions. Finally in 146 the
revolt of the Achaean League ended in the destruction of

Corinth, the dissolution of the League and the subjection of many states to the control of the governor of Macedonia. The full significance of Roman domination in Greece and the hellenistic world generally is, however, a separate issue, which we shall consider in the last chapter.

6 Ptolemaic Egypt

I

When the provinces were shared out at Babylon after Alexander's death

> Ptolemy the son of Lagus was appointed to govern Egypt and Libya and those of the lands of the Arabs that were contiguous to Egypt; and Cleomenes, who had been made governor of this satrapy by Alexander, was subordinated to Ptolemy (Arrian, *Events after Alexander, Fragmente der griechischen Historiker*, 156 F 1, 5).

But Ptolemy very soon did away with Cleomenes, 'regarding him as loyal to Perdiccas and not to himself' (Pausanias, i, 6, 3). From his base in Egypt Ptolemy was from the start a formidable obstacle to anyone seeking to reunite Alexander's empire. But his own aims and those of his successors are far from clear. It seems certain that Ptolemy I had no ambitions of his own to win the whole empire. But in that case what was the purpose of his overseas acquisitions? The problem is raised by a passage in Polybius (v, 34, 2 ff.), describing the position as Ptolemy IV Philopator's acceded in 221. The new king, he says,

> showed himself inattentive to business and difficult of approach, and treated with complete negligence and indifference those charged with the conduct of affairs outside Egypt, to which the former kings had paid much more attention than to the government of Egypt itself. In consequence they had been always able to maintain the respect of the kings of Syria both by sea and land, being

masters of Coele-Syria and Cyprus; and they also exercised pressure on the dynasts of Asia Minor, and likewise the islands, since they had the chief cities, strongpoints and harbours in their hands all along the coast from Pamphylia to the Hellespont and the neighbourhood of Lysimacheia; while by their command of Aenus, Maronea and other cities even further off, they exercised supervision over the affairs of Thrace and Macedonia. With so long an arm and such an advanced fence of client states (dynasties), they were never in any fear for their Egyptian dominions, and for this reason they naturally paid serious attention to foreign affairs.

Ptolemy had seized Coele-Syria in 319 after the conference of Triparadeisus (see p. 49) but soon lost the northern part of it to Eumenes. Soon after Eumenes' death the whole area was in Antigonus' hands. Following Ipsus in 301 Ptolemy seized the southern half of the province and refused to give it up to Seleucus, who being in his debt politically did not press the claim for the present. But Coele-Syria remained an issue between the two kingdoms and was one important reason for the five wars fought between the Ptolemies and the Seleucids in the third century, until in 200 after his victory at Panium Antiochus III became master of Syria and Phoenicia.

Ptolemy I made early contacts with Cyprus, seized the island shortly afterwards and in 310 appointed his brother Menelaus general in charge. After Ipsus he temporarily lost it to Demetrius, but recovered it permanently in 294. It was probably about 310 that he made an alliance with Rhodes, a city which 'got most of its revenues from merchants sailing to Egypt; in general, the city was sustained from that kingdom' (Diodorus, xx, 81, 4), a statement partially confirmed by the large number of Rhodian stamped amphorae found in Alexandria. A little later, probably between 291 and 287, Ptolemy took over the patronage of the Island League, organized originally by Antigonus (see p. 52). Thus Ptolemy's determination to control substantial areas outside Egypt is clear from an early date and, as Polybius indicates, he also held many coastal possessions in Asia Minor.

But Polybius also asserts that these holdings ensured – and, he implies, were intended to ensure – that the Ptolemies down to Ptolemy III Euergetes 'were never in any fear for their Egyptian dominions'. For Polybius, then, Ptolemaic policy was defensively conceived.

This view has to be taken seriously, even though it perhaps over-simplifies or even distorts some of the facts. Polybius believed, not merely that Ptolemy IV neglected foreign affairs – a questionable judgement – but also that when Philip and Antiochus allied themselves against Egypt shortly after Ptolemy IV's death in 204, Egypt itself was to form part of Philip's share in the spoils. (Cf. Polybius, iii, 2, 8: 'Philip laying hands on Egypt, Caria and Samos'. Some scholars have unjustifiably emended the text to read 'the Aegean' in place of 'Egypt'.) Indeed, he criticizes Philip because after winning the battle of Lade against the Rhodians in 201, though 'it was quite possible for him to sail to Alexandria' (Polybius, xvi, 10, 1), he did not do so. As a statesman in his prime Polybius had seen Egypt invaded by Antiochus IV, and this may have influenced his judgement. At any rate he seems to regard Ptolemaic foreign policy as designed primarily and directly to prevent attacks on Egypt. Such attacks would come mainly from Syria and the possession of Coele-Syria and Cyprus certainly served as a defence against attacks from that quarter. But it has also been argued that Ptolemaic control of the Aegean was designed to counter Macedonian influence in Greece. There was indeed an anti-Macedonian aspect to Ptolemaic foreign policy, as is plain in the Chremonidean War (see pp. 94–5), which was instigated and financed by Ptolemy II. But that war seems to have been a response to Antigonus' creation of a fleet and it looks as if what the Ptolemies feared was Antigonid expansion into Asia Minor rather than the Macedonian control of Greece – though as an insurance and a threat they were always ready to subsidize Greek political troublemakers such as Aratus of Sicyon or, briefly, Cleomenes III of Sparta. Ptolemaic action against Macedonia in Greece was in fact generally maintained at a low level.

Syria then seems to have presented the main threat. But the

defence of Egypt against the Seleucids was not to be achieved merely by setting up a buffer zone under Ptolemaic suzerainty. It also required a well-equipped army and navy and for these most essential commodities were notably lacking in Egypt – metals, timber, pitch, money and suitable manpower. Suitable manpower meant, of course, Greeks, Macedonians and Anatolians, and only if money was available would they be forthcoming. There was a little gold in Nubia but by and large the other essentials had also to be imported – as well as many things needed to maintain the level of civilized life which a hellenistic ruler would require, e.g. wool, purple dye, marble, fine wines, horses. We should therefore regard the control of Coele-Syria, Cyprus, the Asia Minor coast and the Aegean islands as serving a further purpose by providing many things absent from the Nile valley and the Delta.

The products of Ptolemaic possessions abroad might reach Alexandria as tribute. But goods from elsewhere, and the hiring of troops, required money. Ptolemy I inherited a useful 8000 talents (Diodorus, xviii, 14, 1) from Cleomenes, who had exploited Egypt intensively but for the continued defence of Egypt and the military occupation of Cyrene, which Ptolemy had attached not to Egypt but to himself personally (rather as Thessaly was attached to the kings of Macedonia), as well as for the protection of the other outside possessions, a continuing source of wealth was essential. It was in order to provide that wealth that some of the most characteristic features of the Ptolemaic regime in Egypt were devised – though once set up, the system tended to become self-perpetuating. It therefore seems probable that in its original form this regime must go back to Ptolemy I, though it is under Ptolemy II (and perhaps thanks to the activities of his chancellor (*dioiketes*) Apollonius) that the full system was developed and refined.It is certainly from his reign that full details begin to be available.

II

This system may be described as a large-scale experiment in bureaucratic centralism and in mercantilism, in as much as it aimed at accumulating precious metals through controlled trade and the subordination of the economy to state power. Such a policy is clearly formulated in a letter of 258 from Demetrius, who was evidently responsible for the mint at Alexandria, to Apollonius the *dioiketes* of Ptolemy II. This letter, after the usual preliminaries, reads:

> I am attending to the work as you wrote me to do, and I have received in gold 57,000 pieces, which I minted and returned. We might have received many times as much but, as I wrote to you once before, the strangers who come here by sea and the merchants and brokers and others bring both their local money of unalloyed metal and the gold pentadrachms (*trichrysa*) to be made into new money for them in accordance with the decree which orders us to receive and remit, but as Philaretus does not allow me to accept, not knowing to whom we can appeal on this subject, we are compelled not to accept.

The letter goes on to say that men grumble because their gold is lying idle, since it can be neither exchanged 'nor sent into the country to buy goods'. Also 'all the residents in the city (sc. Alexandria)' were unable to exchange their worn gold but above all the revenues were suffering. For, says Demetrius,

> I take it to be an advantage if as much gold as possible is imported from abroad and the king's coinage is always good and new without any expense falling on him (*P. Cairo Zen.*, 59021 = *Select Papyri*, no. 409).

It is from this letter that we learn of a measure taken by Ptolemy II some time after 285, as part of a general series of ordinances regulating the taxes of Egypt, to exclude all foreign money from the kingdom and to compel foreign traders to change their money on reaching Egypt. In return they received new Ptolemaic coins struck on a lighter standard than those used elsewhere in the hellenistic world, and close to, though not identical with, the so-called Phoenician standard, in use at Cyrene. Why, shortly after 300, Ptolemy I had adopted this lighter standard is not certain. Some believe that he wanted to make it fit into certain foreign trade areas, while others connect it with a change in the relative value of gold and silver (the value of gold had been declining during the early decades of the third century). But it is perhaps rather to be regarded as a step towards creating in Egypt and its possessions a closed monetary system from which the circulation of foreign currencies was excluded. If that is so, Ptolemy II's regulation to which Demetrius refers in his letter reinforces that concept by giving it the stamp of law. It is interesting to find the Ptolemaic closed monetary system being copied a century later by the Attalids of Pergamum, whose *cistophori* (coins so-called from the sacred box, *cista*, portrayed on them) were also used as an exclusive currency.

Demetrius' remarks on the desirability of accumulating gold illustrate the mercantilist thinking behind Ptolemy II's economic policy. This was backed up by an intensive control of production throughout the whole kingdom with the purpose of maximizing the wealth flowing into Ptolemy's coffers. The first requisite was an effective bureaucracy and here the Ptolemies could build on the Pharaonic system which divided the country into some forty nomes, subdivided into *topoi* (areas) and *komai* (villages) – to use the Greek names – under nomarchs, toparchs and komarchs. Upon this the Ptolemies grafted a more complex system with troops stationed throughout the country under the authority of generals (*strategoi*) and a more elaborate fiscal service under *oikonomoi*. With the passing of time more and more power fell to the *strategoi*, especially during the second century, when their other duties became so great that their purely military functions were taken over by separate officials, with authority over several nomes, called *epistrategoi*. Because Ptolemy's attention was concentrated on the extraction of wealth, his chief functionary in the kingdom was the *dioiketes*, the financial minister at Alexandria, whose authority gradually grew to take in every other branch of state affairs. As we have seen (p. 24), the correspondence between Ptolemy's powerful *dioiketes* Apollonius, who was active from 260 to *c.* 246, and Zenon, his agent in charge of a large estate granted to Apollonius by Ptolemy in the Arsinoite nome in what is now the Fayum, is one of our main sources of information on the functioning of the administrative system at this time. In drawing on the rich volume of material preserved in this dossier the historian has however to remember that he may be dealing with the evidence for a somewhat short-lived experiment rather than a system which lasted through into the later Ptolemaic period. With this caution we can use the Zenon papyri to throw light on a remarkably elaborate system of administration

Under the *dioiketes* were the *oikonomoi*, who had the thankless task of extracting rents and taxes from the population and at the same time preventing the peasants from becoming so discouraged that (as sometimes happened) they abandoned their holdings and fled. A copy of the instructions sent in the third century probably by a *dioiketes* to an *oikonomos* – it may be a standard exhortation sent to each *oikonomos* when he took office – gives some notion of the latter's task:

> In your tours of inspection try as you go from place to place to cheer everybody up and to put them in better heart; and this you should do not merely by talking to them, but if any of them complain of the village scribes or the komarchs about anything to do with farm-work, you should look into it and as far as possible put a stop to such things ... You must regard it as one of your most indispensable duties to see that the nome is sown with the kind of crops prescribed in the schedule. And should any be hard-pressed because of their rents or completely exhausted, you must not let this pass without investigation (*P. Tebt.*, 703 = *Select Papyri*, no. 204).

The letter from which these extracts are taken provides a comprehensive survey of the different forms of official exploitation to which the highly regimented *fellahin* were subjected. It suggests devices which the *oikonomos* should employ to ensure that no source of income escapes his official eye – for instance, he is to use the period of the Nile floods, when the cattle were perforce concentrated on high ground, to carry out a registration of their number for taxation. One cannot withhold a measure of sympathy not only for the peasants but also for the *oikonomos* who had to maintain their goodwill while extracting his pound of flesh.

The taxes and rents imposed were extremely varied in kind and took in every possible source of revenue. They are known to us from a wide range of papyri containing payment-orders, receipts, contracts, tenders and other matters of everyday fiscal or economic life. A typical example is this order for the payment of rent, written perhaps by a general in 244/3:

> To Achoapis. Concerning the holding of Alcetas, one of the prisoners from Asia in the area of Psenarpsenesis, which has been reoccupied by the Crown after the sowing of the fourth year, Apollonius, the keeper of contracts, has submitted to us a contract which he said that Alcetas had made with Heliodorus, the cultivator of the holding, for a fixed rent of 30 *artabae* of wheat, and they have signed the customary oath that it has been leased for this amount. Therefore let the above-mentioned rent be measured out to the Crown (*P. Petrie*, 104 = *Select Papyri*, no. 392).

Here several points require elucidation; and for this we have to consider the system of land tenure in Egypt.

Ptolemy treated the whole of the land of Egypt, no matter how assigned or occupied, as his own possession. After the meeting of Perdiccas' enemies at Triparadeisus in 320 there was, as we have seen (p. 49), a redistribution of satrapies by Antipater who, Diodorus records:

> assigned to Ptolemy the satrapy which he had held up to then, for it was impossible to change this, in as much as he appeared

to be holding Egypt as spear-won land and the fruit of his own bravery (xviii, 39, 5).

However, only part of the land of Egypt was cultivated directly as 'crown land'. Much of it was held by the powerful native temples, whose priesthood was the nearest thing to an indigenous nobility. In theory temple land was also deemed to be the property of the king, and the kings took steps to control its cultivation and to sequestrate its revenues, allowing only what was necessary to revert to the temples themselves. But in this they were only partially successful, and as the power of the monarchy weakened in the second century the priests succeeded in increasing the extent of temple lands and the influence which they themselves exercised. Noteworthy too are the large and impressive temples built, for instance, at Denderah, Karnak, Edfu, and Kom Ombo, in the Ptolemaic period.

Land retained in the king's hands was farmed by crown peasants, who held plots mainly on short leases. It was among these men that the local *oikonomos* was occupied, solicitously nurturing their ability to pay taxes, and in this task he had the assistance of many minor officials, themselves Egyptians, various guards, the komarch and the village scribe (mentioned in the letter). These men at the lower administrative levels were necessarily Egyptians since they had to deal directly, in Egyptian, with the native population. The seed-corn was provided by the crown, but its equivalent had to be returned after the harvest and, as we saw, what the tenants planted was determined centrally and recorded in the schedule of sowing. Other land was made over in gifts, to the temples or to private individuals such as Apollonius, the *dioiketes*, whose estate of nearly 7000 acres in the Fayum has already been mentioned or else it was allotted to reservist soldiers known as *cleruchs* (or sometimes after 217 as *katoikoi*).

In order to hold Egypt securely against all rivals the Ptolemies needed manpower and there is a wealth of evidence indicating a great influx of foreigners of all nationalities during the first fifty years of Ptolemaic control. The Ptolemies encouraged this. After the battle of Gaza (312), for example, 'Ptolemy sent the prisoners to Egypt with instructions that they were to be distributed among the nomes' (Diodorus, xix, 85, 3–4). There were over 8000 of them. It was to cater for the needs of the immigrants that the important category of 'cleruchic land' was introduced. Land allotments, varying in size between three and a half and seventy acres and scattered over the country, were assigned to reservists, who were saddled with the double duty of cultivating the land and serving in the army when called on. These men saved the king a great deal of valuable currency which would have been needed had he employed mercenaries in their place. In some cases the cleruch rented his plot to a tenant–cultivator, either part of it (if the whole was too large for him to cultivate alone), or the whole when he was called up for military duties. In the letter to Achoapis (p. 107), Alcetas, a prisoner of war perhaps taken in the Laodicean War against the Seleucids (246–241), had become a soldier in Ptolemy III's army, had acquired a *kleros* (allotment) and had rented it to one Heliodorus. Having fallen foul of authority Alcetas had had his lot confiscated by the government, which investigated the lease and ordered the rent (payable in wheat, not money) to go to the Crown. Originally allotments were personal but by the mid-third century a papyrus from the Arsinoite nome mentions a cleruch 'to whom and to whose descendants the land belongs' (*P. Lille*, 4), and in an amnesty granted in 118 by Ptolemy Euergetes II, his wife and his ex-wife, we learn that

> they have decreed that all recipients of grants of land and all holders of temple land and of other land *en aphesei* (i.e. released by the government), both those who have encroached on crown land and all others who hold more than their proper portion, shall, on giving up all the excess and declaring themselves and paying a year's rent, be released from responsibility for the period up to the 51st year and have legal possession of the land (*P. Tebt.*, 5, ll. 36–43 = *Corp. Ord. Ptol.*, no. 53).

This document shows that by this time cleruchic land was

beginning to approximate to private property. Whether they farmed their own lots or no, cleruchs did not always live on their *kleroi*. As reserve soldiers they were liable to be called up from time to time. We also hear of soldiers being assigned living quarters, usually at the expense of the native Egyptians. This led to much bitterness. But even more was created when, towards the end of the second century Egyptians began to be settled as cleruchs on the land and, as happened in some cases at Kerkeosiris in the Fayum, ousted the Greek holders of large *kleroi*.

Like the crown peasants the cleruchs were also subjected to the various taxes which helped to swell the royal revenues. We hear of duties on wool and linen; of a succession duty (payable on death); of a 5 per cent tax on house rents; of a tax of 10 per cent on sales and 2 per cent on market sales; of a $33\frac{1}{3}$ per cent tax on the profits on pigeons (at Kerkeosiris this was assigned to the god Soknebtunis); of a $33\frac{1}{3}$ per cent tax on vineyards, orchards and gardens together with $\frac{1}{6}$ of the produce of the vineyards paid in kind and of that of orchards and gardens paid in money (this latter tax, known as *apomoira*, was diverted to maintain the posthumous cult of Arsinoe Philadelphos, wife of Ptolemy II, *P. Rev. Laws*, 37, 15–18); of a tax on cattle and on slaves; of a poll-tax and of a local customs tax. The tax on corn (unlike that on vines, olives and other cash-crops) was in kind and crown peasants who had to pay rent for their lands as well ended up having to surrender, as rent and tax, over 50 per cent of their harvest. What was left, after the cultivator and his family had been fed, would be sold or (more commonly) exchanged for other necessities. It is likely that the crown peasant operated with a mainly barter economy, without much use of currency. The position of the cleruch was a little easier in that he was not called upon to pay so much rent, since part of this obligation was fulfilled in the form of military service.

Not all products could be sold. For in addition to exacting heavy taxes the Ptolemies imposed many monopolies. A noteworthy example is furnished by the oil-producing crops, sesame, castor-oil, linseed, safflower and round gourd, the regulations concerning which are contained in a code of 259 known as the *Revenue Laws of Ptolemy II* (see p. 24) (*P. Rev. Laws*, cols. 38–56 = *Select Papyri*, no. 203). This document shows the government exercising complete control over the oil industry at every stage from the sowing of the plant to the retailing of the oil at fixed prices, after it had been manufactured in state factories supervised by the local authorities. Naturally attempts were made to get round these laws. A papyrus of 114 throws light on the measures taken, sometimes at personal risk, to deal with contraband. Apollodorus, who has contracted to retail oil and collect taxes concerned with it at Kerkeosiris, writes to Menches, the village scribe, describing how, hearing that there was contraband oil in the house of Sisois, he descended upon it accompanied by the agent of the *oikonomos* 'since you and the other officials were unwilling to accompany me', whereupon Sisois and his wife set upon Apollodorus and drove him out. When he later tried to arrest Sisois, a whole gang of his friends overpowered Apollodorus and his supporters, beat them up and wounded Apollodorus' wife in her right hand. Apollodorus claims a loss of ten talents in copper in respect of his contract, which he tries to extract from the appropriate officials. There is, however, no question of compensation for injury (*P. Tebt.*, 39 = *Select Papyri*, no. 276).

Mines, quarries, salt-production and the extraction of nitre and alum (used for fulling) were also monopolies. But in many other branches of the economy we find a strict control which falls short of complete monopoly – for example in the production of linen, papyrus and beer (the national drink of Egypt) – or the use of licences or leases combined with taxes, as in the case of bee-keepers, pig-keepers, fishermen and most kinds of trader. It is probably true to say that no aspect of agriculture or production in Ptolemaic Egypt escaped government attention in one form or another and a combination of heavy taxes of almost every conceivable kind and fixed prices ensured that the real benefits ended up in Ptolemy's treasury. It should be added that this system was applied equally and for the same reasons to Ptolemaic possessions abroad. The state came first and this order of priority was inculcated in the official ideology. 'No one', writes the *dioiketes* to his *oikonomos*, 'has the right to do what he wants, but all is regulated for the best' (*P. Tebt.*, 703, ll. 230–2).

The Ptolemaic system has been characterized as a highly planned economy. This is misleading. In many spheres the Ptolemies simply took over what they found, grafting on to it measures necessitated by the existence of a new Greco-Macedonian ruling class including the cleruchs. The details are often subject to local compromises and there is a great deal of incompetence. As a system of exploitation it was harsh and often illogical, concerned rather to prevent cheating than to secure the most efficient results. But perhaps its main weakness was its single-minded concentration on extracting as much wealth as possible for Ptolemy and its disregard – except for fine words such as the *dioiketes* writes to his *oikonomos* – for the well-being of the native Egyptians.

Naturally the system encountered resistance. It was in the interest of the Egyptian to emphasize his distress and to exaggerate his inability to pay. The officials were met with often exasperating complaints of the sort exemplified in the following letter, written in the mid-third century by Harentotes, a lentil-cook of Philadelphia, to Philiscus, probably the *oikonomos* in Crocodilopolis:

> I give the amount due on 35 *artabae* (sc. of roasted lentils) a month and I do my best to pay the tax monthly so that you have no complaint against me. Now the people in the town are roasting pumpkins. For that reason then nobody buys lentils from me at the present time. I beg and beseech you then, if you think fit, that I be granted more time, just as has been done in Crocodilopolis, for paying the tax to the king. For in the morning they straightway sit down beside the lentils selling their pumpkins and give me no chance to sell my lentils (*P.S.I.*, 402 = *Select Papyri*, no. 266).

Minor officials were deluged with such cajoling complaints; but *their* job was to get the money in.

III

The new element introduced into Egypt under Alexander and then under the early Ptolemies was, as we have seen, a Greek and Macedonian ruling class. The reservist soldiers were scattered about the countryside for the Ptolemies, unlike the Seleucids, did not encourage cities and Egypt possessed few. There was of course Alexandria, a cosmopolitan agglomeration, the heart of Ptolemaic administration, with a large population of Greeks, Macedonians, Jews and native Egyptians. It contained the royal palace and the ministries, but compared with upper Egypt and the Fayum it has revealed almost nothing to the excavator and the moist soil has destroyed any papyri. Thanks to a change in the sea-level much of the ancient city now lies under the water. From the outset the Ptolemies tried to keep the Egyptian peasantry from settling there, but in vain, as we can see from Polybius' description of its population in the second half of the second century.

> It is inhabited by three classes of people, first the native Egyptians, a volatile group, hard to control; secondly by the mercenaries, a numerous, overbearing and uncultivated set, it being an ancient practice there to maintain a foreign force which owing to the weakness of the kings had learnt to rule rather than obey; thirdly there are the Alexandrians themselves, a people also not genuinely civilized for the same reasons, but still superior to the mercenaries [*or* to the other two categories] for though they are mixed they come from a Greek stock and have not forgotten Greek customs (xxxiv, 14, 1–5).

Alexandria was thus a rather special case. It was never felt to be wholly part of Egypt and its official title in Roman times was Alexandria-by-Egypt. As the most important cultural centre of the hellenistic world it will, however, be our concern below in Chapter 10. Besides Alexandria there was also Naucratis, an ancient Greek settlement and an outlet through which for several hundred years the Pharaonic government had regulated trade with the Greek world. In addition there was Ptolemais in upper Egypt, the only Ptolemaic foundation and the creation of Ptolemy I. Clearly the traditions of the highly centralized kingdom of Egypt and the inclinations of the Ptolemaic dynasty were both against founding local centres of even limited autonomy, which is what cities must inevitably have become. A centralized bureaucracy was the best guarantee of complete official control.

IV

Even before Alexander, Greeks and Egyptians had had to adjust to each other's presence in the Nile valley but it was only with the Macedonian conquest that the problem of the two cultures became a central one for both people. During the reigns of the earlier Ptolemies there is little evidence of deep hostility between the two races. The Egyptians kept their own laws and courts, and in the second century there were special tribunals to deal with disputes involving Egyptians and Greeks and royal judges (*chrematistai*) with jurisdiction over both peoples. But we possess a series of royal decrees (*prostagmata*) with the force of law from the reign of Ptolemy II which apply equally to both Greeks and Egyptians. Some of these – and other documents too – reveal a disquieting development, the tendency of the administrative power to encroach on the judicial, as when, for example, in a letter to his *dioiketes* Apollonius, in 259, Ptolemy II sends instructions that

> since certain advocates . . . are taking up fiscal cases to the injury of the revenues, you are to give orders that those who have acted as advocates be made to pay the Crown the ten per cent deposit doubled and forbid them in future to act as advocates in any case (*P. Amherst*, 33 = *Select Papyri*, no. 273).

Clearly the authorities were not to be hampered by complainants with access to legal help.

The Egyptians were at a disadvantage in so far as the new ruling class was entirely made up of newcomers. The upper ranks of the civil service, the Greek priesthoods, the cleruchs, the holders of gift land from the kings, the Greeks of Alexandria and the other cities, and naturally the king's Friends, formed a single caste from which even the richer native Egyptians were excluded. The Egyptian priesthood, which might have maintained itself on equal terms with the newcomers (since the temples were ancient, rich and powerful) failed to resist the pressure which the king exerted in order to incorporate them economically in his general system. Their sources of wealth were now limited to what was necessary for the maintenance of the temples. This at least was true in the third century. Later, as we shall see, their situation improved.

It was, however, in the countryside that the two races came into closest contact. Here friction and hostility surface in the papyri and with them racial resentment. In the Zenon papyri we meet a camel-driver, probably an Arab, who complains that he has not been paid regularly and attributes this to the fact 'that I am a barbarian', and 'I do not know how to behave like a Greek (*hellenizein*)' (*P. Col. Zen.*, 66, ll. 19, 21). A little later, in the reign of Ptolemy III, an Egyptian priest of high standing engaged in a lawsuit involving a cleruch billeted on him – the old grievance – complains that the latter 'despises me because I am an Egyptian' (*P. Yale*, 46, col. i, l. 13). But sometimes the boot was on the other foot. A certain Ptolemy, son of Glaucias, a Macedonian, who lives in the temple-complex of Sarapis at Memphis, complains on several occasions (in 163, 161, and 158) that he is being persecuted because he is a Greek (not a Macedonian!) (*UPZ*, 7, 8, 15), but this was shortly after the revolt of Dionysius Petosarapis, when feeling was tense, and furthermore there may have been personal hostility towards this man. It would therefore be unsafe to draw general conclusions from a few passages of this kind. A Zenon papyrus (*P. Cairo Zen.*, 59610) speaks of the difficulty in getting Egyptians and foreigners to work together; but in the main the two peoples seem to have enjoyed a reasonably satisfactory *modus vivendi*.

The Egyptians, of course, were economically inferior and occupied the lower ranks in the social scale for there was probably no slave class of any dimensions in the countryside. Slavery played a part in the domestic life of Alexandria as in any other Greek city and we know of a weaving establishment belonging to Apollonius, Ptolemy II's *dioiketes*, at Memphis, which may have employed slave labour (*P. Cairo Zen.*, 59142), but the existence of a nominally free peasantry and the fact that all types of manual labour were performed by free men left no real place for slaves outside the towns (except occasionally in the mines). The fortunes of the crown peasants were often desperate, but they had one traditional remedy – to strike by running away, usually in a group (*anachoresis* was the technical term for this well-understood institution) – and the existence of temples with rights of asylum encouraged recourse to it. For example, in the summer of 256 Panacestor, the bailiff of the *dioiketes* Apollonius, and Zenon's predecessor on his gift estate, has to report that the peasants on the estate have rejected the terms of the contract proposed to them and have taken refuge in a temple (*P.S.I.*, 502). To get them back to work he has been obliged to alter the method of assessment. It appears that Panacestor will himself have to make up the shortfall. Grievances of this kind, social in origin, tended to take on a racial aspect simply because the officials, in the upper echelons at least, were Greeks and the peasants or workers Egyptians. The same applies to the grievances over billeting, which find frequent expression in the papyri. Thus in a document of the mid-third century Ptolemy II writes to a subordinate:

About the billeting of soldiers, we hear that some undue violence is used, as they do not receive lodgings from the *oikonomoi*, but themselves break into the houses and ejecting the inhabitants occupy them by force. Give orders therefore that in future this is not to be done (*P. Hal.*, 1, ll. 166–71 = *Select Papyri*, no. 207).

He goes on to elaborate the correct procedures to be observed, insisting on the restoration of billets after their evacuation and imposing a complete ban on all billeting in Arsinoe; if soldiers *must* go there, let them build huts.

By and large the Greeks kept themselves aloof from the Egyptians. There are indeed exceptions. Some examples of inter-marriage by the poorer Greeks, of whom we know less, are attested from 256 onwards. The dedication of a shrine to the Egyptian goddess Thoeris in the Fayum, made on behalf of Ptolemy III and Berenice 'by Eirene and Theoxena, daughters of Demetrius, Cyreneans, whose mother was Thasis and who also have the Egyptian names of Nephersuchus and Thaues' (Wilcken, *Chrestomathie*, 51, ll. 8–12), indicates the Egyptian side of a mixed marriage between a Greek man and an Egyptian woman. The double names mentioned here have quite a different significance from the double names often found being used by Egyptians who are 'on the way up', holders of *kleroi* or men hoping to pass for Greek or to get recognition from Greeks with whom they came into contact – like Menches, the village scribe of Kerkeosiris, who was also called Asclepiades (*P. Tebt.*, 164), or Maron son of Dionysius, a *katoikos*, who was previously called Nektsaphthis son of Petosiris (*P. Tebt.*, 61a). A recently published tombstone (*Bull. Inst. franç. arch. or.*, 72 (1972), 139–67, no. 16) of a Magnesian called Diphilus, the son of Thearus, depicts the dead man's mummy on a funeral bier attended by various supernatural figures, one with a jackal's head. The inscription is in a mixture of Greek and hieroglyphics, and there is also a subsidiary demotic inscription. But this stone, probably from the early-third century, is certainly exceptional and may belong to a family established in Egypt before Alexander. The usual Greek aloofness was reinforced by addiction to the gymnasium (see pp. 60 ff.), which was not only the centre of their education, where as adolescents they studied Greek literature, rhetoric and mathematics, as well as physical training, but also the focus of their social life and culture. Gymnasia existed in Alexandria and also in the nome capitals and even in the countryside. Their *alumni*, 'those from the gymnasium' as they were styled, formed organizations dedicated to the support of the institution and the Greek way of life, serving as a club for those who had received a Greek education – though increasingly 'culture-Greeks' (the ones with the double names) were also admitted. Unfortunately the precise relationship between the *alumni* of the gymnasium and the ethnic groups known as *politeumata* is badly documented for the Ptolemaic period. It is, however, known that Greeks scattered through Egypt formed such *politeumata*, as did other ethnic groups among the mercenaries. A special case is that of the *politeuma* of the Jews settled in Alexandria and placed under their own ethnarch; on this institution see Chapter 12.

V

So far we have been considering conditions in Egypt mainly during the first hundred years of Ptolemaic rule. But towards the end of the third century a change took place in the relative positions of the two races. Speaking of the period following Ptolemy IV's victory over the Seleucid king Antiochus III at Raphia in 217, Polybius (v, 107, 1–3) tells us that

> the king, by arming the Egyptians for his war against Antiochus, took a step which was of great service for the time, but which was a mistake as regards the future. For they, highly proud of their victory at Raphia, were no longer disposed to obey orders, but were on the look-out for a leader and figure-head, thinking themselves well able to maintain themselves as an independent power, an attempt in which they finally succeeded not long afterwards.

The situation is more complicated than Polybius here suggests. The growth in influence of the Egyptian element, which undoubtedly took place after 217, was due to more than the arrogance of the 20,000 native troops who had for the first time been included in the phalanx. Their enrolment was itself motivated to some extent by financial embarrassment; this is at any rate indicated by a deterioration in the Ptolemaic currency under Ptolemy III (246–221). But Ptolemy IV may also have found it necessary to compensate for the desertion of several of his mercenary captains. After the war financial difficulties increased as a result of the cost of the war itself, and they led in turn to increased financial pressure and growing resistance to this pressure by the peasantry. To mobilize the country to its defence Ptolemy IV had moreover been forced to make concessions to the priests, who now pressed their advantage. In a Greek, demotic and hieroglyphic inscription which records the decree of the synod of priests which assembled at Memphis in November, 217, to celebrate the victory (the so-called Pithom *stele*), not only is Ptolemy IV given the full titulature of a Pharaoh, but this is true for the Greek as well as the Egyptian versions. Subsequently the inclusion of these titles is normal and can be seen in the famous Rosetta inscription (*OGIS*, 90) of 196, which celebrated the coronation of Ptolemy V in autumn 197 (see p. 21).

This growth in Egyptian influence and self-confidence coincided with a long-drawn-out civil war, in which upper Egypt broke away and was from 207 to 186 governed by separate Pharaohs of Nubian origin, and with the onset of almost endemic brigandage in lower Egypt, including the Delta. These signs of governmental weakness or even collapse may be partly due to nationalist feeling, but primarily they reflect growing social distress which takes nationalist forms simply because the exploiting class is made up of Greeks. Since the flow of Greek and Macedonian immigrants had long ago dried up, the king and his court felt themselves weakened, and hence were led to make repeated concessions to the temples and to publish amnesties (euphemistically termed 'benefactions' (*philanthropa*)) for the peasantry. But these very concessions reduced their ability to raise adequate revenues for the future and so still further weakened the government; it was a vicious circle.

Fiscal concessions did not, indeed could not, rule out the resumption of pressure but the general pattern began to favour the Egyptians, rich and poor. Land allotments were now made available to Egyptian soldiers (*machimoi*). Non-Greeks found a way into the bureaucracy, especially if they acquired a Greek education. An example is Paos, who was 'one of the First Friends' and general in the Thebaid under Euergetes II (170–163, 145–116). Greeks and men of Greek background increasingly took to worshipping Egyptian gods whom they often identified with those of Greece. For instance, a late-second-century dedication on behalf of Ptolemy VIII Euergetes II and Cleopatra and their children from the island of Dionysus (Setis) at the Cataract (mod. Essehel) by Herodes son of Demophon of Berenice, chief bodyguard and general, and an association of soldiers devoted to the worship of the royal house, is made to

> Cnoubis who is also Ammon, Satet who is also Hera, Anuket who is also Hestia, Petempamentes who is also Dionysus, Petensetis who is also Cronos, Petensenis who is also Hermes, the great gods and the other powers who look after the cataract (*OGIS*, 130).

The gods named are all local divinities who needed to be placated, especially since some members of the association were Egyptians. There was also a general increase in intermingling and intermarriage between the races, though the higher one goes in the social scale the less the contact. According to Plutarch (*Antonius*, 27), Cleopatra VII was the first of her house to learn the native language, but she was exceptional, for she spoke at least nine languages.

VI

Herodes' dedication raises the question of religion, which was obviously an important aspect of the relations between the Greeks and the Egyptians. The Greek immigrants of course brought their native gods with them, but the Ptolemies were from the outset careful to pay respect to the traditional gods of Egypt (though this did not prevent their taking the temple lands and trying to break the power of the priesthood). Of the Greek pantheon Dionysus was given special honour by Ptolemy IV (see p. 211). But two developments owe their origins especially to the Ptolemies, the cult of the royal house and the worship of a new god, Sarapis.

The dynastic cult can be traced back to Alexander's attempt to secure deification, though indeed there are earlier precedents for the worship of great men in Greece and it is likely that Alexandria possessed a cult of Alexander as its founder from an early date. But the growth of the dynastic cult of the Ptolemies, the beginnings of which are to be found under Ptolemy I, are best considered in the general context of ruler cult, an institution common to most of the hellenistic kingdoms. Its development and significance will therefore be left for fuller treatment in Chapter 12.

The other religious innovation for which Ptolemy I was responsible was the cult of Sarapis. Several contradictory accounts of the origin of this cult are extant but the probability is that it arose out of a cult at Memphis, where the sacred bull, Apis, was after death identified with Osiris and worshipped as Osor-Hapi (hellenized as Oserapis: *UPZ*, 1). Sarapis at Alexandria was another version of Osor-Hapi at Memphis; and according to Plutarch (*On Isis and Osiris*, 28) the Athenian priest Timotheus and the hellenized Egyptian priest Manetho (who wrote a history of Egypt in Greek) advised Ptolemy I on the institution of the new cult. Its purpose was probably to provide the Greek population and especially that of Alexandria with a new patron deity – though the earliest evidence for a cult of Sarapis as a specifically Alexandrian god dates to the Roman empire. Sarapis was never popular among the Egyptians, but his cult had an unexpected success abroad, appearing at Delos with an Egyptian priest before the end of the third century (*IG*, xi, 4, 1299), and then quickly spreading throughout the Greek, and later the Roman, world. Sarapis was associated with the underworld, but he also had some of the attributes of a god of healing.

VII

Ptolemaic Egypt was the last of the hellenistic monarchies to fall to Rome but long before Octavian took over the land from Cleopatra and Antony in 30, conditions had become anarchic. The papyri present a picture of widespread corruption and of a population wholly hostile to the bureaucracy and frequently resorting to flight to evade the increasing demands made upon them by the royal officials. The kings have lost all real control over these. In their hope of maintaining goodwill they issued a series of amnesties (*philanthropa*) like that of Euergetes II in 118 (p. 109); the latest known is one of *c.* 60 making concessions to the cavalry cleruchs (*katoikoi*) of the Heracleopolite nome (*Corp. ord. Ptol.*, no. 71) and confirming their hereditary possession of their lots and the right of their nearest kin to inherit should they die intestate. The power that the Crown has lost has fallen into the hands of the priests and of certain influential individuals, whose ability to offer protection (*skepe*) to runaways and others in distress seems to anticipate the conditions of the declining Roman empire half a millennium later. For this collapse of Ptolemaic rule there are many causes, some of which have been examined above, but to those must be added a disastrous foreign policy, the loss of markets abroad, the wastage caused by internal unrest and civil wars, incompetent government at home, bureaucratic corruption and currency depreciation. In considering the whole sorry tale it is difficult not to echo the judgement of E. Will that Ptolemaic Egypt fell a victim to its own wealth employed in the service of interests which were never its own.

7 The Seleucids and the East

I

In Egypt the Ptolemies and a Greek elite confronted a native population with a powerful priesthood and national traditions going back four millennia. The country was a compact whole based on the Nile valley and the Delta. The lands which constituted the rival kingdom of the Seleucids were in almost every way a contrast to this. In the first place their area fluctuated violently between 312, when Seleucus seized Babylonia (p. 52), and 129, when the losses following the death of Antiochus VII left the dynasty rulers over a small area in northern Syria. By 303 the far east was added to Seleucus' dominions (but India was lost), and in the next twenty years he and his successor, Antiochus I, acquired most of Syria, Mesopotamia and Asia Minor. But from the middle of the third century Bactria broke away and Parthian power grew, with the result that everything east of a line from the eastern end of the Caspian Sea to the mouth of the Persian Gulf was lost. Nor did the eastern campaigns of Antiochus III between 210 and 205, which made a deep impression in Greek lands (and led him to take the title of 'the Great'), have any lasting effect in the far east, though they reasserted Seleucid power in Media.

In Asia Minor Seleucid power was seriously shaken when Seleucus II (246–226) became involved in war with his brother Antiochus Hierax, whom he had put in charge at Sardes, and Hierax called on the help of the Galatians (see p. 59) with disastrous results. The chaotic conditions which ensued were exploited by Attalus I, who had inherited the principality of Pergamum from his uncle Philetaerus, a eunuch, half-Paphlagonian, who had made himself independent in the reign of

Antiochus I. Attalus achieved great prestige from his defeat of the Galatians and in the second century, after some vicissitudes, the Attalids, largely through their early alliance with Rome, became a major force in Asia Minor, profiting from the weakened position of the Seleucids. For after seizing Coele-Syria in 200 Antiochus III in 188 lost most of Asia Minor, after which Seleucid power was gradually whittled away, not least through the Jewish rising under the Maccabees (see pp. 224–6). It can indeed be argued that the height of Seleucid power came under its founder, Seleucus I.

The second characteristic of this kingdom is the variety of its peoples and cultures. Babylonia possessed an ancient civilization comparable to that of Egypt but there was little in common between the Greek cities of western Asia Minor and the Iranian peoples of the eastern satrapies, or between the Arabs of southern Palestine and the new foundations in Bactria. Any unity which the Seleucid realm might possess the king had to impose on it with the aid of the bureaucracy and the army. Antioch-on-the-Orontes, in northern Syria, was nominally the capital, corresponding to Alexandria. But Sardes-on-the-Hermus in Lydia and Seleuceia-on-the-Tigris supplemented Antioch as important administrative centres sharing the responsibility for this vast and sprawling kingdom. In particular the governor in Seleuceia had also to keep an eye on the upper satrapies of Media, Susiana, Parthia and areas still further east, so long as they were still under Seleucid control.

Like the Ptolemies the Seleucids regarded their possessions as spear-won territory. This principle was clearly enunciated by Antiochus III at a conference with the Romans at Lysimacheia in 196. Asked why he had crossed over into Thrace he replied, Polybius tells us,

> that he had crossed to Europe with his army for the purpose of recovering the Chersonese and the cities in Thrace, for he had a better title to the sovereignty of those places than anyone else. They originally formed part of Lysimachus' kingdom but when Seleucus went to war with that prince and

conquered him in the war, the whole of Lysimachus' kingdom came to Seleucus by right of conquest . . . At present he (Antiochus) was repossessing himself of those territories by right as well as by might (xviii, 50, 3–6).

Like Ptolemy and other hellenistic kings, the Seleucids ruled with the help of their Friends, and a Greco-Macedonian elite quite separate from the native populations whom they governed. Analysis of the composition of this ruling class reveals the fact that Syrians, Jews, Persians and other Iranians are completely excluded for about two generations, and even afterwards, as we saw (p. 65), they never amount to more than 2·5% of the whole – a figure based on a sample of several hundred names (cf. Habicht, *Vierteljahrschrift* (1958), pp. 5 ff.). The few who do appear are mainly commanders of bodies of native troops. One exception who virtually proves the rule is Hannibal, the exiled Carthaginian leader, who was a member of Antiochus III's war-council during the war with Rome but his position was anomalous and relations did not run smoothly.

The exclusive use of Greeks and Macedonians indicates very clearly Seleucus' idea of how he hoped to bring cohesion to his heterogeneous dominions. In rejecting the Persians as partners in rule he was probably going along with the general sentiments of his Friends and his soldiers. Alexander's policy of joint authority (p.36) had never been popular with his army. The later Seleucids grew more exclusive. Antiochus I was Seleucus' son by his Bactrian wife Apama, but no later dynastic marriages were made with Iranians. Indeed, as Momigliano has remarked (*Alien Wisdom*, pp. 137 ff.), the Seleucid world showed a profound indifference to the Iranians, which may have contributed to the ease with which the Parthians annexed all Iran up to the Euphrates before the end of the second century.

Confronted with a variety of indigenous cultures, the Seleucids chose to rest their power on what was familiar – the civilization of Greece and Macedonia. For this immigrants must be attracted to and settled on the lands of Asia, and the Seleucids encouraged this by granting land and planting cities in an area where social traditions and the economic system were both quite different from those of Greece and equally of Macedonia. It is dangerous to generalize from circumstances which may vary considerably from area to area, but a number of inscriptions give us a glimpse of the conditions under which the peasants of Asia lived and of the grants of land which successive kings made to their Friends and other recipients. Some of these date to the third century when Antigonus held Asia Minor, but there is no reason to think that Seleucus brought any substantial change to the system he found Antigonus operating. Evidence from the kingdom of Pergamum can also be applied without great risk of error to the Seleucid territories.

An inscription from Sardes of uncertain date describes in detail an estate granted by Antigonus to one Mnesimachus:

> These are the items of which the estate consists: to wit, the villages named as follows: Tobalmoura, a village in the Sardian plain on the hill of Ilos, and as appurtenances thereto other villages also that of Tandos, as it is called, and Combdilipia; the dues payable by the said villages to the chiliarchy of Pytheus . . . are 50 gold staters a year. (Other villages and their dues are then listed.) Now from all the villages and the allotments (*kleroi*) and the dwelling-plots thereto appertaining, and from the *laoi* with all their households and belongings, and from the wine vessels and the dues rendered in money or in labour, and from the revenues of other kinds accruing from the villages, and still more besides these, when the division took place, Pytheus and Adrastus received as separate property a farmstead at Tbalmoura (*sic!*); and apart from the farmstead are the houses of the *laoi* and *oiketai*, and two gardens . . . and at Periasasostra dwelling plots . . . and gardens . . . as well as *oiketai* dwelling at that place (Buckler and Robinson, *Sardis*, vii, 1, no. 1).

This estate (*oikos*) contains five villages, several allotments (*kleroi*), a farmstead and various gardens, together with the peasants; there is also reference to slaves (*oiketai*), probably supervisors. But what are the dues mentioned in this inscription, evidently as evidence for the value of the estate? The usual view is that they represent the payment which Mnesimachus, the grantee, would have to make to the government (through several chiliarchs, since the estate is in separate parts coming under their several jurisdictions); he would have to extract these sums (and as much more as he could) from the tenants, that is, the occupants of the *kleroi* and the *laoi* (peasants) living in the villages. But it has been argued by the French scholar P. Briant (*Actes du Colloque*, 1971, pp. 93–133) that the *laoi* continued to pay their dues directly to the chiliarchs, who handed them on to Mnesimachus. On this view the latter is the recipient, not of the land (with its people), but merely of the revenues derived from it; and the *laoi* remain royal peasants.

There are, to be sure, instances of royal peasants continuing to live in villages which have been assigned to individuals. An example occurs in an inscription recording three letters to Meleager, the governor (*strategos*) of Hellespontine Phrygia, from Antiochus I (*c*.275) about grants of land made to Aristodicides of Assus 'because as our Friend he has rendered services with all goodwill and enthusiasm'. The first of these letters contains an instruction to Meleager that:

> if the crown peasants of the region in which Petra lies wish to live in Petra for protection, we have ordered Aristodicides to let them do so (Welles, *R.C.*, no. 11, ll. 22–5).

But this letter merely indicates that *laoi* living on land near Petra which remained in the king's hands after Petra was transferred to Aristodicides normally resided in that place and were to continue to do so. It tells us nothing of the status of the *laoi* living on the land actually assigned to Aristodicides and it therefore does not help us with the situation of the *laoi* on Mnesimachus' estate.

A certain amount of information about the status of *laoi* in Asia Minor and Palestine is furnished by inscriptions; evidence is lacking for areas further east. They lived in villages, perhaps under a *komarch* (though this position is attested only for the early-fourth century, in Xenophon, and later in Roman times). If, as has been plausibly suggested, the so-called 'satrapic economy' sketched in ps.-Aristotle, *Oeconomica*, ii, 1 is based on that of Asia Minor in the early-third century, the *laoi* there paid a tithe, whereas in Coele-Syria they appear to have paid a fixed impost. One important inscription bearing on the position of the *laoi* is from the temple of Apollo at Didyma and contains a letter dated 254/3 from Antiochus II to Metrophanes, probably governor of the Hellespontine satrapy. In this Antiochus reports:

> We have sold to Laodice [his divorced wife] Pannu Kome and the manor house (*baris*) and the land belonging to the village, bounded by the land of Zelia and by that of Cyzicus and by the old road which used to run above Pannu Kome, but which has been ploughed up by the neighbouring farmers so that they might take the place for themselves – the present Pannu Kome was founded later – and any hamlets (*topoi*) there may be on this land, and the *laoi* who live there with their households and all their property, and with the income of the fifty-ninth year, at a price of thirty talents of silver – and likewise any people who, being *laoi*, have moved from this village to other *topoi* – on the terms that she will pay no taxes to the treasury and that she will have the right to join the land to any city she wishes (Welles, *R.C.*, no. 18, ll. 1–14).

This transaction, which was very favourable to Laodice and probably represents a divorce settlement, clearly included the *laoi*, who evidently went with the village, even if they had moved elsewhere. There is no suggestion that such removal was illegal, as in the cases of *anachoresis* encountered in Ptolemaic Egypt, but by moving they did not break the ties with their place of origin nor rid themselves of the obligations which that link carried with it. On the other hand, this inscription offers no support for the view that it was only the revenues that were transferred by the king for it opens unambiguously with the words 'we have sold to Laodice' and the *laoi* are included in the sale, not merely the taxes which they pay. On the whole therefore this inscription is against the view that Mnesimachus was not in possession of his estate, but only of the income from it.

Antiochus' letter to Metrophanes further informs us that Laodice may join her new estate to any city she wishes. There is a similar provision in Antiochus I's first letter to Meleager (see p. 127), which states that the land assigned to Aristodicides (the exact situation of the second piece is left to the decision of Meleager himself) is to be attached to the city territory of Ilium or Scepsis and a further letter, sent by Meleager to Ilium, indicates that the beneficiary opted for the former. Taken along with the letter concerning Laodice's estate this suggests that it was usual for recipients of estates to be required to attach them to cities. But it would be rash to deduce that *all* privately held land had necessarily to be attached to a city. An inscription found not far from Beth Shean (Scythopolis) in Israel shows Ptolemy, the first Seleucid governor of Coele-Syria and Phoenicia after its seizure by Antiochus III in 200, owning several villages, 'some as private property, some on hereditary tenure and some which you (i.e. Antiochus III) ordered to be assigned to me' (Y.H. Landau, *Israeli Exploration Journal* (1966), pp. 54–70). There is no suggestion in the text of the inscription that any of these villages was attached to the territory of any city, e.g. Scythopolis. It is of course possible that conditions in Palestine were different from those in Asia Minor. Whether, when an estate was attached to a city (as in the case of Laodice's estate or of that granted to Aristodicides), the attachment effected any change in the juridical status of the *laoi* is unknown. A great variety of patterns and statuses is apparent in inscriptions and no doubt over decades many villages gradually acquired a corporate existence. A recently published inscription shows the *laoi* of two villages meeting in an assembly and passing a decree (in 267); this is merely one of many possible forms of development which might, as M. Woerrle, who published this inscription (*Chiron*, 5 (1975), pp. 58–87), observes, eventually end in the foundation of a city.

In addition to grants of land to individuals there is also evidence of grants to temples. There were many ancient temple states in Asia Minor, with lands, temple *laoi*, a hereditary high priest, and often eunuchs and temple prostitutes. Book xii of Strabo gives a list of the more important with their tabus and main characteristics. An inscription from Icarus (the island of Failaka off Kuwait at the head of the Persian Gulf), which contained a temple of Artemis (probably really a semitic goddess), shows the king carrying out a synoecism, moving the temple and generally treating the temple land as if it were his own (*SEG*, xx (1964), 411). But on other occasions royal land was transferred to a temple. Thus an inscription from Roman imperial times on the north gate of the precinct of Zeus (Ba'al) of Baetocaece near Apamea in northern Syria includes a letter from an Antiochus (which one remains uncertain) assigning the village of Baetocaece, which had formerly belonged to a certain Demetrius (probably a Macedonian), to the temple 'with all its property and possessions', a phrase which probably includes the *laoi* (Welles, *R.C.*, no. 70). Whether this land, including the village, had earlier belonged to the temple (that is the view of the German scholar H. Kreissig) and had been granted to Demetrius, we do not know; if so, presumably since Demetrius' death it had reverted to the crown. It appears now to have been ceded with full possession to the temple. There is thus some ambiguity concerning the ultimate ownership of temple land but it seems likely that, as in Egypt (see p. 128), the rights of the temples grew stronger with the passing of time.

II

The appearance of a 'phalanx of Macedonians' 16,000 strong at the battle of Magnesia in 189 (Appian, *Syriace* 32, 1) implies the presence in the Seleucid kingdom of regular 'Macedonian' troops – though whether they were all Macedonians of ethnic origin we cannot be sure. The march past by at least 20,000 'Macedonians' in the great pageant staged at Daphne in 166 by Antiochus IV (Polybius, xxx, 25, 5) furnishes less convincing evidence, for on such an occasion numbers could have been made up with oriental troops unsuitable for placing in the battle line.

The likelihood is that these Macedonians were established on the land in military settlements known as *katoikiai*. Some may indeed have been settled individually like the Egyptian cleruchs and the *kleroi* on the lands granted to Mnesimachus (p. 126) may have been of this character; if so, the king had evidently retained ownership, since they were included in Mnesimachus' estate. Cleruchic settlements are found in the kingdom of Pergamum; a fragmentary inscription (Welles, *R.C.*, no. 51) of uncertain date is concerned with the size and hereditability of *kleroi*, and it seems likely that the soldiers granted them were often grouped in settlements called *katoikiai* as under the Seleucids. A group of three documents from Smyrna record complicated negotiations with Magnesia-by-Sipylus which ended in the granting of Smyrniote citizenship first to Seleucid *katoikoi* (probably simply soldiers in this case) stationed in Magnesia and in the open outside the city and subsequently the extension of the agreement to take in a group of *katoikoi*, including a troop of Persians, who were formerly stationed in Magnesia, but are now in a fort nearby called Palaemagnesia (*OGIS*, 229). The third of these documents lays down, in relation to the group in Palaemagnesia, that:

> it was decreed that they should be citizens and possess all the rights the other citizens possess; the two allotments (*kleroi*) which the saviour god Antiochus (I) granted them and about which Alexander (probably a Friend of Antiochus I) wrote, shall remain free of tithe, and should the land which those who were formerly *katoikoi* in Magnesia possess be included within the boundaries of our city, the three allotments shall remain free and their present tax immunity shall continue (ll. 100–2).

The *katoikoi* in Palaemagnesia are occupiers of *kleroi* which had clearly been assigned to them as a group, not as individuals, and the presence of Persians indicates that such settlements were not restricted to Greeks and Macedonians. Indeed, as time passed that would have been impracticable. In a letter to his commander

Zeuxis, quoted by Josephus, Antiochus III writes:

> Learning of sedition in Lydia and Phrygia, I thought the
> matter required great care; and having taken counsel with my
> Friends on the necessary course of action, I decided to move
> 2000 Jewish families with their effects from Mesopotamia and
> Babylonia to the forts and most essential places (Josephus,
> *Antiquities of Judaea*, xii, 3, 4).

He goes on to give instructions for allotting plots of land to build
houses and for cultivation, the granting of seedcorn and a ten-
years immunity on the crops grown. Whether this letter is
genuine or not, it provides a convincing account of how a military
katoikia might be set up.

   Such military settlements fulfilled a threefold purpose. Unlike
Alexander's settlements they consisted mainly not of veterans,
but of active soldiers. They therefore furnished a military reserve
of trained men on whom the king could draw in the event of war.
In peacetime their members acted as garrisons maintaining order
and defending vulnerable points against invasion and they also
pursued their civilian occupations, primarily in the cultivation of
the land. However, not every Anatolian *katoikia* is a military
settlement. There are records of several dozen civilian *katoikiai*,
many if not most of whose members were drawn from the
indigenous population and were no doubt liable, if the need
arose, for call-up like the military *katoikoi*. Unfortunately in
many cases it is not possible to be certain with which sort of
katoikia one is dealing. Identifiable military *katoikiai* are found
mainly in western Asia Minor in both Seleucid and Pergamene
territory. The Attalids settled various mercenaries in this way,
including Gauls. Thus in 218 Attalus, alarmed at the un-
collaborative behaviour of his Galatian mercenaries,

> promised for the present to take them back to the place where
> they had crossed (sc. from Europe) and give them suitable
> land for a *katoikia* and afterwards to attend as far as he could
> to all reasonable requests they made (Polybius, v, 78, 5).

In organization, especially if the *kleroi* were held in common, the *katoikiai* were very like the villages, which constitute the main units of social structure and production throughout the Anatolian countryside. Villages were of course inhabited by peasants, *laoi*, paying taxes in kind to the landowner; normally they were tied to the village, but the possibility that they might be allowed to move has been discussed above (p. 128). Some villages stood on city land, in which case there was the possibility (but not any certainty) of an improvement in the status of the inhabitants (as happened to the *katoikoi* in Palaemagnesia). Others further east formed the nucleus of a temple estate or were situated on land belonging to a temple. The *katoikiai* approximate in many ways to the village but, especially when they are made up of Macedonians, could themselves hope to be promoted to the status of a city. If this occurred, it brought with it a new administrative structure and many special advantages which we must now consider.

III

The foundation of a chain of new Greek cities extending over the whole of their dominions to Bactria and Sogdiana in the far east is the most striking accomplishment of the Seleucid dynasty. Unlike the old cities of Greece and western Asia Minor they were commonly laid out on a rectilinear grid-pattern, taking account of course of the topography of the site; a good example is Priene, refounded about 350 and laid out along those lines. The more successful of the new cities offered too a high level of amenity. A long inscription from the Attalid capital, Pergamum, details the duties of the *astynomoi*, magistrates responsible for the condition of the streets, the water supply and the public lavatories, with details of fines for contraventions of the regulations (*OGIS*, 483).

The greater part of this colonizing work was carried out during the reign of the first three Seleucid kings, Seleucus I (312–281), Antiochus I (281–261) and Antiochus II (261–246). Some foundations in the east belong to Antiochus IV (175–164), though fewer than has often been supposed. In fact most of the details of the colonization are unrecorded. The importance of the Greek and especially of the Macedonian element can however be deduced from the names of the settlements, many of which are taken from regions and cities of Macedonia and northern Greece. Thus in northern Syria, which Seleucus I chose to make the heartland of his kingdom, we find regions named Pieria and Cyrrhestice, together with cities called Europus, Beroea, Edessa, Cyrrhus, Perinthus, Maronea, Apollonia; in Palestine Dium and Pella; in Mesopotamia Anthemusia, Ichnae and Aenus; in Media Europus (an alternative name to Rhagae); in Persis Tanagra and Maitona (if that is in fact the same as Methone); in Bactria or Sogdiana Thera, Rhoetea and perhaps Argos; and on the Arabian shore of the Persian gulf Arethusa, Larissa and Chalcis. The existence of these names has sometimes been taken to show that the Seleucids deliberately sought to create a 'Macedonian' kingdom but that conclusion is hazardous. Many of these names may be the spontaneous nomenclature of soldiers anxious to remind themselves of home, like countless place-names in North America. The purpose of the dynasty can be more clearly seen in the dynastic names attached to the more important foundations and to many others besides.

First there were the four great cities of northern Syria: Antioch, the capital, which continued to grow down to the time of Antiochus IV and was famous for its park at Daphne; Seleuceia-in-Pieria, the harbour; Laodiceia-on-Sea; and Apamea on the middle Orontes, a great military centre where the Seleucids kept their cavalry and elephants. Seleucus' earliest foundation was in Babylonia at Seleuceia-on-the-Tigris, which served as a centre of administration and of Greco-Macedonian influence throughout Mesopotamia. In addition to these major foundations a host of dynastic names taken from those of Seleucid kings and their queens are recorded from all parts of the kingdom. In Syria for instance there is Laodiceia-on-Lebanon and Antioch-in-Cyrrhestice; an Apamea controlled the Euphrates crossing at Zeugma, and in northern Mesopotamia there was Antioch-Nisibis in Mygdonia and Antioch-Edessa (its native name was Orrhoe) in the bend of the Euphrates. Further east many ancient cities were given a Greek look and a dynastic name. Susa was named Seleuceia-on-the-Eulaeus, and later under Antiochus IV Babylon was refounded (as we know from an inscription of 167/6 (*OGIS*, 253) from that city, which calls the king 'saviour of Asia and founder and benefactor of the city'). There were many other dynastic foundations, some of them now mere names: Seleuceia-in-Susiana, Seleuceia-on-the-Erythraean Sea (i.e. the Persian Gulf), Apamea-in-Mesene, Antioch-in-Persis (mod. Bushire) and many Alexandrias refounded as Antiochs. Asia Minor had Laodiceia-the-Burnt, Apamea-Celaenae, Seleuceia-on-the-Calycadnus, Laodiceia-on-the-Lycus and many more. Taken together they indicate very clearly the determination of the Seleucids to emphasize the personal character of their rule and the role of the king and his family as the unifying influence in the kingdom.

Whether they bore Macedonian or dynastic names, these cities varied tremendously in character. We must distinguish between the ancient Greek cities of the Aegean coast, such as Smyrna and Ephesus, new foundations like Seleuceia-on-the-Tigris, native cities which acquire dynastic names, like Jerusalem renamed Antioch (2 Macc., iv, 9: see on this pp. 224–6), and native cities which are fully hellenized to become administrative centres with functionaries and a garrison. The extent of Greek or Macedonian influence in the original foundation varied very much from city to city. A second-century inscription (Roussel, *Syria* (1942–3), pp. 21–32) shows that there were magistrates at Laodiceia-on-Sea called *Peliganes*. The word *Peligan* connects with a word found in Epirus and Macedonia meaning 'old' (Strabo, viii, 329, fg. 2),and this suggests a strong Balkan element in the original population of Laodiceia. The same conclusions may be drawn for Seleuceia-on-Tigris since the word *Adeiganes*, which occurs in a passage in Polybius (v, 54, 10) naming the magistrates of that city, can now be safely emended to read *Peliganes*. Both cities however are likely to have contained orientals too, as did Apamea in Asia Minor; for, according to Strabo, 'it was from Celaenae that Antiochus (I) Soter made the inhabitants move to the present Apamea, the city which he named after his mother Apama' (xii, 8, 15). Some cities were founded or reinforced by colonists sent at the king's request from one of the old Greek cities; an example is Antioch-in-Persis which received colonists from Magnesia-on-the-Maeander (see p. 62). But, as we have seen, Smyrna gave its citizenship to a body of Persian troops from Palaemagnesia (p. 131) and Stratonicea in Caria contained some Carian demes.

Being a city implied possessing the forms of organization normal in Greece – tribes, a council, magistrates, a territory (usually divided into demes), a code of law and some provision for finances. A wall was generally necessary for defence, and an assembly was usual, if not universally found. The economic basis of life was generally agriculture, whether practised by the citizens or by a subjected peasantry, but there seems to have been some increase in trade and industry in the eastern cities, though mainly in quantity rather than anything fundamentally new in character (see Chapter 9). Outwardly the cities of which we have clear records behave as if they were sovereign states, passing decrees and exchanging envoys with other states and cities, and it has often been argued that at any rate the older cities of the Aegean seaboard were in fact genuinely independent. This, however, is a dubious assumption. Alexander, as we saw (pp.39–40), could declare Priene 'free and autonomous' yet interfere extensively in her affairs and collect 'contributions' from her; and Antigonus I at Tyre in 314 (p. 51) declared all Greeks 'free, ungarrisoned and autonomous' and later in his letter to Scepsis claimed the securing of this as his main concern at the time of the peace of 311 (p. 53), yet experienced no embarrassment in ignoring the declaration whenever it suited his purpose. For example, he intervened at Cyme to set up a court (*OGIS*, 7) and he sent detailed instructions to Teos (*c.* 303) regulating a synoecism between Teos and Lebedus (Welles, *R.C.*, nos. 3–4) which, as we can see from references to delay in the letters, was unpopular in both cities. Already earlier, we learn from Strabo 'the Scepsians were incorporated in Alexandria (Troas) by Antigonus; then they were released by Lysimachus and went back to their own home' (xiii, 1, 52). Probably Lysimachus intervened similarly to upset the Teos-Lebedus synoecism.

Arbitrary acts of this kind did not, however, prevent Antigonus and the Seleucids after him from repeating the claim to be liberators. It was a claim to which the Greeks themselves not unnaturally made repeated appeals. Thus according to a decree passed some time after March 268, the Ionian League sent envoys to Antiochus I, who were to exhort him 'to exert every care for the Ionian cities so that they may for the future be free and democratic and firmly governed according to their ancestral laws' (*OGIS*, 222, ll. 15–16). In an inscription from the temple of Apollo at Didyma (*OGIS*, 226) there is a reference to Hippomachus of Athens 'who brought back freedom and democracy from King Antiochus (II) the God' and in the inscription dealing with the agreement between Smyrna and the *katoikoi* at Palaemagnesia (p. 131) it is stated that Seleucus II 'had assured autonomy and democracy for the people (sc. of Smyrna)' (though it seems fairly certain that the complicated negotiations with Magnesia and Palaemagnesia had been undertaken on his orders). The agreement made with the various *katoikoi* also involves oaths to maintain 'the autonomy and democracy' of Smyrna (*OGIS*, 229, ll. 67 ff.). Likewise a decree of Delphi (*OGIS*, 228) praises Seleucus II for declaring Smyrna to be 'holy and free from reprisals' (*asylos*) and 'free and tribute-free'. A decree of the Delphic Amphictyony from the end of the third century (*OGIS*, 234) praises Antiochus III 'for preserving democracy and peace for the people of Antioch' (sc. of the Chrysaorians, a new name for Carian Alabanda). Examples could be multiplied with ease. The difficulty is to determine what is meant by 'freedom', 'democracy', and 'autonomy' in these various contexts, for to some extent the words are interchangeable, so that 'democracy' in some decrees appears to be the equivalent of 'free'. But 'freedom' is something very much less than it would have been in the fifth or fourth century. In his letter to Meleager (see p. 127) Antiochus I refers to 'cities in his territory and alliance', thus implying a distinction between these and other cities. But cities 'within the alliance' – the term 'alliance' was also favoured by the Attalids – had to bend their policy to fit that of the king and freedom which was 'conceded' could scarcely be regarded as genuine freedom. Thus Antiochus II, writing to Erythrae (*c.* 260), remarks:

> We praise you for being grateful in all things – for you seem generally to pursue this as your policy . . . Since Tharsynon and Pythes and Bottas (sc. the envoys) have shown that under Alexander and Antigonus your city was autonomous and tax free . . . we grant you exemption not only from other taxes but even from contributions towards the Galatian fund (i.e. a special tax to meet the cost of war or defence against the Galatians) (Welles, *R.C.*, no. 15, ll. 14–15, 21–3, 27–8).

Grants of freedom from taxes and garrisons are something separate from grants of 'freedom and autonomy' or 'autonomy and democracy' but in the absence of the former it becomes difficult to see what the latter can have meant. For in fact the payment of royal tribute was the normal lot of all cities not specifically exempt. It later provided a precedent for the Romans when they stepped into the shoes of the hellenistic kings. One notable right, indicative in the past of genuine city freedom, is missing – the right to coin – and when under Antiochus IV (and in Macedonia under Philip V) a municipal coinage emerges, it is something new, suggesting a fresh attitude towards the cities. But, as E. Will remarks (*Le Monde grec et l'orient*, Vol. II, p. 458), though there are hints of a move towards a new definition of the relations between the Seleucids and the cities, based on royal liberalism and mutual goodwill, time ran out before this could take effect. Basically, throughout the history of the Seleucid dynasty – and of the other royal houses no less – relations with the cities were based on relative power rather than on law.

It goes without saying that the new cities of the east were never independent and it is only in 109, when the Seleucid dynasty was reduced desperately in power and territory, that our sole surviving example of a grant of freedom to one of these cities occurs, in a letter from Antiochus VIII or IX to Ptolemy IX concerning Seleuceia-in-Pieria. The relevant clause reads:

> The people of Seleuceia-in-Pieria, the city holy and *asylos*, from of old supported our father and throughout maintained firmly their goodwill towards him . . . Now, being anxious to reward them fittingly with the first [and greatest] benefaction, we have decided that they be for all time free (Welles, *R.C.*, no. 71, ll. 4–6, 11–13).

(The title 'holy and *asylos*' appears on Seleuceian coins of the late-second century.) Fundamentally, however, the new cities and the old were in the same situation; they were merely exposed to different degrees of subjection. At the best a city was without garrisons and tax-free; at the worst it had a royal garrison in its citadel and a royal governor (*epistates*), whose duties were primarily military, but often included judicial powers (as in the case of Cleon, the Attalid representative on Aegina: *OGIS*, 329), and indeed other powers according to the place and circumstances. How the cities responded to these burdens and pressures will be considered in Chapter 8.

IV

The new cities were the basis and instrument of hellenization, the spread of Greek culture, institutions and ideas and the Greek language as far as Afghanistan and India. As we have seen, they varied greatly in origin (the genuine foundations belonging mainly to the early part of the third century before the flow of men from Macedonia and Greece began to run dry) and they varied vastly in size. According to Polybius (v, 70, 5) Antiochus III felt confident after taking possession of Philoteria (on Lake Galilee) and Scythopolis (Beth Shean) 'as the territory subject to them was easily capable of supplying his whole army with food'. Others, like Aspendus, were quite small. Nor were they spread evenly over the Seleucid territories. Asia Minor and northern Syria received the bulk of the colonists, but further east they are also to be found in large numbers, especially in Bactria, so that there hellenism lasted well beyond the date when the Seleucids lost political control about the middle of the third century.

The political history of the Greeks in Bactria and India is an obscure story resting on (for the most part) second-rate sources and some remarkable coins (which have been used to support some over-bold hypotheses). It seems, however, that a little before 250 Diodotus, probably the satrap of Bactria, revolted from the Seleucids in order to set up an independent kingdom, and that a little later the Parthians seized the area east of the Caspian Sea and, when Seleucus II tried to recover the province, defeated him and asserted the independence of Parthia. In Bactria, Diodotus and his homonymous son reigned for a considerable time but when Antiochus III invaded the far east he found a certain Euthydemus on the Bactrian throne; he had probably killed and supplanted Diodotus II. Euthydemus and his son Demetrius extended and consolidated Bactrian territory against the Parthians and later kings crossed the Hindu Kush and set up a Greek kingdom in Paropamisadae and Gandhara. There were Greeks ruling in India until well into the first century. Eventually this interesting outpost of the hellenistic world was overthrown by three barbarian peoples—the Sacas (the Sai of certain Chinese records), the Scytho-Parthians (or Pahlava) and the Yuëh-Chih. The Aśoka inscriptions and the excavations at Ai Khanum (see pp.60–2) go to show that there is still much to be learnt about these eastern Greeks under the soil of central Asia and northern India. But though they clearly maintained their hellenic culture, they were cut off before long from the main body of the hellenistic world, which, as we have seen (pp. 66–7), therefore became more Mediterranean based. It was in the hellenizing of the Syrian coastline and much of Asia Minor that the great achievement of the Seleucid kingdom lay, an achievement that was to endure until the coming of Islam, and in some areas still longer.

8 Inter-city Contacts and Federal States

Most Greeks in the hellenistic world still lived in cities. But the city itself had changed and the new monarchies often made its role precarious. The defeat of Athens and Thebes by Macedonia at Chaeronea (338) had demonstrated the weakness of the city-state when it was faced with a powerful professional army and a capable monarch. The resources of the monarchies now dwarfed those of the cities; only an exceptional city like Rhodes on its island could hope to follow an independent policy and even Rhodes was closely linked with the Ptolemies. For most cities political independence was circumscribed by the power of neighbouring kings. The much-prized right to settle disputes with one's rival by going to war was less attractive when it might bring down the intervention of a king, with loss of face or, worse, of freedom. Besides the threat which the kingdoms constituted, life was also at the mercy of a good deal of more or less institutionalized violence in the form of reprisals for real or alleged injuries, brigandage and piracy. Hence increasingly cities sought to negotiate agreements with each other and with the kings in order to secure protection against these varied forms of violence. These agreements were an inroad on freedom but the alternative was worse. The kings were open to some forms of pressure. For example, declarations of freedom to cities within their domains made as a political gesture (see pp. 137 ff.) could often be exploited to bring genuine advantages. The kind of political activity to which this led was very different from that of the days when the Greek *polis* was really independent. But the Greeks adjusted to it and were not slow to find new fields in which to exercise their patriotism and ambition.

Thus for many reasons, ranging from the search for greater security to the creation of new civic values, the cities of the hellenistic world were compelled to change the pattern of public life. More time was now spent on activities which were not indeed new – individually they can mostly be paralleled from the fifth and fourth centuries – but which acquired an increased significance in the new atmosphere. More and more of men's political energies now went into formalized exchanges of various sorts, which enabled rich citizens to spend their money and their effort on the city's behalf as self-financing envoys or as generous benefactors. An outstanding example of such a patron is Protogenes, the list of whose gifts to the impoverished city of Olbia, at the mouth of the Hypanis (Bug) in southern Russia, towards the end of the third century, occupies nearly 200 lines of an inscription now in Leningrad (*Syll.*, 495). But many other cities were in the debt of local benefactors who lent money to pay for corn in time of famine, endowed charities, shouldered the cost of public buildings and exercised their influence with kings on their city's behalf. This is true both of the new foundations within the monarchies and of the old 'independent' city-states. All alike now devoted much time and effort to sending and hearing embassies about religious festivals, to securing the recognition of immunity from reprisals (*asylia*), to requesting or granting privileges and citizenship, to solving judicial problems and to settling boundary disputes.

Of the decrees passed in response to all this activity, some were purely formal, but many also dealt with real and important issues like ownership of land and the demarcation of frontiers. In order to publicize the decision this was usually engraved on a pillar either in the city in question or at some public sanctuary such as Olympia or Delphi, and from surviving inscriptions together with remarks by authors, it is possible to build up a picture of the society in which these multifarious exchanges played so vital a part.

I

To avoid unnecessary wars and to mitigate the hardships if war came was a major object of city policy, and to achieve this cities would frequently call in the help of kings – or indeed have it imposed, since a king might well regard a war which he had not planned as either embarrassing or ill-timed. Inscriptions reveal a substantial growth in the use made of arbitration, carried out by either an invited third party or one of the kings. Most disputes continued to be about the ownership of land lying on the border between two cities. A typical example is the quarrel between Corinth and Epidaurus, both members of the Achaean League (see p. 154), over the ownership of the promontory of C. Spiraeum on the Saronic Gulf. Some time between 242/1 and 238/7 the adjudication of this matter was delegated to another constituent member, Megara, which lay across the gulf opposite the disputed territory, and its findings were set up in the Asclepieum at Epidaurus, since the Epidaurians, in whose favour the decision went, had a clear interest in publicizing this. The inscription reads:

> The Megarians decided as follows for the Epidaurians and Corinthians concerning the land which they contested and concerning Sellanys and Spiraeus, sending a tribunal of 151 men in accordance with the decree of the Achaeans. When the judges reached the territory in question and adjudged the land to belong to the Epidaurians, the Corinthians challenged the delimitation, whereupon the Megarians again sent from among their judges 31 men to define the boundaries in accordance with the decree of the Achaeans; and these men came to the territory and delimited it thus (there follows a full delineation of the boundary) (*Syll.*, 471).

Such decisions did not always prove lasting, where land was scarce or feelings were strong. For example, in about 140 the Milesians acted in a dispute between Messene and Sparta over the so-called Denthaliate territory on the western slopes of

Mount Taygetus (*Syll.*, 683). From other evidence we know that this decision turned out to be merely one chapter in a long and contentious quarrel which lasted at least from 338, when Philip II had assigned the land to the Messenians, to a similar decision by the Roman emperor Tiberius in AD 25 (Tacitus, *Annals*, iv, 43). In the arbitration of 140 'a tribunal was formed from the whole people (sc. of Miletus), the largest allowed by law, consisting of 600 judges' (*Syll.*, 683, ll. 68–9). The large numbers involved in this and in the Megarian arbitration, with its 151 judges, were presumably intended to minimize the risk of corruption. But there was no fixed rule about numbers, for in another arbitration involving Epidaurus and, this time, Hermione, the Milesian judges, who appear to have been in the Peloponnese on other business, were only six in all (Moretti, i, no. 43).

It was not only to settle disputes beween one city and another that foreign judges were called in. Many cities, for a mixture of reasons, managed to get their internal legal affairs into a state of confusion, so that there was often a backlog of unheard cases in the courts. Polybius (xx, 6, 1) reports that in 192 'public affairs in Boeotia had fallen into such a state of disorder that for nearly twenty-five years justice, both civil and criminal, had ceased to be administered there'. Often, in such circumstances (though not in this instance), a friendly city, or one or two cities acting in conjunction, would be invited to send a small commission to decide outstanding cases. Where such cities fell within the dominions or control of a king he would normally be associated with the invitation. Thus a panel of Coan judges was sent to settle cases at Naxos 'in accordance with the instructions of King Ptolemy (I)'. They included Bacchon, the *nesiarch* (chief officer) of the Island League, to which both Cos and Naxos will have belonged (*OGIS*, 43). Such commissions presuppose the availability of men with a wide legal knowledge, able to master and apply the law of cities not their own; perhaps too they suggest a tendency of the legal systems of different cities to approximate closely to each other. For, although often these men simply applied conciliation, there were many occasions requiring a judicial decision based on equity or strict law and the activity of such commissions helped to bring together the legal systems of various cities and to create something like a common Greek law. Certainly, though each city had its own code, Theophrastus in his book *On Contracts* was able to construct a theory of sales of general application. On the other hand, marked differences in such matters as laws of inheritance or sanctions against debtors existed between one city and another. Difficulties therefore arose but some cities such as Rhodes and Priene acquired reputations for the skill and impartialityof their arbitrators, who were in great demand.

Acts of arbitration diminished the likelihood of war breaking out between neighbours. But war was not the only disturbance to which cities were liable. A practice which could disrupt peaceful intercourse and prove disastrous to innocent citizens was the exercising of *syle* – the legitimate use of reprisals by city A against any citizens of city B, a member of which was adjudged to have given rise to a grievance. In the hellenistic period there is a notable growth in the number of successful attempts by cities to have themselves declared *asylos* – immune from the exercise of *syle,* reprisals. This is really an extension of a privilege earlier accorded to temples, and it is often solicited after a god or goddess has made an appearance (*epiphaneia*) or has delivered an oracle indicating his, or her, wish that the territory of the city (and not merely the temple) shall be declared 'holy and immune from *syle*' (*hiera* and *asylos*). If a king's support could be obtained, so much the better. This happens in one of the earliest requests for city immunity, that of Smyrna, in which, probably in 246, Seleucus II 'wrote to the kings, dynasts, cities and peoples urging them to recognize the temple of Stratonicis Aphrodite as immune (*asylos*) and our city as holy and *asylos*' (*OGIS*, 229, ll. 11–12). A newly discovered inscription shows that attempts by Teos in 204/3 to have immunity accorded also owed a great deal to the support of Antiochus III, who after taking over the city from Pergamum, initiated the move,

coming into the assembly and personally declaring our city

and territory holy, *asylos* and free from tribute and promising that we should be freed by him from the other contributions which we had made to King Attalus (P Herrmann, *Anadolu* (1967), p. 13, ll. 17–20).

This Tean appeal for immunity from reprisals, *asylia*, was directed especially to the cities of Aetolia and Crete, which were renowned for their practice of piracy and so a manifest danger to any maritime city. There can be little doubt that requests for *asylia* made in Crete and Aetolia were concerned not so much with restraining the exercise of legitimate *syle* but rather with the limitation of piracy and later in the second century (probably around 160) a second series of Tean inscriptions shows the Teans once again approaching Cretan cities to request the 'renewal' of the grants of *asylia* (which had evidently become a dead letter) and to secure some kind of procedure through grants of *isopoliteia*, nominally a potential exchange of citizenship but in this instance a means of obtaining access to the courts in the Cretan city, where piratical outrages might (it was hoped) be brought to book (on *isopoliteia* see further pp. 150ff.).

The Tean request of 204/3 was unusual in not being associated with any divine epiphany or oracle or with the *asylia* of a temple. But all these feature in one of the best recorded attempts to secure immunity from attack, that made in 207/6 by the city of Magnesia-on-Maeander, on its own behalf and on that of its temple of Artemis Leucophryene. A fragment of a sacred history of Magnesia recorded on the stone wall of a portico in the city describes epiphanies of both Apollo and Artemis Leucophryene, the latter in 221/0. Apollo was thereupon consulted at Delphi, where an oracle declared 'that it was better and more desirable that those reverencing Pythian Apollo and Artemis Leucophryene should regard the city and the territory of Magnesia-on-Maeander as holy and *asylos*' (*Syll.*, 557, ll. 7–10). Fourteen years later – the delay can be explained in various ways – in 207/6 we know from a series of inscriptions that in response to Magnesian embassies many cities, peoples and kings granted this recognition together with that of the games held in Artemis' honour every fourth year. These were declared to be equal in rank with the Pythian games at Delphi and to be *stephanitai* or 'crowned', i.e. games at which as an indication of their prestige the victors received wreaths, sometimes instead of, but in this case as well as, cash prizes. Of the kings whose replies are preserved only Ptolemy IV, however, grants the requested *asylia*, Antiochus III, Philip V (almost certainly) and Attalus I making no reference to this. It certainly looks as if those kings were keeping open the option of annexing Magnesia, should a suitable occasion arise – in which case a previous grant of *asylia* would have been an embarrassment.

The festival of Artemis Leucophryene was only one of many which were set up at this time. Already in Chapter 4 we have glanced at some of those frequented by the *technitai* of Dionysus based on Teos and (pp. 71–2) at other festivals at which Onasiteles of Cedreae won prizes. Between Alexander's death and the Roman defeat of Antiochus III in 189 five smaller annual festivals, including that of Artemis Leucophryene, were converted into four-yearly celebrations with wreaths as prizes. In 248 the *technitai* of Dionysus centred on the Isthmus and Nemea recognized the *Museia* of Thespiae as a 'crowned' festival (*Syll.*, 457) and (as we know from the Athenian reply to the Thespian envoys) equal in rank to the Pythian games. In 276 the Aetolians had celebrated their victory over the Gauls who were attacking Delphi by establishing a Delphic festival called the *Soteria*. Probably in 246 they made this quadrennial and 'in the musical section equal to the Pythian games and in the athletic and equestrian sections equal to the Nemean games in its age-groups and prizes' (*Syll.*, 402, ll. 15–16, Chios; cf. *Syll.*, 408, ll. 16–18, Athens). The change in the form and prestige of this festival had the political purpose of registering throughout the Greek world the Aetolian control of the panhellenic shrine of Delphi. Festivals at Cos and Miletus were also similarly transformed. In such cases there was often an economic motive, for an enhanced festival would bring many visitors to its contests. Kings too valued the political advantage and prestige which came from setting up special festivals, a noteworthy example of royal activity being the

Ptolemaieia, inaugurated in 280/79 by Ptolemy II in honour of his father, who had died three years earlier. In a decree of the same year the Island League, controlled from Alexandria, recognized the new festival as equal in prestige to the Olympic games (*Syll.,* 390). Another royal festival of importance was the Pergamene *Nicephoria,* a 'crowned' festival with 'the musical section equal to the Pythian games, the athletic and equestrian sections equal to the Olympic games' (*Syll.,* 629, l. 9) and there were countless *Romaia* in honour of Rome set up from 189 onwards. These festivals offered competitors the chance to win glory for themselves and their cities, and by bringing large numbers of people together in a peaceful milieu they helped to break down the old exclusiveness of the city-state.

Another feature of hellenistic life which tended to blur the sharp lines between one community and another was the growing custom of making grants of citizenship, *proxenia* and *asylia* to individuals from other states; sometimes these grants were made to whole cities or peoples. An example already noted is the granting of *proxenia* at Lamia (p. 73) to Aristodama of Smyrna and her brother in recognition of her poetic displays. A *proxenos* was originally granted that status by another city and charged with the duty of looking after the interests of its citizens when they visited his. *Proxenia* was closely linked with the ancient institution of guest-friendship. It implied personal links and obligations and was usually hereditary. But already by the fourth century we find grants of *proxenia* being made in recognition of services rendered, as when, for example, in 386 the Athenians passed a decree for Phanocritus of Phanium and his descendants to the effect that

> whereas he informed the generals about the ships sailing past and, had the generals listened to him, the enemy triremes would have been captured, for these services he be granted *proxenia* and the status of benefactor (*Syll.,* 137)

a decree which can hardly have pleased the generals in question. Later, by the third century, grants of *proxenia* become more frequent and were often linked with other honours, including grants of citizenship, which strictly speaking were inconsistent with the original concept of *proxenos*. Thus the city of Ilium honours a doctor, Metrodorus of Amphipolis, for his services to King Antiochus (probably Antiochus I) after he had received a wound in the throat. He is declared *proxenos* and benefactor of Ilium, but in addition is granted 'citizenship, the right to acquire land in Ilium (a valuable concession) and access to the council and people first after the sacrifice' (*OGIS*, 220, ll. 14–19). An inscription of *c.* 266 from Histiaea in Euboea lists 31 *proxenoi* from various towns which are known to have had close trading relations with Histiaea (*Syll*, 492). It is unlikely that all these men were expected to fulfil the traditional duties of *proxenoi*; the grants will be marks of goodwill designed to facilitate relations in the future. From such large-scale concessions it is only a small step to declaring whole groups or communities *proxenoi*. Thus 266 mercenaries, many of them barbarian Mysians, serving in a body of troops sent by Attalus I of Pergamum, are granted *proxenia* by the Phocian town of Lilaea in 208, and at the same time *asylia*, citizenship and the status of benefactor (*Fouilles de Delphes*, iii, 4, 132–5). These men were of various nationalities but in the later part of the third century the Molossian community of the Aterargoi renews mutual friendship and *proxenia* with the Pergamioi and their descendants 'for all time' (*SEG*, xv (1957), 411). This grant establishes a close and lasting link between two neighbouring communities. In some cases *proxenia*, like *isopoliteia* (p. 146), had a practical use in giving its recipient access to the courts of the city conferring the right but increasingly *proxenia* grants were merely intended to honour the recipient and were associated with other specific privileges.

We have noted *asylia*, the status of benefactor, access to the council and the people, and the right to acquire land. Other similar associated grants are freedom from taxation (*ateleia*), the right to be taxed on the same basis as citizens (*isoteleia*), freedom to enter and leave the city and to import and export goods, legal privileges in the use of the courts, access to common land, the right to cut timber, a place of honour at the games, and dining rights in the town hall during visits. Grants of marriage rights are rare (but in practice intermarriage seems to have been fairly common without such grants). The total effect of all these privileges was to create in every city a large group of foreigners who enjoyed a variety of rights which they shared with citizens.

Among these we have noted citizenship and this clearly outweighed the rest. Many cities suffering from depopulation made use of such grants to replenish their own citizen bodies (see p. 167). Often the impetus came from a king. Thus Larissa in northern Thessaly, a city strategically placed in relation to the southern frontier of Macedonia, received two letters in 217 and 215 from Philip V, urging the adoption of new citizens. In the second of these Philip reveals his interest at that time in the Romans (against whom he was very soon to be fighting).

> It is a fine thing that as many as possible may share in the citizenship, so that the city is strong and the countryside is not, as at present, shamefully deserted. This I think no one of you would deny; and it is possible to observe others who similarly enrol citizens, including also the Romans, who admit to citizenship even slaves when they manumit them, and grant them a share in the offices; and in this way they have not only enlarged their own city, but have also sent out colonies to nearly seventy places (*Syll.*, 543).

The accuracy of Philip's information did not equal his interest: manumitted slaves were not allowed to hold office in Rome and the number of colonies is considerably exaggerated. A similar example of citizen-enrolment from about the same period, as we saw earlier (p. 68), comes from Dyme in Achaea, which enrolled fifty-two soldiers, probably mercenaries, as citizens.

In cases such as these citizenship was granted for internal reasons but many grants took the form of *isopoliteia*, which had a rather different purpose, since it involved the bestowal of a potential citizenship which became actual only if the recipient took up residence in the city making the grant. This kind of concession is clearly defined in a joint decree of the peoples of Temnus and Pergamum, dating from the time of Lysimachus or of Philetaerus, the ancestor of the Attalids, in the early-third century, which reads:

> Resolved by the people of Temnus and Pergamum . . . that the Temnites shall enjoy citizenship in Pergamum and the Pergamenes in Temnus, and they shall share all the rights shared by the other citizens and the Temnites shall have the right to own land and a dwelling in Pergamum and the Pergamenes in Temnus (*OGIS*, 265) – where however the 'right to vote' in the other city is a restoration of a lacuna in the text and is to be rejected: see Robert, *Opera minora selecta*, vol. I, pp. 204–9.

The details of such exchanges of citizenship were often spelt out at length. An inscription recording such an agreement between Miletus and Heraclea-by-Latmus, from about 180, amounts to over 125 longish lines (*Syll.*, 633).

Grants of *isopoliteia* are sometimes made to individuals and sometimes conferred by one state upon another, as when in 200 the Athenians, in gratitude for naval help, 'voted *isopoliteia* for all Rhodians' (Polybius, xvi, 26, 9). But we also find grants of *isopoliteia* accompanied by economic concessions, and the motive behind the grant seems often to have been commercial rather than political. In other cases, as we have seen (p. 146), *isopoliteia* could also be a means of allowing citizens of a city which has been accorded *asylia* access to the courts of the city making the grant, and this is true especially of grants by Cretan cities, since it is unlikely that many Greeks from elsewhere would wish to exchange their citizenship for that of a city in that troubled island.

A yet further stage in the uniting of cities comes when two communities are completely merged to form a single state, thus creating what is described as *sympoliteia*. An example is that of the two Phocian towns of Stiris and Medeon at some date in the second century, of which an inscription records:

The Stirians and Medeonians became members of one state, having their sacred buildings, city, land, harbours and all things free (sc. from mortgages), upon these terms: the Medeonians shall all be Stirians with equal and like rights, and shall share in the assembly and election of magistrates along with the city of the Stirians, and those who have reached the age shall judge in all the law-cases in the city (*Syll.*, 647).

The inscription continues with provision for a 'steward of sacred rites' to be elected from the Medeonians to see to the religious rites of that city (since a synoecism with Stiris could not be allowed to interfere with these) and to count as one of the magistrates of the joint city in receipt of the appropriate pay. Finally provision is made that no one who has held office or priesthood in Medeon shall lose any exemptions from liturgies (i.e. public appointments to specific duties to be financed by the man appointed), which have thereby accrued.

There were many such cases of *sympoliteia* in this period, some incorporating several towns (as when Lysimachus transferred the inhabitants of Colophon and Lebedus to Ephesus: Pausanias, i, 9). The harsh fact was that small towns were too vulnerable. Such unions were not, however, always immutable. A boundary commission delimiting the bounds of the new city formed by the union of the two Aetolian townships of Melitaea and Perea in Phthiotic Achaea lays down that 'if the Pereans leave the union they shall in leaving keep one councillor' (*Syll.*, 546B, ll. 16–18), a passage which incidentally provides evidence that cities sent representatives to the council of the Aetolian federation in proportion to their size.

II

The Aetolian federation is itself an example of an important form of *sympoliteia* which grew in strength and influence in Greece proper during the third and second centuries. Federalism, that is, the merging of a group of cities in a larger organization to which they have surrendered some (but not all) of their independent rights, in order to strengthen themselves, was a reasonable and, one might think, obvious development in a world in which large territorial monarchies dwarfed individual cities and the disadvantages of the old city-state exclusiveness had already begun to be apparent. In fact however it was primarily in those areas of Greece where the city-state had not hitherto found strong roots or developed a history of traditional independence and even hegemony that the more important federal states arose. The two most influential were in Aetolia and Achaea. Aetolia was still a tribal state in the fifth century but by 367 an Athenian inscription (Tod, 137) shows the assembly referring a breach of 'the common laws of the Hellenes' by Trichonium, which had arrested the Athenian envoys sent to announce the sacred truce for the Greater Eleusinian Mysteries, to the *koinon* (common-alty) of the Aetolians (which had already accepted the truce). It is perhaps appropriate that what is at present our earliest reference to the Aetolian confederation should concern a breach of generally accepted convention, for throughout their history the Aetolians were renowned for lawlessness and piracy. The Aetolian League had a primary assembly consisting of all men of military age, meeting twice a year, in spring and autumn. Its chief magistrate, elected annually, was the General and there was also a council (*boule* or *synedrion*) which seems to have seen to government between the meetings of the assembly but not to have been associated with the latter's decisions in the normal Greek fashion. This council, composed of city representatives elected in proportion to populations (see p. 152), amounted to several hundred men. Day-to-day business was conducted by a small committee of the council, the *apokletoi*, something over thirty in number, who met under the presidency of the General, but vital issues of foreign policy were decided by the assembly.

The Aetolians were at pains to exploit the great prestige which they had won by saving Delphi from the Gauls in 279 (see p. 147) and subsequently they extended their federation across central Greece. As they took over more and more peoples they were able to exercise their votes in the Amphictyonic Council controlling

Delphi, a fact which enables the stages of their expansion to be followed and dated. The citizens of these peoples and cities were either incorporated in Aetolia as full members or they received a grant of *isopoliteia* (see pp. 150–1). *Isopoliteia* was also used to attach more distant states such as Chios (*SEG*, ii (1925), 258 combined with *SEG*, x, viii (1962), 245), Vaxos in Crete (*Insc. Cret.*, ii, Vaxos, nos. 18 (=*SVA*, 585) and 19), or Lysimacheia, Cius and Calchedon (though Polybius, xviii, 3, 11, uses the word *sympoliteia*, probably in a general, non-technical sense). By expansion of this kind the Aetolians became a power of some account, which the king of Macedonia had to take seriously. They later became allies of Rome against Philip V, with dire consequences for Greece.

Still more important for the history of Macedonia and mainland Greece was the Achaean League. From early times the cities of the Achaean people on the northern coast of the Peloponnese had enjoyed some kind of federal association, but under Alexander and his successors this had fallen apart. In 280 the cities of Dyme, Patrae, Tritaea and Pharae came together in a new federation which was later joined by Aegium, Bura, Ceryneia, Leontium, Aegira, Pallene and perhaps later Olenus (though by the time Polybius was writing in the second century Olenus, like Helice, no longer existed). In 251 a young Sicyonian named Aratus expelled the local tyrant and brought Dorian Sicyon into the Achaean League, and in 243 he seized Corinth from Antigonus Gonatas (see p. 95). Between 243 and 228, thanks to Aratus' successful policy of aggression against them, most of the Isthmus states, Arcadia and Argos became federal members. But the rise of Cleomenes III at Sparta threatened the League with disruption and in the winter of 225/4 the decision was taken to call in the help of Antigonus III. The political background of this *volte-face* has already been examined (see p. 97) and we shall later be looking at the revolutionary movement in Sparta which drove Aratus to take this step (see pp. 172 ff.). The outcome was that from 224 until 199 Achaea, after rising to power largely through a policy of opposition to Macedonia, was now tied closely to the king as a member of an alliance of federal states established by Antigonus and for some time operative under his successor Philip V (see p. 97). Membership of this wider organization brought Achaea into collision with Rome in the First Macedonian War (215–205) and when the Second Macedonian War broke out in 200, Achaea perforce switched its allegiance to Rome. As a Roman 'ally' it was permitted to expand to take in the whole of the Peloponnese but Sparta was never reconciled to League membership and it was finally a quarrel with Sparta which in 147/6 led to a Roman ultimatum, a short and ruinous war and the dissolution of the League. The history of Achaea illustrates both the advantages that federation could bring and the limitations felt by a federation even as strong as Achaea in confrontation with the Macedonian monarchy and even more with Rome.

The historian Polybius, born at Megalopolis in Arcadia, grew up a citizen of Achaea and played an active role as a statesman in its service. His account of the merits of this federal state, though prejudiced in its favour, illustrates the ideals which to some extent actuated those who administered it.

> In the past many have tried to unite the Peloponnesians in a single policy of common interest, but no one was able to achieve this since each was striving, not in the cause of general freedom, but for his own power. But in my own time this object has been so much advanced and so far attained that they not only constitute an alliance and friendly community, but they have the same laws, weights, measures and coinage, as well as the same magistrates, council-members and judges, and almost the whole Peloponnese only falls short of being one city through the fact that its inhabitants do not possess one single walled refuge (ii, 37, 9–11).

There is some exaggeration here. The separate cities kept their own laws in addition to those of the federation and the coins were those of the separate cities until the early-second century, when from about 190 federal coins were first issued. The League did however possess a single general (after 255), ten *damiurgoi*, and various other magistrates such as the cavalry-commander, secretary, sub-general and admiral.

There was also an assembly, the role and composition of which has been the subject of long controversy. The evidence is not entirely clear but in the present writer's opinion, throughout the third and second centuries down to 146 a primary assembly open to all male adult citizens met four times a year at meetings known as *synodoi* to transact normal business. At those meetings the council (*boule*) which was open to men aged thirty and over, and the magistrates, were also present. But, at any rate in the second century, the laws laid down that questions of war or alliance and the receipt of messages from the Roman senate had to be dealt with at a special assembly, which usually but not invariably was also open to attendance by the whole adult male population, but at which voting was probably by cities. This rule, designed to ensure that certain business was reserved to specially convened meetings, was probably introduced once the appearance of the Romans on the scene made foreign policy a more delicate matter, and provides a good example of how the presence of the Romans changed both the principles and the practice of government within the Greek states.

For rather more than a hundred years the Achaean League played an important role in Greek politics. Polybius asks himself the reason for its success and answers the question in idealistic terms.

It is clear that we should not say that it is the result of chance, for that is a poor explanation. We must rather look for a reason, for every event, probable or improbable, must have a reason; and here it is more or less as follows. One could not find a political system and principle more favourable to equality, free speech and in short genuine democracy than that existing among the Achaeans. This system has found many of the Peloponnesians ready to join it voluntarily and many have been won over by persuasion and argument; while those who at the appropriate moment were compelled by force to join rapidly changed their attitude and became reconciled, since by reserving no privileges to the original members and putting all new adherents on the same footing, the League quickly reached the goal it had set itself, being aided by two powerful factors, equality and humanity. This then we must consider to be the initiator and cause of the present prosperity of the Peloponnese (ii, 38, 5-9).

The sanguine and optimistic tone of this passage – clearly written before the disasters of 146 – ignores the very real weaknesses of the League. Politically it may have been democratic, in as much as vital decisions were taken by an assembly open to all adult males. But its officers seem to have come from a fairly small group of families based on a few cities; and its collapse before the assault of Cleomenes, which forced Aratus to reintroduce the Macedonians into the Peloponnese, reflects a fundamental weakness for which Plutarch alleges these causes:

> There had been agitation among the Achaeans and their cities were eager for revolt, the common people hoping for land distribution and the cancellation of debts, and the leading men in many places being dissatisfied with Aratus, and some of them being angry with him for bringing the Macedonians into the Peloponnese (*Cleomenes*, 17, 5).

The first of these causes we shall consider in Chapter 9. But the opposition of the upper class to his Macedonian policy suggests that many would have preferred to go with Sparta. One can hardly therefore resist the conclusion that the Achaean League had not won the allegiance of the cities it had incorporated by force to the extent that Polybius asserts.

Nevertheless, despite these weaknesses, in a world of monarchies the federal states of Achaea and Aetolia exemplify the continuing ability of the Greeks to respond to a new political challenge with new solutions. One is bound to ask whether, given another century without Rome, federalism might not have developed fresh and fruitful aspects, for despite the use of force (and that Polybius admits) these federations grow out of an internal response of the Greeks themselves and are in consequence quite different in character from the leagues imposed upon Greece by Philip II, Antigonus I and Demetrius Poliorcetes, and Antigonus Doson. Federalism offered the possibility of transcending the limitations of size and relative weakness of the separate city-state. But time ran out.

9 *Social and Economic Trends*

I

We have already seen, in Chapter 4, how shaky were the foundations on which the apparent homogeneity of the hellenistic world rested. This becomes even more apparent when one considers the social and economic basis of life in the huge area involved. The working of the land was of course inevitably of paramount importance both to the new Greek cities and to the native populations among whom they were established. But there the similarity ended. The cities were not only centres of Greek culture but economically they were organized after the manner characteristic of the Greek city-state, in which a closely-defined citizen body, which might be a large or small proportion of the total population, owned the land and worked it with the help of slave-labour, and in which resident aliens shared in social, cultural and economic life but not in government. Cities run on these lines remained alien units embedded in the vast areas of the east, where ultimately the land was the king's (though quite often assigned to a privileged group of estate owners) and was worked by peasants living in villages. In Chapters 6 and 7 we have already considered some of the variants of this basic social and economic pattern, to which the hellenistic influx brought no substantial change.

One reason for this inertia was the fact that the hellenistic age was not characterized by any substantial transformation of the forces of production. We hear indeed of specific improvements to irrigation and drainage. 'Alexander', writes Strabo (xvi, 1, 9), 'paid careful attention to the canals' (sc. of Babylonia) and he gives details of methods used to build dams and prevent silting. We know from Theophrastus of similar works in Thessaly (*On the causes of plants*, v, 14, 2) and recent excavations have revealed a network of canals in the Crimea (see Préaux, *Le Monde hellénistique*, p. 476, quoting information from J. Pečirka). The Ptolemies too introduced new fruits and crops, as did their rivals in Pergamum and Antioch. More use was made of iron ploughs and there were some improvements in farm equipment, for example, the introduction of the Archimedean screw, used for irrigation, and new oil- and wine-presses – perhaps even a threshing-machine (if a third-century papyrus has been correctly interpreted: *BGU*, 1507). But the total result of all this was not very significant. Irrigation could quickly deteriorate through neglect, as happened at Kerkeosiris in the Fayum in the second century, where at one stage dykes collapsed and land returned to desert. Indeed, except for a new quick-growing wheat which gave a double harvest and a higher yield (*P. Cairo Zen.*, 59155), most of the novelties were intended to provide luxury products for a small minority without making undesirable payments abroad.

Another result of Alexander's campaigns and the Seleucid colonization which followed was the spread of a money economy to the cities of Asia. Alexander's conquests had released large quantities of precious metals from the treasuries of the east and this both sent down the value of gold and silver and increased the amount of coinage in circulation. The hellenistic world fell into several zones within which coinage minted on different standards circulated. Continental Greece, for example, including the Peloponnese, coined on a reduced 'Aeginetan' standard with a drachma weighing 5g. whereas Euboea and the islands used a Rhodio-Phoenician standard, with a drachma of 3·25–3·75g. But these were mainly local coinages. Of far greater importance was the adoption of the Attic standard by Alexander himself and later by Lysimachus, who issued large numbers of silver coins with Alexander's head, which circulated throughout Asia Minor. The drachma of this series weighed approximately 4·25g. and the highly popular tetradrachm 17g. Many cities coined to this standard, which was employed by the Antigonids and Seleucids and thus became the basis for what was virtually an international coinage. The chief exception was Ptolemaic Egypt and its possessions, where a coinage based on the lighter, so-called Phoenician standard, with a tetradrachm of 13–15g., was employed to enforce a monetary monopoly within a closed economy (see pp. 104 ff.)

This spread in the use of money did not however have much effect on the natives living in their villages and the use of barter and the payment of dues in kind were still characteristic of most areas outside the immediate influence of a city. Governments had a special interest in grain and foodstuffs, for urbanization placed an additional burden on the capacity of the land to feed everybody and many cities created special magistracies responsible for the buying and distribution of corn. Thus the letter of Antigonus I regulating the union between Lebedus and Teos (see pp. 136–7) shows that it was only with reluctance that the king gave permission to set up a special fund in the city for grain (perhaps in this case to tide over the period of the synoecism).

> Previously we were unwilling that any city should undertake the importation of grain or maintain a (sc. subsidized) grain-supply, for we were unwilling to have the cities spend for this purpose large sums of money unnecessarily; and we did not wish even now to give this permission, for the crown land is near and if a need of grain arose we think that whatever was needed could easily be brought from there (Welles, *R.C.*, no. 3, ll. 30 ff.).

But the cities preferred, if possible, to avoid such dependence. Samos, in the second century, set up a fund, the capital of which was then loaned out and the interest on the loans, collected by special magistrates called *meledones,* was devoted to the annual purchase of corn, which was then distributed free to the citizens. The corn itself was mostly bought from that paid as tithe to the goddess Hera, who possessed lands on the mainland opposite Samos (*Syll.*, 976). Grain shortage was clearly a general fear and its causes are not easily divined. Bad harvests and distortion of the market by war and speculation no doubt both played a part and the high cost and difficulties of land transport together with the dangers of sea transport sometimes hindered attempts to alleviate a local shortage.

II

If there was no fundamental change in the level of agricultural production during the hellenistic age, the same also applied to trade and industry. As before, some cities managed to prosper and to base a successful economy largely upon trade, in particular the island city of Rhodes, organized under a naval aristocracy, which has left its record in many honorific inscriptions. Down to 168, when it fell foul of Rome, the Rhodian ruling class was successful in preserving peace and prosperity abroad and fending off any social problems within the city by a kind of institutionalized charity.

> The Rhodians are concerned for the people in general, although their rule is not democratic; still they wish to look after their multitude of poor. Accordingly, the people are supplied with corn and following a certain ancestral custom the needy are supported by the well-to-do; and there are certain liturgies that supply provisions so that the poor man gets sustenance and at the same time the state does not run short of useful men, especially to man the fleet (Strabo, xiv, 2, 5).

There is also evidence for the development of industry in the east, of metalwork, textiles, building construction. It was typical of Antiochus IV's idiosyncratic behaviour that he would escape from the court and 'be chiefly found at the silversmiths' and goldsmiths' workshops (sc. in Antioch) holding forth at length and discussing technicalities with the moulders and other craftsmen' (Polybius, xxxvi, 1, 2 = Athenaeus, v, 193d). Tyre and Sagalassus were famous for their dye-works, Sidon for its glassware, Tarsus for its linen. We lack firm evidence about the type of labour used in these enterprises, but it seems unlikely that we have to do here with an increase in scale on what went before. There is no sign of anything like 'mass-production'. The typical unit remained small – probably the owner and one or two slaves, with a good deal of domestic production. In this respect the hellenistic age merely continues the conditions of the earlier city-states.

Some states such as Rhodes, as we saw, derived the bulk of their wealth from commerce. But commerce was handicapped by an undeveloped technology. At sea the steering apparatus was still primitive and though sailing into the wind appears to have been known, it was not commonly used. But worse was the danger from pirates, a profession that flourished in times of war and disorder; indeed Strabo (x, 4, 10), speaking of Crete, one of the areas where piracy was endemic before the Romans took the island over, speaks of 'the mercenary soldiers in the island, from whom the piratical bands were also wont to be recruited'. Piracy and mercenary service are thus treated as two alternative outlets in time of distress, hard conditions and war. The pirates were among the main providers of slaves; their captives could be either ransomed or sold according to circumstances. As we have seen, slaves were an essential component of the economic life of the older Greek cities.

In discussing urban life in the hellenistic age we are largely restricted to those cities which existed before the reign of Alexander, since evidence for the new foundations is still slender. The main political changes brought about by his career and what followed have already been considered. Most cities were now no longer truly independent. Economically, this brought both advantages and disadvantages. Among the latter was the obligation not only to make regular payments of tribute (except where a town was specifically exempt from this) but also to furnish occasional special contributions for war or other specified purposes. The Athenians, Plutarch reports, were especially incensed with Demetrius Poliorcetes because

after he had ordered them to procure speedily 250 talents for his use, and after they had levied the money rigorously and inexorably, when he saw the money had been collected, he commanded that it should be given to Lamia and her fellow-courtesans to buy soap (*Demetrius*, 27, 1).

The story may be untrue or at least exaggerated, but it illustrates the resentment felt at such arbitrary exactments, which were in their turn swelled by the need to furnish so-called voluntary 'crowns' (actually sums of money) demanded in connection with the celebration of various festive occasions. Frequently cities had to fall back on rich benefactors to tide them over such payments, for example Boulagoras who paid for the 'crown' demanded from Samos by Ptolemy III (*SEG*, i (1923), 366), or Protogenes of Olbia, clearly a man of almost fabulous wealth, who among other benefactions furnished 900 gold pieces, which were owing to the Scythian (or Sarmatian) king Saitapharnes as a sort of danegeld, 'because there was no money in the revenues' (*Syll.*, 495, ll. 86 ff.; date *c.* 230). Protogenes and later Niceratus (*Syll.*, 730) of Olbia, or Agathocles of Istria (*SEG*, xxiv (1969), 1095) – such men as these can hardly have gained their immense wealth except in the profitable slave-trade of the Black Sea area and it has been suggested that they enjoyed a convenient symbiosis with the adjacent barbarians, with whom they traded and negotiated.

It was however some compensation for these depredations that the kings themselves – the hellenistic kings, that is, not the barbarians from across the northern frontiers – often ministered to their own prestige by making gifts to the cities, helping out with loans in time of famine, or paying for the building of temples, porticoes and theatres. An outstanding example of this occurred following a disastrous earthquake at Rhodes in 227. Polybius tells us that:

On this occasion the Rhodians dealt with the matter in such a way that by stressing the extent of the calamity and its appalling character and by conducting themselves in public audiences and in private intercourse with the greatest serious-ness and dignity, they had such an effect on cities and especially on kings that not only did they receive most lavish gifts, but the donors themselves felt that a favour was being conferred on them (v, 88, 4).

Such gifts to cities were possible only in a society which enabled kings and certain private individuals to amass vast fortunes and these were devoted, not to investment in any enterprise which might have increased productivity (and so ultimately made possible a general improvement in the quality of life), but rather to ostentatious expenditure or usury – and of course, where rulers were concerned, to meeting the cost of defence or aggressive warfare. Conditions in Boeotia in the early-second century were perhaps more generally typical of those in central Greece than Polybius (who disliked Boeotia) was willing to admit. After describing the chaotic situation in this state, where the law-courts had been in abeyance for twenty-five years (see p. 144) and demagogues had set up schemes for state payments to the indigent (perhaps by paying out wages to troops mobilized unnecessarily), Polybius adds that

> childless men, instead of leaving their money to their nearest relatives, as had formerly been the custom here, employed it in feasting and drinking and so made it the common property of their friends (xx, 6, 5–6).

The reference to childlessness strikes a note heard elsewhere. In a general indictment of contemporary second-century Greece Polybius tells us that

> in our own time the whole of Greece has been subject to childlessness and a general population shortage, as a result of which cities have become deserted and the land has ceased to yield fruit, though there have been neither continuous wars nor epidemics (xxxvi, 17, 5 ff.)

This he attributes to refusal to marry and the use of infanticide, and he castigates the attitudes of mind which led to these practices. But such attitudes hardly arose *in vacuo*. Rather they were a response to the uncertainty of life amid war, revolution and piracy, all of which increased following the arrival upon the scene of the Roman legions. These same conditions may well have contributed to the situation in Boeotia described by Polybius. But one should beware of interpreting such accounts too generally. In his reference to childlessness and conspicuous spending, the historian is probably thinking and writing mainly of his own class, that of the richer landowners. His complaint that there were no men to till the soil is partly refuted by the widespread revolutionary demand for a redivision of the land, which implies a shortage of land rather than of men and the vast number of men enlisting for mercenary service from areas like Crete tells a similar story. The drop in population was probably characteristic only of certain classes and certain districts.

There was to be sure widespread distress in the countryside in many parts and this links up with both land-shortage and indebtedness, ills endemic in Greece for many centuries. The details are often obscure and the causes uncertain; they may also have varied from place to place. But a low living standard, the absence of any margin to meet lean years or upsets due to mobilization and war will have played a large part in reducing peasants to a condition of dependence from which it was virtually impossible to emerge. In extreme cases men would abandon their holdings altogether to take refuge in towns or try their fortunes abroad as mercenaries; alternatively they might resort to piracy, as so often happened in Crete and Aetolia. Diodorus for example, describes how in about 307, when the Macedonian officer Ophellas set out from Cyrene to join Agathocles of Syracuse in his war on Carthage, many Athenians gladly joined his expedition:

> and not a few of the other Greeks too were eager to share the enterprise, hoping to divide up between them the finest part of Africa and to plunder the wealth of Carthage. For owing to the continuous wars and the struggles of the rulers against

each other Greece had become poor and miserable; consequently they believed that they would not merely gain many benefits but would escape from the misfortunes of the times (xx, 40, 6–7).

This kind of attitude may help to explain why many cities suffered from a dearth of citizens and were obliged to make up their numbers by enrolling new men. We have already seen examples of this at Larissa and Dyme (pp. 68, 150–1); the same procedures are to be found at Pharsalus and Phalanna, both, like Larissa, in Thessaly (*IG*, ix, 2, 234 and 1228 and *add.* = Schwyzer, 567, 612).

III

Economic distress and great extremes of poverty and wealth were a recipe for class conflict and led to threats of social revolution in Greece proper and in the lands around the Aegean. There is no evidence that this was also true in the settlements of the new kingdoms but it is perhaps unsafe to build too much on records that are still scanty. In Egypt, as we saw (p. 119), risings due to social distress took on a nationalist colour because the ruling class was Greek but the Egyptian peasant often merely tried to escape from a desperate situation by running away. It was mainly in the cities of old Greece, which had less to gain from the hellenic expansion in Asia, that social revolution was a serious threat.

Evidence for this goes back well beyond Alexander. A speech falsely attributed to Demosthenes (ps.-Demosthenes, xvii, 15) 'On the Athenian treaty with Alexander', alleges that

> it says in the treaty that the delegates and those charged with general surveillance shall ensure that no executions or banishments occur in the cities which share in the peace contrary to the city laws, nor confiscations of property nor division of land nor cancellation of debts nor liberation of

slaves with a view to revolution.

Similar phrases seem to have been included in the foundation document of the Hellenic League set up by Antigonus I and Demetrius I in 302 (*SVA*, 446, l. 43) and they spell out the classic formula of social uprising, which constantly recurs in inscriptions. Thus an oath of loyalty taken, probably by new citizens, at Itanus in Crete contains the pledge: 'I will not bring about any division of land. . . or cancellation of debts' (*Syll.*, 526, ll. 22 ff.)

This preoccupation with revolution directed towards social and economic change clearly reflects a real threat. Partly that was because the discontented were potential traitors if any enemy attacked. In the fourth century Aeneas the Tactician had pointed out (*Poliorcetica*, 14) that if perils threatened a city, debtors should be relieved of part or even the whole of what they owed 'since such men are many in number and on the watch for an opportunity, and exceedingly dangerous'. A century later the Cynic writer Cercidas of Megalopolis wrote a virulent poem on the contrast of riches and poverty, asking

> Why has not heaven made poor the extravagant Xenon and caused to flow in our direction the wealth which he squanders on useless things? And since it is easy for a god to accomplish everything that crosses his mind, what, one may well ask, is there to prevent him relieving this dirty usurer, who'd die for a ha'penny, who lets his money out only to take it back, this destroyer of property, of his swinish wealth and giving a perishing hand-out to the fellow eating a bare minimum and filling his cup from the common bowl? Surely the eye of Justice has been blinded! (Meliambi, fg. 4 in Powell, *Collectanea Alexandrina*, pp. 203–4.)

He goes on to urge the rich to practise charity before disaster overtakes them.

In this case the trouble Cercidas foresees is revolution; but in reality revolution and foreign coups could hardly be separated.

Giving the background to a disastrous and bloody coup carried out by the Aetolians in an Achaean city, Polybius writes:

> The people of Cynaetha, who are Arcadians, had been for many years vexed by never-ending and embittered factional strife; there had been constant massacres, expulsions, confiscations of property and division of the land (iv, 17, 4).

This social conflict had no doubt been partly fuelled by the events of Cleomenes III's reign at Sparta (which we shall be looking at shortly: see pp. 172 ff.) – though Polybius, somewhat idealistically prefers to attribute it to the failure of the Cynaethans to humanize themselves by the practice of music – but the social issues had inevitably been absorbed into the struggle between pro-Achaean and pro-Aetolian parties in the town. The Aetolians were merely exploiting social discontent for their own ends. But in 205 after the First Macedonian War they proposed revolutionary legislation in their own country. Commenting on the growth of debt in Aetolia, Polybius relates how

> being naturally fond of making innovations in their constitution [a great fault in Polybius' conservative eyes] they chose Dorimachus and Scopas to draw up laws, as they saw that both these men had revolutionary tendencies and that their fortunes were compromised in many private transactions. Having been invested with this authority they drafted laws (xiii, 1).

But they were opposed by Alexander, elsewhere described as the richest man in Greece, and it is not clear whether the legislation went through; both lawgivers subsequently took service in Egypt (on Scopas see pp. 77–8).

In general, the revolutions of which we are informed were unsuccessful for various reasons. In the first place they were mainly directed simply towards reversing roles, putting the poor where the rich had been and vice versa – and indeed without an increase in the level of production this was inevitable. Secondly, the most oppressed element, the slaves, were excluded from the movement, which never included the liberation of slaves as part of its stated programme, though as a matter of expediency slaves were sometimes given or sold their freedom in order to furnish additional manpower. An example of this (see p. 173) was provided by the Spartan king Cleomenes, who let some of the helots buy their freedom and, as we saw, in the treaty quoted by ps.-Demosthenes (p. 167), liberation of slaves was a fear of the land-owning class. Failure to incorporate the slaves is not, however, very surprising, since in ancient Greece status was a potent concept and the economic misery common to poor free men and slaves counted for little in comparison with the gap which the free man was conscious of between himself and the slave; a relevant parallel from modern times is the attitude of the poor white in the southern states of North America. Finally, the arrival of the Romans on the scene from the late-third century onwards exerted a distorting influence, supported very often by force and violence, in favour of the stability which seemed to be offered by the established ruling class.

That the number of revolutions recorded in Greece during this period is in fact not very large, even when compared with those in Italy and Sicily, perhaps indicates that the upper class in the Greek cities was fairly successful in its use of palliatives, cheap or free corn and other philanthropic measures, which kept the revolution at bay except when the discontented found a rallying point (and sometimes material help) abroad.

IV

The most striking example of a temporarily successful revolutionary movement in the hellenistic world was that led by the two Spartan kings Agis IV (244–241) and Cleomenes III (235–222; died 219) and by their late-third-century and early-second-century successors. Our main source for the careers of Agis and Cleomenes is Plutarch's *Lives* of the two kings. His account, derived from the lost, pro-Spartan historian

Phylarchus, presents both men in a rather philosophical and idealized light. Our other main source, Polybius, in his excerpts and (for the later revolutionary leaders) in the account of Livy, who followed him, is hostile to the Spartan kings whom he describes as tyrants.

The accumulation of wealth at Sparta had been especially disastrous because of the peculiar agrarian economy of that state, where full Spartiate citizens each possessed their own plot of land manned by helots, state slaves, assigned to do the work, while other branches of the economy were in the hands of the *perioikoi*, the 'dwellers-around', who were not citizens. At an uncertain date

> a certain powerful man came to be ephor who was headstrong and of a violent temper, Epitadeus by name, and he had a quarrel with his son and introduced a law permitting a man during his lifetime to give his estate and allotment to any one he wished or in his will and testament so to leave it. This man, then, satisfied a private grudge of his own in introducing the law; but his fellow citizens welcomed the law out of greed, validated it and so destroyed the most excellent of institutions (Plutarch, *Agis*, 5, 2–3).

The result was a concentration of land in the hands of a few (especially heiresses). By the middle of the third century

> there were left of the old Spartan families not more than seven hundred, and of these there were perhaps a hundred who possessed land and an allotment; while the ordinary throng, deprived of resources and civic rights, lived in enforced idleness, showing no zeal or energy in warding off foreign wars, but constantly on the watch for some opportunity to subvert and change affairs at home (Plutarch, *Agis*, 5, 4)

The traditional training, the common messes, all that had produced the traditional Spartan, had been abandoned and Sparta had sunk to relative obscurity, the loss of Messenia in the fourth century having accentuated the decline.

Agis, on his accession, decided to restore what was understood to be the ancient regime with its land allotments and equality of Spartiates, in short the 'system of Lycurgus', the semi-legendary lawgiver to whom the traditional ways were attributed. Having had a supporter elected to the ephorate, Agis had him introduce a bill

> the chief provisions of which were that debtors should be relieved of their debts and that the land should be divided up, that which lay between the water-course at Pellene and Taygetus, Malea and Sellasia (i.e. the city land proper) into 4000 lots and that which lay outside this into 15,000; that this latter should be apportioned among those of the *perioikoi* and resident aliens who had had the education of free men and were besides physically vigorous and in the prime of life (Plutarch, *Agis*, 8, 1–2).

The public messes and the strict regime associated with these were also to be restored. At first all appeared to be going well. When his fellow-king Leonidas opposed him he was forced to withdraw into exile at Tegea. But at the vital moment Agis' plan failed. Having secured the cancellation of the debts which hung over many estates, his supporters, including his uncle Agesilaus, prevented the carrying through of the measure to divide up the land. Agis was called away to a campaign against the Aetolians, and on his return was assassinated. His failure sprang from his inability to persuade a sufficient number of rich and poor to accept a regime of traditional austerity with the object of ensuring Sparta's survival. Most revolutions appealed to greed and envy: Agis' idealism raised too many enemies.

Six years elapsed before the accession to the throne of Cleomenes III, the son of Agis' opponent, Leonidas. Cleomenes had married Agis' widow and our tradition attributes a good deal to her success in winning him over to the programme of reform but Cleomenes' conversion was directly linked with an aggressive policy aimed at taking over the Peloponnese, which brought him into direct opposition to the Achaean League led by Aratus, who had similar ambitions. In 229 the Aetolian League made over to Cleomenes the Arcadian towns of Tegea, Mantinea, Orchomenus and, probably, Caphyae, and soon afterwards he attacked a fortress on the frontiers of Megalopolis. In 227 he carried out a coup d'état eliminating the ephorate (which was declared 'non-Lycurgan'), exiling eighty of his opponents and putting through a new version of Agis' reforms, with fresh lots and a new phalanx of 4000 citizens, a number made up from the *perioikoi*, and the old training was reintroduced.

With this new force Cleomenes won some striking military successes and the Achaean League began to crumble. Quite mistakenly the masses throughout the Peloponnese saw Cleomenes as a possible saviour. 'There had been agitation among the Achaeans,' writes Plutarch (*Cleomenes*, 17, 3), 'and their cities were eager for revolt, the common people expecting division of land and abolition of debts'. And in his *Aratus* (39, 4) he describes the Achaean leader as 'seeing the Peloponnese shaking and its cities everywhere stirred to revolt by restless agitators'. But the Spartan revolution was not for export. Faced with the disintegration of the League, Aratus sacrificed his anti-Macedonian policy to strike a bargain with Antigonus III, who marched south and soon penned Cleomenes in Laconia. In this crisis

> Cleomenes set free those of the helots who could pay down five Attic minas (thereby raising a sum of 500 talents) and armed 3000 of them in the Macedonian fashion (Plutarch, *Cleomenes*, 23, 1).

This was a desperate measure forced on him by circumstances. In 222 he was defeated by Antigonus at Sellasia in northern Laconia – a battle in which almost the whole Spartiate force was annihilated – fled to Egypt and perished there three years later, leading a revolt against Ptolemy IV.

'Antigonus', says Plutarch (*Cleomenes*, 30, 1), 'treated the Lacedaemonians humanely and did not insult or mock the dignity of Sparta, but restored her laws and constitution', and Polybius (ii, 70, 1) confirms that he 'restored the ancient form of government'. Polybius regarded Cleomenes' government as a tyranny and these references to restoring the ancestral government seem to mean a return to the situation before the reforms. But the phrase is elastic, for though the ephorate was restored, Sparta was left without kings. Later, in the second century when Sparta was compelled to join the Achaean League (in 189), Livy (xxxviii, 34, 3), echoing Polybius, gives as the conditions imposed: 'that they should abolish the laws and traditions of Lycurgus and accustom themselves to the laws and institutions of the Achaeans'. This may mean that after Sellasia some of the social aspects of Cleomenes' reforms were allowed to persist; on the other hand they may have been introduced under one or other of Cleomenes' successors.

The revolutionary movement at Sparta is remarkable for its persistence under a series of later leaders. Still in the third century there were Lycurgus and Machanidas (who was killed by the Achaean leader Philopoemen in person at a battle fought at Mantinea in 207) and later Nabis, who is praised on a Delian inscription as 'King Nabis son of Damaratus, a good man in his relations with the shrine and the Delian people' (*Syll.*, 584). Polybius, however, tells us that

> he utterly extirpated the remaining (members of the royal house?) who survived in Sparta and banishing those citizens who were distinguished for their wealth and illustrious ancestry gave their property and wives to the chief of those who remained and to his mercenaries, who were for the most part murderers, housebreakers, brigands and burglars (xiii, 6, 3).

Elsewhere (xvi, 13) he accuses him of liberating slaves (probably helots). Judging by the details that have come down to us, and even allowing for Polybius' Achaean prejudice, Nabis seems to have lacked all the idealism of Agis and even Cleomenes, his career approximating to that of the worst sort of tyrant. With his murder in 192 the revolution dissipated itself, fragmenting into groups of exiles intriguing against each other and appealing constantly to Rome. Incorporated in the Achaean League Sparta remained an alien body and eventually by its secession in 149/8 precipitated the Achaean War and the destruction of the League. But by this time the social aspects of what was, for all its panache, a backward-looking and ultimately impotent movement had disappeared, leaving only a political conflict. At the end the Roman denouement is symbolic of the way Rome took over decision-making in Greece and the Greek world. Henceforth the hellenistic social structure and the problems it engendered are mainly significant as one of the factors affecting Roman provincial government.

10. Cultural Developments: Philosophy, Science and Technology

I

Greek expansion during the early hellenistic period led to a wide diffusion of Greek creative energy. But for several reasons, of which the most important were their security, their wealth and the ambitions of their rulers, there was also a contrary current leading to a concentration of cultural activity in the great royal cities such as Pergamum and Alexandria. Monarchic patronage was of course nothing new. Sicily had attracted Pindar, Aeschylus and Plato, and Macedonia Euripides but now the patrons were even richer and more impressive. In particular Alexandria dominated the intellectual life of the Greek world, especially under the first three Ptolemies (323–221), and this was largely thanks to the creation of the famous Museum – literally, the Muses' sanctuary – and Library. Perhaps foreshadowed in the Museum and Library of the Lyceum, Aristotle's school at Athens, the Alexandrian institutions may have been inspired by Demetrius of Phalerum under Ptolemy I (though another tradition attributes the great library to Ptolemy Philadelphus).

Vast sums were expended on buying books and attracting scholars to Alexandria; eventually the library contained 500,000 scrolls. The Museum which operated in close conjunction with the Library was in effect a research institute and Alexandria especially encouraged the systematic study of philology, that is, of language and letters. Under scholars such as Zenodotus of Ephesus, Aristophanes of Byzantium and Aristarchus of Samothrace, Homer's text was analysed in detail. The great problem, whether there was one Homer or several, was only one

of the issues which exercised the
with the historical and geograpł
By their commentaries and the
language, these men laid the fc
modern scholarship. The finaɪ
patronage also brought many pc
the Syracusan writer of pastoral
he preferred his own city and
Egyptian capital, or perhaps he fa
sought there. His *Syracusan Women* (*Iayʊ* 15), a racy con-
versation between two Syracusan ladies, resident in Alexandria
and out for the day to watch the festival of Adonis, gives a lively
picture of the great city. Apollonius of Rhodes, who was for a
time librarian, published an epic on the Argonauts marked by
Euripidean sentiment and a strong feeling for landscape. He
came into collision with Callimachus, the poet perhaps most
typical of what we style Alexandrianism, in that he combined
wit and learning with a mastery of metre, language and
mythological allusion to create verses appealing almost wholly to
the intellect.

In Pergamum (especially in the second century) the Attalid
kings exercised a similar patronage. Their library was the
greatest after that of Alexandria, and at their court there
flourished a group of artists and scholars known to us especially
through the work of Antigonus of Carystus, who not only
practised sculpture and wrote on art, but also published a
number of biographies full of anecdotal material. He was
attacked by Polemon of Ilium, a great collector of information on
works of art, some of which he assembled during extensive
travels from Asia Minor to Sicily and Carthage. Another famous
Pergamene figure was the Homeric scholar Crates of Mallus, who
tried to explain away difficulties in the poet by assuming
allegorical meanings and so often succeeded in importing
anachronistic Stoic concepts. Crates broke his leg in an open
sewer while visiting Rome in 168 and, staying on to convalesce,
aroused interest in scholarship by lecturing there. Another
Pergamene scholar was the historian Neanthes of Cyzicus but

...ranch of literature which on the whole flourished
...he great royal capitals. Hieronymus of Cardia, it is
... up residence at Pella (see pp. 17–18); but Timaeus
...at Athens and Polybius at Rome (through no choice of his
...) and in Megalopolis.

II

Athens remained a centre of importance, despite the attractions
of royal patronage; and other cities with a strong cultural
tradition were Rhodes, Cos and (at the very end of our period)
Tarsus. Athens was especially renowned as the home of
philosophy. It was there that Socrates, Plato and Aristotle had
taught and during the period after Alexander the most
distinguished philosophers from all parts of the Greek world
chose to migrate to that city and set up their schools there. The
Academy, established by Plato just before 369, had become less
important under the direction of Speusippus and Xenocrates,
who turned the interest of the school mainly to questions
of ethics. 'The reason for discovering philosophy', wrote
Xenocrates, 'is to allay that which causes disturbance in life'
(F. Heinze, *Xenocrates* (1892), fg. 4), a point of view close to
that of Epicurus (see p. 179). Under Polemo, who took over
the direction of the school in 314, this ethical bias became
more marked. 'A man', he wrote (*Diog. Laert.*, iv, 18), 'should
train himself in practical matters and not in mere dialectical
exercises' – a breach with Plato, who like Socrates had laid great
store on dialectic as a source of knowledge and so of virtue.
From the mid-third century onwards however the Academy took
on a new complexion and a new vitality under Arcesilaus of
Pitane in Asia Minor, who rejected all kinds of dogmatism –
he is said for that reason to have published nothing – but
instead developed the doctrine of 'suspended belief', which
strongly recalls the scepticism of Pyrrhon of Elis (d. 275/0), who
believed that happiness sprang from the equanimity which was
the result of a refusal to make any positive judgements. To

Arcesilaus scepticism was not however a mere attitude of mind to ensure imperturbability but rather a positive philosophical position.

After a period in the Academy and several years spent abroad in Asia Minor and Macedonia Aristotle had returned to Athens, where he taught in the Lyceum. After his death this was bought and converted into a regular school by his successor Theophrastus, who was to be its head until his death *c.* 283/4. Theophrastus kept up the full Aristotelean programme of research and his successor Strato was exceptional among hellenistic philosophers for his interest in problems of natural science. Both sustained the high prestige of the Lyceum. But after Strato's death (*c.* 270) its reputation declined. Indeed the great philosophical schools which brought distinction to Athens from the third century onwards were those of the Epicureans and the Stoics.

Epicurus (341–270), a native of Samos, set up his school at Athens about 307/6. His followers formed a close community which included women and slaves and, despite the austerity of their way of life, its privacy and the doctrine of hedonism which Epicurus taught aroused quite unjustifiable suspicion and hostility, for to the Epicureans 'pleasure' had a special meaning.

> When we say that pleasure is the goal we do not mean the pleasures of the dissipated and those which consist in the process of enjoyment . . . but freedom from pain in the body and from disturbance in the mind. For it is not drinking and continuous parties nor sexual pleasures nor the enjoyment of fish and other delicacies of a wealthy table which produce the pleasant life, but sober reasoning which scarches out the causes of every act of choice and refusal and which banishes the opinions which give rise to the greatest mental confusion (*Letter to Menoeceus*, 131–2, trans. Long).

'Pleasure' consisted in having one's desires satisfied rather than in the act of satisfying them and the pleasure to be derived from a mind at rest, from imperturbability (*ataraxia*), was to be set far above the pleasures of the body. This *ataraxia* was to be ensured by the realization that the universe ran of its own volition according to the atomic theory of Democritus, that there was no personal survival after death and the dissolution of one's constituent atoms, and that the gods, distant and aloof, had no part or interest in our world. Men should abstain from all political action and avoid all situations which might arouse emotion. A gentle friendship in a low key within a closed circle was the true ideal.

Epicureanism never became wholly respectable (except for a short time at Rome towards the end of the republic), and in both popularity and influence it was outstripped by the teachings of the Stoa. This school, set up in the Painted Hall (Stoa Poikile) by Zeno of Citium in Cyprus (335–263), taught a complete philosophical system which with certain modifications was to flourish throughout the hellenistic period and to become the most popular philosophy during the first two centuries of the Roman Empire. It had several main tenets. The only good is in virtue, which means living in accordance with the will of god or nature – the two being more or less identified. One's knowledge of what that is depends on an understanding of reality, which (contrary to the view of the sceptics) can be acquired through the senses by a 'perception conveying direct apprehension' (*kataleptike phantasia*), as the Stoic jargon described accepting the evidence of the senses. Such virtue is the only good: all else (if not positively evil) is indifferent. These doctrines, easily grasped by many more than the initiates of the school (though not without their contradictions when pressed to their logical conclusion), were widely taught and strongly and emotionally felt, as we can see from the *Hymn to Zeus* composed by the Stoic Cleanthes (331–323), who succeeded Zeno as head of the school.

> Nothing occurs on the earth apart from you, O God,
> nor in the heavenly regions nor on the sea,
> except what bad men do in their folly;
> but you know how to make the odd even,

and to harmonize what is dissonant; to you the alien is akin.
And so you have wrought together into one all things that are
   good and bad,
so that there arises one eternal rationale (*logos*) of all things,
which all bad mortals shun and ignore,
unhappy wretches, ever seeking the possession of good things
they neither see nor hear the universal law of God,
by obeying which they might enjoy a happy life
(H. von Arnim, *Stoicorum veterum fragmenta* i (1903), 537 ll.
11–21, trans. Long).

Like the Epicureans the early Stoics were firmly convinced that
by reason man could detect and choose the true path to follow;
they were not cast down by the doctrine that only true virtue was
good. But later, in the second century, Panaetius of Rhodes (*c.*
185–109), who became head of the school, taught a modified and
more human doctrine which offered hope to those who had not
achieved virtue but were trying hard to make some progress
towards it.

Thus Athens remained an important centre of philosophical
teaching long after she had lost all political power. But elsewhere
throughout the hellenistic world more popular forms of
philosophy flourished in the diatribes of the wandering Cynics or
in such works as the *Phaenomena* of Aratus of Soli, a metrical epic
version of the astronomical treatise of Eudoxus of Cnidus, which
made its appeal not so much as a work of science but as a
demonstration of the providential character of the Stoic cosmos.
Like the Cynic philosophers, sculptors and painters also tended
to move from place to place, since they relied, even more than
literary artists, on the open purses of the kings.

III

It will be apparent from what has so far been said that the hellenistic cultural world drew much (but not all) of its stimulus from the patronage provided by the royal courts, but its talent mainly from the Greek cities (including those of the near east) where it was fostered by the tradition of Greek education. This tradition was expressed by way of the teaching provided for the children of the well-to-do (and sometimes those of slender means as well) in the gymnasium. Primarily an athletic institution (see pp. 71 ff.), the gymnasium had always attached importance to musical training, and it now developed into a secondary school. As for example in the gymnasium at Pergamum, built on three levels to cater for boys, ephebes and young men, there were generally lecture-rooms, porticoes and libraries adapted to this now central function. The curriculum was mainly literary, with the chief emphasis on poetry, especially that of Euripides and Homer. The life of the gymnasium is illuminated by many inscriptions and in particular by one of which nearly 70 lines survive from Teos, which contains the regulations for the spending of a sum of money given to the gymnasium by a certain Polythrus (*Syll.*, 578). From this we learn of the appointment of 'three teachers of letters to give instruction to the boys and girls' (for Teos, rather unusually, provided co-education), two *paidotribai* (gym-masters) and a lyre-player, who was not only to teach the lyre, but also to give a general musical education. The status of the teachers was not very high, but the regard felt by the upper-class citizens for the gymnasium was expressed in the many decrees honouring the higher officials in charge, the *paidonomoi*, who looked after the classes of boys, and especially the gymnasiarch who was in effect the headmaster.

These higher officials were holders of unpaid posts carrying great prestige, and it is clear from the inscriptions that it was usually the gymnasiarch who provided the funds for sacrifices, to endow and support contests and even at times to repair or extend the school buildings. For example a late-second-century decree from Salamis states that:

> whereas Theodotus son of Eustrophus of Piraeus, having been elected gymnasiarch for the year of the archon Ergocles, sacrificed oxen at all the appropriate sacrifices, and entertained all the youths receiving training in gymnastics, and carried out the rites of the Hermaea and entertained everybody, spending on this no small amount; and whereas he supplemented the amount assigned to him for oil with additional expenditure from his own resources . . . (the list of his benefactions continues for a further fifteen lines) . . . the council decided to recommend to the people that Theodotus be praised and crowned with a gold crown according to the law in recognition of his munificence towards the people of the Salaminians, and that the award of this crown be announced on the stage at the next celebrations of the Dionysia at Salamis, and at the gymnastic contest at the festival of the Aiantes (*Syll.*, 691).

In an age when the political life of the cities had languished, the role formerly filled by prominent magistrates now often fell to the officials of the gymnasium.

The importance of the institution was also recognized by the kings, who frequently subsidized or endowed the gymnasium itself or the many activities connected with it. For the pupils the great day was that of the competitions, which combined the characteristics of a modern sports day with the annual examinations. The winners had their names inscribed on columns; thus a second-century list records the victors in the boys' class at Magnesia-on-Maeander:

> . . . the son of Artemidorus, . . . the son of Aeschylinus and — —emus the son of Anasicrates . . . for composing songs. For lyre-playing: Mandrocles son of . . ., Ariston son of An— —, Lycomedes son of Charichius.

For singing to the lyre: Dionysius son of Apollodorus, Cteatus
son of Morimus, Pythagoras son of Apollophanes.
For painting: Apollonius son of Apollonius, Callistratus son
of Zopyrus, Alcis son of Zopyrus.
For arithmetic: Neoptolemus son of Admetus, Demetrius son
of Anaxicrates (*Syll.*, 960).

Brought up in this atmosphere of literature, music and physical
exercise, the middle- and upper-class Greek boy, whether he
lived in Athens, in Pergamum or on the Oxus, inherited the
culture of Greece and with it the traditional feelings of inherent
superiority over all other races.

IV

Though its education was primarily literary, the hellenistic age
also saw some noteworthy developments in both pure and
applied science, here too largely under the stimulus of Alexandria
and Pergamum. A contributory factor may have been that now
for the first time science ceased to be the private preserve of
philosophers, as it had been hitherto. Philosophy remained at
home in the city-state, primarily in Athens, but science migrated
to the new world of the monarchies. This does not imply that
science changed its character. The hellenistic world like that of
the city-states never took a decisive step in the direction of
harnessing scientific discoveries to the practical use of human
communities and the achievement of material progress – for
reasons we shall shortly consider. That the extension of scientific
knowledge was a matter of degree and not of kind can be asserted
with confidence, although first-hand evidence is lacking and we
have to rely mainly on late writers to discover what was actually
achieved in the fields of, for example, mathematics, astronomy,
biology and medicine.

Scientific thought in the hellenistic age profited from the
mental stimulus which came along with the general shake-up in
ideas and the cross-fertilization of different cultures – even

though most of its practitioners were Greeks. Still more it benefited from the leisure and resources made available by royal patrons, and by the amenities provided in the great teaching and research centres which they endowed. But not all scientists were in receipt of patronage: 'well-propped pedants who quarrel without end in the Muses' bird-cage', as Timon of Phlius satirically styled the scholars in the Museum (Athenaeus, i, 22d). Many had private incomes or earned their living by their professions, as doctors, architects or engineers, and this was all to the good, since it helped to bridge the gap between theory and practice. It would be impossible within the scope of this chapter to consider in any great detail the achievements of men whom we should now call scientists of various sorts. The most one can hope to do is to glance briefly at the accomplishments of some of the most important figures and then to ask some general questions about the successes and the limitations of hellenistic science.

V

It is perhaps not surprising that an age distinguished by so vast an expansion in men's horizons also displayed a particular interest in astronomy and in the relationship of the earth to the heavenly bodies. Aristarchus of Samos, who lived in the early-third century and wrote a treatise on the size of the sun and moon and their distance from the earth, also propounded the striking thesis that the sun was the centre of the universe. According to Archimedes,

> Aristarchus of Samos brought out a book of certain hypotheses in which it follows from what is assumed that the universe is many times greater than that now so called. He hypothesizes that the fixed stars and the sun remain unmoved, that the earth is borne round the sun on the circumference of a circle . . . and that the sphere of the fixed stars, situated about the same centre as the sun, is so great that the circle in which

he hypothesizes that the earth revolves bears such a proportion to the distances of the fixed stars as the centre of the sphere does to its surface (Archimedes, *Sand-reckoner* introd., tr. Lloyd).

It is not entirely clear whether Aristarchus put forward his heliocentric hypothesis as a fact or merely as an axiom, on which to base certain further conclusions; on the whole, the latter seems more likely. But in any case his theory did not win general support. For a variety of reasons a rival hypothesis proved more acceptable. This hypothesis, which appears to have been largely the work of Apollonius of Perge (late-third century) and Hipparchus of Nicaea (early-second century), sought to explain the apparent movements of the heavenly bodies by a combination of epicycles – an epicycle is the movement of a body in a circle, the centre of which itself moves along the circumference of another circle – and eccentric circles, such as one gets for instance if the sun moves around the earth along the circumference of a circle of which the earth is not the centre. Not only did this theory keep the earth at the centre of the universe (thus avoiding the offence of impiety imputed to Aristarchus), but it provided an explanation of observed phenomena which was not open to certain objections, which seemed strong to contemporary astronomers, against the heliocentric hypothesis. These were in particular the observed movement of heavy objects by gravity towards the centre of the earth, the fact that objects move through the air at the same speed and for the same distance whether they are going in the direction of the earth's postulated movement or against it, and the inability of observers to detect any difference in the relative position of the fixed stars at opposite ends of the earth's postulated orbit round the sun (stellar parallax). There are of course valid answers to all these objections, but they were not known or not even available to hellenistic astronomers. For one thing, there were not yet optical instruments capable of detecting the minute changes caused by stellar parallax or indeed the phases of the planets.

Both Apollonius and Hipparchus made great contributions to scientific knowledge, the former with his work on conic sections and the latter, as we learn from Ptolemy and Proclus, by his use of the *dioptra*, a device consisting of a rod with two sights used for observation and the taking of bearings. With the aid of this and other instruments

> he dared to do something that would be rash even for a god, namely to number the stars for his successors and to check off the constellations by name (Pliny, *Natural History*, ii, 24, 95).

He also discovered the precession of the equinoxes, the process by which the equinoctial points gradually move along the track of the earth's orbit round the sun at the rate of 50 seconds of angle a year, and so return to the same point in *c.* 26,000 years. Ptolemy describes the basis of this discovery.

> Hipparchus in his work *On the Displacement of the Solstitial and Equinoctial Points*, comparing the eclipses of the moon on the basis both of accurate observations made in his own time and of those made still earlier by Timocharis (an astronomer active about 160 years earlier) concludes that the distance of Spica (a star in the constellation of Virgo) from the autumnal equinoctial point, measured from east to west, was in his own time 6°, but in Timocharis' time 8° (*Almagest*, vii, 2).

The rate of displacement implied by these figures is within 6 seconds of an angle a year from that calculated by modern astronomers, a remarkable achievement.

Perhaps even more renowned than Hipparchus was Eratosthenes of Cyrene (275–194), the librarian at Alexandria under Ptolemy III, and his nickname of Beta was an ironical pointer to his supposed success in several fields without reaching absolute pre-eminence in any. His most striking accomplishment was to measure the earth's circumference by recording the angle of shadow cast by a stick at Alexandria ($7\frac{1}{5}°$) on the day of the summer solstice, when there was no shadow at Syene (Aswan), which he assumed to lie on the same line of longitude as Alexandria. It was a simple matter to show by geometry that $7\frac{1}{5}^{\circ}$ must also be the angle subtended by the arc Syene-Alexandria at the centre of the earth, and then by multiplying the distance between the two places by the appropriate figure $\left(\dfrac{360}{7\frac{1}{5}} = 50\right)$ to arrive at the length of the earth's circumference.

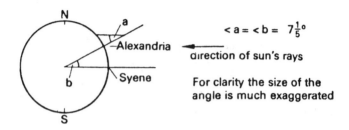

$$< a = < b = \ 7\tfrac{1}{5}^{\circ}$$

direction of sun's rays

For clarity the size of the angle is much exaggerated

Eratosthenes' main difficulty lay in accurately measuring the distance from Syene to Alexandria, which he took to be 5000 stades. The accuracy of his figure of 250,000 stades for the length of the whole circumference depends on the length of stade he was using, and this is not known for certain. On the usual reckoning at an eighth of a Roman mile (185 m.) it would come to 46,250 km. compared with the modern calculation of 40,009 km., but other lengths of stade are possible and in any case the importance of his achievement lies less in the accuracy of the result than in the imaginative use of simple geometry to solve the theoretical problem.

The geometrical knowledge presupposed by this calculation was largely the legacy of Euclid, who flourished around 300 under Ptolemy I, and whose *Elements* brought together a great deal that had already been discovered and proved, but in a highly systematic form in which all the later proofs are derived by logical deduction from a number of assumed 'axioms'. It was in this systematic exposition that the importance of Euclid lay. A little later, at Syracuse, Archimedes (287–212) produced work of great originality on the geometry of spheres and cylinders. It was he who established the value of π. But Archimedes was also distinguished for his work on optics, statics, hydrostatics, astronomy and engineering. His screw – if it was indeed his invention – used a simple principle to construct a machine invaluable for irrigation. Archimedes perished in the Roman sack of Syracuse in 212 after many noteworthy contributions to the defence of his native city.

VI

Another branch of science which made great headway in this period, especially at Alexandria, was that of medicine and biology. The two great names in Alexandrian medicine were those of Herophilus of Calchedon and Erasistratus of Ceos, both active in the early-third century. Herophilus greatly extended Greek knowledge of the brain, the eye, the duodenum (which he so named), the liver, and the reproductive organs. His work was facilitated by the use of dissection and G. E. R. Lloyd, *Greek Science after Aristotle*, (p. 76) quotes Celsus' account of the extension of this practice even to the living:

> Moreover, since pain and various kinds of disease arise in the internal parts, they (sc. the so-called Dogmatists) hold that no one who is ignorant about those parts themselves can apply remedies to them. Therefore it is necessary to cut open the bodies of dead men and to examine their viscera and intestines. Herophilus and Erasistratus proceeded in the best way: they cut open living men – criminals they obtained out of prison from the kings – and they observed, while their subjects still breathed, parts that nature had previously hidden, their position, colour, shape, size, arrangement, hardness, softness, smoothness, points of contact and finally the processes and recesses of each and whether any part is inserted into another or receives the part of another into itself (Celsus, *On Medicine*, 23 ff., tr. Lloyd).

That human vivisection was really used in Alexandria has been questioned, but there seems no good reason to reject Celsus' statement. Erasistratus made important discoveries, especially in relation to such processes as digestion, and the vascular system, for which he adopted a mechanical explanation. He did not of course understand the circulation of the blood and in fact he believed that the arteries normally contained air (which was only replaced by blood when an incision took place and the air escaped).

After the deaths of the two masters their schools seem to have degenerated into sects and the practice of dissection was discontinued. By the later second century the reputation of Alexandrian doctors had deteriorated greatly, if we can believe the historian Polybius, who asserts that

> not a few invalids indeed who had nothing serious the matter with them have before now come very near losing their lives by entrusting themselves to these physicians, impressed by their rhetorical powers (xii, 25 d, 5).

VII

In mechanics and the application of technology the hellenistic age made some progress, but on the whole its achievements were disappointing. By 300 several of the more outstanding technical devices – the lever, the pulley, the wedge and the windlass – were already known; only Archimedes' screw was added in the third century. For our knowledge of hellenistic improvements in the field of technology we are dependent directly or indirectly on four writers, two of them of the hellenistic period itself, one at its very end and the fourth from the first century AD. Ctesibius of Alexandria (fl. c. 270) is credited with a large number of mechanical inventions, among them a pump, a water-clock and improvements to artillery; his own work is lost. Part of the *Mechanical Collection* of Philo of Byzantium (c. 200) survives, and we have *On Architecture* by Vitruvius (c. 25) and (in Greek and Arabic) works by Hero of Alexandria (*c.* AD 60) *On Pneumatics, On Artillery Construction* and *On the Construction of Automata.* Altogether these writers give a picture of considerable available skill and ingenuity and undoubted curiosity about how machines can be developed. Why in spite of this there was nowhere any co-ordinated programme for the development of applied science is a question which obtrudes itself, but is not easily answered.

Pappus of Alexandria, a writer of the fourth century AD, has a significant passage (it is quoted by Lloyd, *Greek Science,* pp. 91–2) in which he indicates the fields where a writer of the late empire regarded mechanical devices as important. After discussing the distinction between the theoretical part of mechanics (geometry, arithmetic, astronomy and physics) and the practical part (metal-working, building, carpentry, painting and the manual activities connected with these), Pappus lists the following as the most necessary of the mechanical arts in relation to practical needs:

1. The construction of pulleys which 'use a lesser force to raise high great weights against their natural tendency'.

2. The making of instruments necessary for war: 'missiles of stone, iron and the like are hurled a great distance by the catapults they make'.

3. The making of machines proper: 'water is easily raised from a great depth by the water-lifting machines that they construct'.

4. 'The ancients also called wonder-workers mechanicians. Some invented pneumatic devices, as Hero in his *Pneumatics,* others seem to imitate the motions of living things by sinews and ropes, as Hero does in his *Automata* and *On Balances,* and others use floating objects, as Archimedes in his work *On Floating Bodies,* or water-clocks, as Hero in his work *On Water-Clocks,* which is evidently connected with his study of the sun-dial.'

5. The making of spheres, i.e. 'the construction of a model of the heavens by means of the uniform circular motion of

water' (*Mathematical Collection*, viii, 1–2).

Other similar lists agree with Pappus in placing the needs of warfare and the production of 'wonder-working machines' as being among the main and most essential functions of mechanical science; to these he adds weight-lifting, irrigation and some kind of primitive planetarium. It is a curiously limited view of a field capable, when developed, of transforming the whole pattern of material life. Why is the Greek view of the possibilities open to technology so restricted?

First, it is only fair to note that technological progress depends on the interplay of many factors: advance in one field is often stimulated by, but also dependent on, advances in another. For example, Hero of Alexandria was awake to the possibilities of steam and even used it in a primitive way to rotate a ball by allowing the steam to escape from bent pipes inserted in it. But the effective use of steam as a form of power depends on the ability to make strong metal cylinders and some kind of piston to convert the direct force into circular movement, and that without serious leakage. To do this required a technology which Hero's age did not command. But perhaps no less important a factor was the cheapness of labour, which made the saving of it seem a matter of small account. Whether the labour was that of the slave or free man does not seriously affect the issue. This lack of incentive was reinforced by a generally conservative attitude, which made men unwilling to invest money in developing inventions requiring a considerable capital outlay. Lloyd (*Greek Science*, p. 108) effectively illustrates this point by contrasting the speed with which the simple rotary mill worked by donkeys or horses spread throughout the western Mediterranean in the second century with the slow diffusion of the more costly water-mill, the principles of which were known by the beginning of our era, but which spread only slowly during the first three centuries AD.

The attitudes of mind which this implies can be traced back to various causes. One is the classical contempt for manual labour and the crafts, which, according to Herodotus (ii, 166–7) first

5 The Rosetta Stone, a large slab of black basalt, now in the British Museum, contains a bilingual inscription in Greek and Egyptian, the latter in both demotic and hieroglyphic versions. This inscription records a decree of the priests of Upper and Lower Egypt, assembled at Memphis on 27 March 196, in the ninth year of Ptolemy V Epiphanes, honouring the king with a *set* festival and celebrating his accession in 204 and his visit to Memphis in November 197. The discovery of the stone in 1799 made possible the decipherment of Egyptian hieroglyphs by the French scholar Champollion.

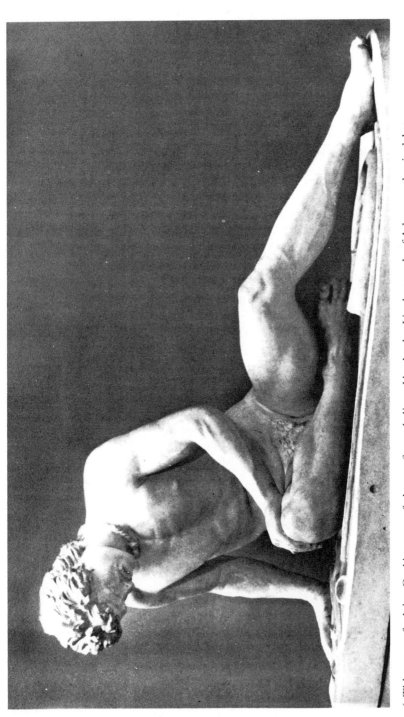

6 This statue of a dying Gaul is a copy of a bronze figure dedicated by Attalus I in the temple of Athena on the citadel at Pergamum, and forming part of a monument erected to celebrate Attalus' victory over the Galatians.

7 Some second-century hellenistic rulers: all the coins shown are silver tetradrachms. These coins, from the collection of the Fitzwilliam Museum, Cambridge, are reproduced by permission of its Department of Coins and Medals.

(c) Ptolemy V Epiphanes, from Egypt.

(a) Seleucus IV Philopator, from Antioch-on-the-Orontes.

(b) Antiochus IV Epiphanes, from Antioch-on-the-Orontes.

(d) Eucratides I, a second-century king of Bactria, who extended his power to Paropamisadae, Gandara and Arachosia; from Bactria.

(e) Philip V, from Macedonia.

(f) Perseus, from Macedonia.

8 Part of a model of the citadel of Pergamum. In the centre is the enclosure containing the Great Altar, now in Berlin; its sculptures link the mythical past of Pergamum with the services of the Attalids to hellenism by their defeat of the Galatians. To the right of the Altar is the market-place, and in the left foreground can be seen the highest seats of the theatre.

manifested itself in the fifth century, having been taken over, he thinks, from the barbarians. Whatever its real origin, this contempt is noteworthy in Aristotle, who remarks that

> doubtless in ancient times the artisan class were slaves or foreigners and therefore the majority of them are so now; the best form of state will not admit them to citizenship (*Politics*, iii, 5, 3, 1278 a).

It is interesting to find Plutarch attributing this attitude to Archimedes himself, the Syracusan scientist and engineer (see pp. 188–9).

> Archimedes possessed such a lofty spirit, so profound a soul, and such a wealth of scientific theory that although his inventions had won for him a name and fame for superhuman sagacity, he would not consent to leave behind him any treatise on this subject, but regarding the work of an engineer and every art that ministers to the needs of life as ignoble and vulgar, he devoted his earnest efforts only to those studies the subtlety and charm of which are not affected by the claims of necessity (*Marcellus*, 17, 3).

Before assigning great importance to this factor we should however perhaps bear in mind that the views expressed here may be those of Plutarch himself rather than Archimedes, and further that although these attitudes no doubt persisted among the upper classes in the city-states, they may well have been much less evident among scientists and the practitioners of the crafts themselves and that in any case they are less characteristic of the new monarchies, especially in the field of military science (see below).

Nevertheless, contempt for practical matters and 'arts that minister to the needs of life' continued to exist and will no doubt have had a part in inhibiting technological progress. Cultivated and expressed by the rich, it fits into a set of values which regarded wealth as a route to status and prestige, and these as desirable attributes best acquired through the ownership of land. There was no concept of 'increasing productivity' and so no likelihood of a systematic programme of research to secure this. The inventor himself was inclined to value knowledge for its own sake rather than for the benefits it might bring to mankind generally or even, more particularly, his own fellow-citizens.

VIII

There was however one area in which remarkable technological advances were made in quite a short time. Their constant preoccupation with warfare led the hellenistic kings to encourage their military engineers to devise more and more powerful and accurate artillery and, in consequence, ever stronger and more sophisticated defences to counter this. Already in Alexander's army the chief engineer Diades was responsible for many inventions such as mobile, transportable siege-towers and improved grappling-engines, and another engineer, Poseidonius, built a highly complex siege-tower; these men were working within a department of the Macedonian army set up by Philip II and already responsible in his reign for great progress in torsion catapults.

Later Alexandria became a centre for the development of these engines and in his study of the history of ancient artillery E. W. Marsden has shown that the problem of devising formulae for the calibration of machines so as to obtain accuracy at the desired range for a specific weight of missile was tackled and solved at Ptolemy's court, probably by about 275. The passage in Philo's *On Artillery Construction* describing this is of considerable interest.

In the old days, some engineers were on the way to discovering that the fundamental basis and unit of measure for the construction of engines was the diameter of the hole (sc. through which the twisted skein which acted as a spring passed). This had to be obtained, not by chance or at random, but by a standard method that could produce the correct proportion at all sizes. It was impossible to obtain it except by experimentally increasing and diminishing the perimeter of the hole. The old engineers, of course, did not reach a conclusion, as I say, nor did they determine the size, since their experience was not based on a sound practical foundation; but they did decide what to look for. Later engineers drew conclusions from former mistakes, looked exclusively for a standard factor with subsequent experiments as a guide, and introduced the basic principle of construction, namely the diameter of the circle that holds the spring. Alexandrian craftsmen achieved this first, being heavily subsidized because they had ambitious kings who fostered craftsmanship (50, 14–29, tr. Marsden).

This passage provides evidence for a concerted effort in communal research directed to a specific end. For the kings fighting-power was essential at least to maintain (or if possible to disturb) the *de facto* balance of power. They were actuated by no mere theoretical principles but by the urgency of vital matters of state. Warfare was basic and fundamental to all the major powers of the hellenistic age and it is not surprising that this was reflected in the patronage and direction of military technicians.

IX

In other fields however technology made only limping progress and eventually regressed. The reasons for this are complex and one is undoubtedly the fact that, as we have seen, there was only a feeble commitment to technology in the first place. But a contributory factor may have been a general weakening during the later hellenistic period in the rational outlook which seems essential for progress in both theoretical science and technology, a development which will be considered in more detail in Chapter 12. Greek philosophy at this time was not equipped to help the scientist. As we saw above (pp. 179–81), both

Epicureanism and Stoicism, the two leading philosophies of the period, subordinated the problem of understanding the world of nature to that of achieving peace of mind: their goal was ethical, and they sought to bring a personal advantage to their followers. Whereas the earlier philosophers before Socrates had taken the whole range of knowledge as their field, most (though not indeed all) of those of the hellenistic age restricted themselves to narrower aims which were in fact inimical to scientific progress.

Indeed science itself at this time frequently becomes the hand-maid of pseudo-science. Poseidonius of Apamea, a polymath of the first century (*c.* 135–*c.* 50), who eventually settled in Rhodes (see p. 19), is comparable in some respects to Eratosthenes but his interest in astronomy is as an aid to the astrological ideas which were firmly entrenched in his philosophical system – though it is perhaps salutary to recall that even Hipparchus (see p. 181) believed in astrology. A nice example is recorded by Augustine:

> Cicero relates that Hippocrates, the famous doctor, left an account of how, when two brothers fell ill at the same time and their illness became more serious and then was alleviated at the same time, he suspected that they were twins; but the Stoic Poseidonius, who was much addicted to astrology, was wont to insist that they were born – and conceived – under the same configuration of the stars. Thus what the doctor believed to be related to a highly similar mixture in their bodily constitution, the astrologer believed to be related to the power and configuration of the stars existing at the time of their conception and birth (*City of God*, v, 2 = Edelstein and Kidd, *Poseidonius*, fg. 111).

Today most informed opinion would regard both explanations as inadequate: but the difference in approach reflects two wholly different ways of looking at the natural world and the position of man in it. The change from the one to the other was a development detrimental to science.

X

In this chapter we have considered briefly some of the achievements of the hellenistic age in theoretical and practical science. These were indeed very considerable. As Lloyd has pointed out (*Greek Science*, pp. 177–8), two vital principles of investigation had already been discovered in the period before Aristotle, namely the use of mathematics as a method of investigating natural phenomena and the idea of empirical research to discover the truth. The hellenistic age is important for its development of these concepts and its application of them in various fields of scientific activity. A great deal was done and if one is sometimes surprised by unexpected limitations, the cause lies not in any failure of intellectual grasp or lack of creative imagination, but rather – despite such institutions as the Museum at Alexandria – in the absence of a concerted organizational drive by society as a whole. That, for the reasons we have considered, was not possible.

The Frontiers of the Hellenistic World:
Geographical Studies

The hellenistic age brought a vast extension to the areas occupied, in greater or lesser density, by Greeks. But to the east and south-east these shaded off without clearly defined frontiers. The three centuries we are considering were distinguished by a great deal of exploration and trade well beyond the regions of Greek occupation, and the cultural interchange which we have observed in Asia Minor, Iran, Bactria and Egypt was also experienced to a lesser degree in Arabia and India.

I

The motives behind Greek exploration were mixed. There was an element of scientific curiosity but also a search for wealth, for new commodities and new areas of trade. Alexander's campaigns had themselves stimulated interest in the more distant parts of the earth, and the results achieved under him were amplified by his successors. The early loss of the eastern provinces to the Mauryan empire did not cause the Seleucids to lose interest in the far east and its products. They maintained these and in addition sought to strike up connections with some areas which Alexander had never controlled. Under Seleucus I (d. 281) or Antiochus I (281–261) we hear of an expedition to the region of the Jaxartes (mod. Syrdarya) under the command of Demodamas of Miletus, who there 'erected altars to Apollo of Didyma' (Pliny, *Natural History*, vi, 49), and, following a plan of Alexander, there was an attempt to explore the Caspian under another Seleucid officer, Patrocles, who published a geographical work about 280. Later writers refer to this mainly for distances, but it also contained descriptive passages. Since however he believed that the Oxus ran into the Caspian Sea (Strabo, xi, 7, 3) and that this was a branch of the northern ocean (Strabo, ii, 1, 17), Patrocles' trustworthiness should perhaps not be rated very highly.

A little earlier Seleucus I had sent Megasthenes as his representative to visit the Mauryan emperor Candragupta at Pataliputra on the Ganges. Megasthenes wrote a book on India which, despite Strabo's assertion that he was a liar (ii, 1, 9), assembled a great deal of reliable information, including a description of the caste system, which has come down to us in a version in Diodorus (ii, 40–1). He also mentioned Ceylon (Taprobane). With the fall of the Mauryan empire in 184, Greeks once more crossed over into India from Bactria but knowledge of the sub-continent did not become more widespread, since the Parthian conquests soon reduced this contact by driving a wedge between the Greeks of the far east and the Seleucid kingdom.

India was important to the west for trade in spices and precious goods, and both Seleucids and Ptolemies alike were interested in securing these commodities and the profits to be made out of them. The main route from India was by sea from the Indus along the shores of Baluchistan and up the Persian Gulf to Seleuceia-on-the-Tigris, which was also a terminal point for caravans coming west via the Hindu-Kush and the cities of Bactra and Hecatompylus in what is now northern Iran. From Seleuceia there was a choice of routes using either the Euphrates or the Tigris to strike the Mediterranean at Antioch. From Antioch goods went on by land through Tarsus and Apamea in Phrygia to reach the Aegean at Ephesus. This trade route was under Seleucid control, but was subject to some pressure from the Ptolemies until Antiochus III's victory at Panium in 200 made Coele-Syria a Seleucid province. The Ptolemies for their part had access to goods from the east by a sea-route, and after Panium they depended entirely on this. It involved a voyage along the whole south coast of Arabia as far as the Gulf of Aden where Indian commodities merged with the spice trade of Arabia proper. 'The Sabaeans', writes Strabo (xvi, 4, 19), 'are a very large tribe in whose country myrrh and frankincense and cinnamon are produced; and on the coast is found balsam.' The Sabaeans inhabited what is now the Yemen, and during the third and second centuries both Sabaean and Indian goods were brought by caravan from Adana (mod. Aden) north through Arabia to the Nabataean town of Petra, whence they continued to Rabbatamana, Gerasa and Ptolemais in Palestine or to Suez and Alexandria. The loss of Coele-Syria in 200 deprived the Ptolemies of access to the northerly land section of this route, which now served Damascus and Antioch, and that compelled them to look in a different direction and to exploit routes which had been opened up to the Red Sea during the previous century.

Under the Ptolemies the southern boundary of Egypt lay much further north than had been the case under the native Pharaohs. The frontier lay at Aswan, with lower Nubia as a kind of buffer zone between Egypt and the Ethiopian kingdom of Meroe (south of the second cataract). Strabo (ii, 1; 20) records an expedition as far as Meroe under a certain Philo early in the third century but later, between 206–5 and 187–6, native risings cut off the whole of southern Egypt and the areas beyond from Alexandria. This secession was brought to an end with the defeat of the last of the Egyptian pretenders, Chaonnophris, in 186. More important to Ptolemaic trade however was the expansion and exploration which took place in the south-eastern desert towards the Red Sea.

This began early and continued throughout the reigns of the first four Ptolemies. It was linked partly with the search for trade-routes which would by-pass the exclusive and secretive Arabs of southern Arabia, but even more with the hunting of elephants. Ever since Alexander's battle with Porus on the Hydaspes (Jhelum), the value of elephants as a military arm had been recognized, and prestige required a body of elephants in any up-to-date army. The Ptolemies were debarred from obtaining their elephants from India, like Seleucus I, and so had to make their own captures of African elephants in Somaliland. Under a series of explorers the western shore of the Red Sea was settled with a line of ports. There was Philotera, 'a city in Trogodytice, founded by Satyrus who had been sent to investigate the Trogodytic country and to hunt elephants' (Strabo, xvi, 4, 5). This general of Ptolemy II is known also for his dedication to the queen Arsinoe Philadelphus found at Redesije in the Thebaid (*OGIS*, 30). The founding of Philotera was followed by that of a series of other cities, mainly bearing dynastic names – Arsinoe Trogodytice, Berenice Trogodytice, Ptolemais of the Elephant Hunts – though Myus Hormus, the most northerly, was an exception. Eventually there was a string of settlements on this coast reaching as far as the Straits of Bab-el-Mandeb.

The elephant-hunters have also left dedications. One found at Edfu is to Ptolemy IV (221–204) and his queen:

> To King Ptolemy and Queen Arsinoe, the Fatherloving Gods, and to Sarapis, and Isis, Lichas son of Pyrrhus, an Acarnanian, having been sent for the second time as commanding officer of the elephant hunt [set this up] (*OGIS*, 82).

In his account of the battle of Raphia fought between Ptolemy IV and Antiochus III in 217, Polybius describes how the elephants on both sides joined battle and in some cases fought forehead to forehead.

> But most of Ptolemy's elephants declined the combat, as is the habit of African elephants; for unable to stand the smell and trumpeting of the Indian elephants and terrified, I suppose, also by their great size and strength, they at once turn tail and take to flight before they get near them (v, 84, 5).

For many years this statement – it was the orthodox ancient view, perhaps going back to the historians of Alexander's expedition – was rejected as erroneous, since it was generally agreed that African elephants are larger than Indian. But since 1948, when Sir William Gowers published a classic article on the subject in *African Affairs* (1948), pp. 173 ff., it has been recognized that Ptolemy's elephants were not of the large bush variety but were the smaller so-called forest elephants, which are about a foot shorter in height. Polybius' account is therefore vindicated.

Ptolemaic expansion down the Red Sea coast served the needs of commerce as well as providing elephants for the Ptolemaic armies. The new ports were connected by roads and could be used to unload goods from the east which were then conveyed westward to the Nile by caravan and down that river to Alexandria. An inscription on a pillar at Pithom also informs us that in 270/69 Ptolemy II Philadelphus reopened an old Pharaonic canal running from the Nile at Bubastis to the Red Sea at Pithom (*ZäS*, 40 (1902), 66–75) along the line of the modern Sweetwater Canal, thus providing an alternative route by water, but this seems not to have been much used. After the loss of Coele-Syria Egypt depended wholly on the southern route for its far-eastern trade, and this trade later received a stimulus from the discovery, in a series of steps over a period between the end of the second century and the beginning of the Principate (30), of the monsoon winds. Pliny's account (*Natural History*, vi, 100–1) traces four stages in the development of the monsoon sailings to India and back but unfortunately these cannot be dated with any certainty. Nor is it easy to tie them in closely with two famous anecdotes which are generally associated with the discovery of the winds. The first of these, which Strabo (ii, 3, 4–5) attributes to Poseidonius, concerns a Cyzicene called Eudoxus who, having originally been guided by a shipwrecked Indian, made two journeys to India, the first in the reign of Ptolemy Euergetes II (d. 116), the second under Cleopatra (II or III) and Soter II (116–108); in both cases he was deprived of his cargo under the Ptolemaic laws. The second anecdote is related in an anonymous work of the first century AD, *The Coastal Voyage of the Erythraean Sea*, which is the name the Greeks gave to what is now the Red Sea, the Arabian Sea and the Persian Gulf. It tells how:

all the way from Cane and Arabia Felix they used to sail along the coast in smallish boats, and Hippalus, a pilot, was the first to discover the location of the ports and the formation of the ocean, and thus discovered the direct ocean route. For when the Etesian winds are blowing with us, in the Indian ocean the south-west wind arises, which is called the Hippalus (§57).

It seems likely that Hippalus' discovery of the direct route across the ocean belongs to a later stage, perhaps the last of those indicated by Ptolemy. But Eudoxus' second voyage appears to coincide with the period of greater interest in the eastern trade which is signalled by a change in the titulature of the *epistrategos* of the Thebaid.

It is known from inscriptions that from the early part of the first century and perhaps from the end of the second this important Ptolemaic official was given the additional title of 'general of the Red Sea and Indian Sea' and this new style seems to have been introduced to take account of a growth in the importance of the maritime trade with India – although the absence of positive evidence has led scholars to disagree strongly on the volume of trade taking this route. Eventually it was possible, making the fullest use of the monsoon in each direction, to do the round trip to the Malabar coast within the year but this was probably not done on a large scale until the early years of the Roman empire.

Meanwhile trade in and through the Red Sea continued to be considerable. A mid-second-century papyrus (*SB*, 7169) records a maritime loan made to finance a voyage 'to the spice-bearing lands' by a certain Archippus son of Eudemus, and arranged through an Italian banker, no doubt resident in Alexandria, called Gnaeus. We may perhaps leave this aspect of Ptolemaic trade and exploration with a glance at a dedication made in 130:

On behalf of King Ptolemy (Euergetes II) and Queen Cleopatra his wife, the Benefactor Gods, and their children, Soterichus son of Icadion of Gortyn, one of the chief body-guards, dispatched by Paos, kinsman and general of the Thebaid, to take charge of the gathering of precious stones and of navigation and to provide security for those conveying incense and other cargoes of foreign goods from the direction of Coptos [made this dedication] (*OGIS*, 132).

Soterichus, evidently a mercenary captain from Crete, is responsible for supervising the caravan routes from the Red Sea ports of Berenice, Myus Hormus and Leukos Limen via Coptos to the Nile and for securing the safety of Red Sea commerce.

II

So far we have been considering exploration and trade to the east and south-east. But at the very outset of the hellenistic period, perhaps in about 320, an astounding piece of navigation was carried out on the Atlantic by Pytheas, a sea-captain from Massalia (Marseille). Our knowledge of his voyage depends on references in several authors but especially on Strabo, who however discusses it in a context of polemic against Polybius, whose account was Strabo's own source. Thus many details of the voyage remain controversial and in particular the where-abouts of a mysterious land called Thule, which Pytheas either heard of or, more probably, visited. Concerning Thule Pytheas himself wrote:

> The barbarians showed us where the sun keeps watch at night, for around these parts the night is exceedingly short, sometimes two and sometimes three hours, so that only a short interval passes after the sun sets before it rises once more (Geminus, 6, 9).

A midsummer night of two to three hours corresponds to a latitude of about 65°, but whether Thule was Iceland, the Faroes, Shetland or the Norwegian coast is disputed. Pytheas had more to say on the arctic region where

> there was no longer any proper land nor sea nor air, but a sort of mixture of all three of the consistency of a jelly-fish in which the land and sea float, this medium in which one can

neither walk nor sail holding everything together, so to speak (Strabo, ii, 4, 1, based on Polybius).

It is difficult to see what exactly Pytheas was describing. Hypotheses have ranged from a muddy mixture of ice and water to phosphorescence, the aurora borealis, shallow water or an illusion experienced by men rowing in a sea-mist.

Though we cannot be quite certain about the details it looks as if Pytheas, setting out from Gades (mod. Cadiz) sailed north along the coast of Spain and Gaul to the island of Ushant off Brittany and from there reached Belerion, the western promontory of Cornwall (Land's End), in four days. From here he continued north to circumnavigate Britain in a clockwise direction. On the way he gathered information about the Outer Islands, the Orkneys and the Shetlands and, as we have seen, reached latitudes very near to those of the midnight sun. Before returning home he probably crossed the Channel from South Foreland and continued his voyage up the coast of Europe – perhaps as far as Jutland, but this is uncertain. Though a merchant, Pytheas was interested in scientific cartography and took bearings throughout his voyage, later recording these together with distances in a book entitled *On the Ocean*.

Like many pioneers, Pytheas met with much disbelief. His findings were accepted and used by Dicaearchus, Timaeus and Eratosthenes but the more usual reception was a hostile one and in this respect Polybius' contemptuous remarks about the unlikelihood that 'a private individual and a poor man should have traversed such vast distances on shipboard and on foot' (Polybius, xxxiv, 5, 7 = Strabo, ii, 4, 2) are typical. Polybius in fact had his own reasons for challenging any rival explorer in the Atlantic. For he himself made an important contribution to exploration there and, indeed, liked to picture himself as a second Odysseus, and one moreover who had ventured outside the Pillars of Hercules (at Gibraltar). Our knowledge of Polybius' voyage, which he undertook under the patronage of the great Roman general Scipio Aemilianus, immediately following the latter's destruction of Carthage in 146, depends on a passage in

Pliny (*Natural History*, v, 9) which tells us that

> when Scipio Aemilianus was in command in Africa the
> historian Polybius went round in a squadron furnished by the
> general for the purpose of exploring that continent.

Unfortunately some (but not all) of the manuscripts of Pliny
include a phrase mentioning Agrippa (the friend of the emperor
Augustus) which, if accepted as genuine, would make virtually
the whole of Pliny's account of the west African coast derive from
Agrippa and not from Polybius. If that is so we know virtually
nothing of Polybius' voyage. If however Pliny's account is taken
from Polybius – and it would be a little odd if he led in with the
sentence I have quoted about Polybius' voyage and then
proposed to make no further reference to it – it would seem likely
that he sailed down the west coast of Africa as far as Cape Juby in
southern Morocco. Full knowledge of the Atlantic coasts of
Spain and Gaul had however to wait for the Roman conquest of
those areas. Landmarks in this process were the conquest of
Galicia by D. Junius Brutus in 138/7 and Caesar's campaigns in
Gaul and Britain during the decade 59–50; but these events lie
outside the purview of the hellenistic world and belong rather to
the Roman period which supervened.

III

The vast expansion of the horizon brought about first by
Alexander and later by the exploration which we have been
considering was reflected in books of travel and accompanied by
an impressive development of geographical theory, mainly by
scholars at Alexandria and Rhodes. Of the former I have already
mentioned some of the writers who accompanied Alexander
and recorded their experiences – Callisthenes, Nearchus,
Onesicritus and Aristobulus (see Chapter 1). A later example is
the work *On the Red Sea*, written by Agatharchides of Cnidus in
the reign of Ptolemy Euergetes II (145–116) when, as we have

seen, there was an upsurge of interest in the route to India; unfortunately this work is lost, and survives only in the summaries of Photius, Diodorus and Strabo. More important than these, however, was the development in the theoretical aspects of geography and speculation about the terrestrial globe, its size and its zones and the relationship of the known world to the total area, which occurred in the third and second centuries. By about 300 Dicaearchus of Messene had devised a map of the world based on a central line of latitude running from the Pillars of Hercules along Mount Taurus in Asia Minor, and eastward following the Imaus range into further Asia, and on a meridian drawn through Lysimacheia on the Hellespont. This map was later criticized by Polybius for its dimensions, but the Straits of Messina, Cape Malea and Rhodes were to become canonical points supposedly on a central line.

Dicaearchus' map was revised and a new geographical synthesis attempted by Eratosthenes (see pp. 187–8). Even without his brilliant estimate of the length of the earth's circumference, Eratosthenes represents in many respects the high point of Greek geographical theory. He probably published two separate works, *On the Measurement of the Earth* and *On Geography*; it is the latter, consisting of three books, that contained his physical geography. It began with a general survey of the work of his predecessors including Homer, and then went on in the second book to a full discussion of all aspects of geography – the shape, size and position of the earth, the climatic zones, and the distribution of land and water. The last book described a projection of the world and the details essential for the construction of a world map, based on a combination of astronomic data, observations such as those of Pytheas and Alexander's bematists (who measured and recorded the distances covered on the march) and information taken from later geographical writers. Like that of Dicaearchus, his map contained a main line of latitude based on his and intersecting a meridian passing through Rhodes. But Eratosthenes also added six further meridians drawn at intervals between the western and eastern boundaries of the inhabited world and six further parallels running through Meroe, Syene, Alexandria, Lysimacheia, the mouths of the Borysthenes (Dnieper) and Thule.

Hipparchus of Nicaea added to his many scientific achievements (see pp. 186–7) an informed interest in geographical theory. He strongly criticized Eratosthenes for using unscientific methods, for example for arguing from similarities in vegetation to identity of latitude, but in addition he made a critical analysis of Eratosthenes' world-map, section by section. In his third book, without actually producing a map of his own, Hipparchus laid down a series of scientific principles on which such a map might be constructed. A novel and valuable feature of these was the concept of regular divisions (of 700 stades, i.e. about 80 miles) into which the whole map might be divided. In addition, he was the first man to suggest that longitude might be determined by observing the time of an eclipse at different points. But he underestimated the difficulties involved in organizing the necessary teams of observers and the lack of accurate chronometers was an additional obstacle.

Apart from a minor work no writings of Hipparchus have survived directly and our knowledge of his theories is derived from the *Almagest* of Claudius Ptolemaeus, who wrote in the second century AD. But from this work the outstanding character of his speculations emerges clearly. In Hipparchus the brilliance of Greek geographical theorizing seems to have outstripped the possibilities and resources of the times. His tables of latitude and longitude were a step towards a new conception of the scientific organization of knowledge but his work also brought geography to an impasse, which may help to explain the subsequent reaction and move towards purely practical work. Mathematics and astronomy were henceforth neglected in favour of descriptive geography and this culminated at the very end of the period we are considering, during the principate of Augustus, in the great geography of Strabo, which not only brought together critically a great deal of earlier work, but is today one of our main sources of knowledge for many of the writers we have been considering.

I

From the fifth century onwards the Olympian religion had been under attack. The sophistic movement had engendered a mood of scepticism about most accepted beliefs and at the same time many foreign cults had found a home in Greek cities. Worship of the traditional gods had often come to be associated with that of abstractions such as Friendship, Peace, Wealth or Democracy. Furthermore, the distinctions between god and man had been partly whittled away with the setting up of cults to outstanding men and to some extent by the claims made by some philosophers that with the aid of reason men could live like gods.

> We must not think only in mortal terms but as far as we can make ourselves like immortals and do all with a view to living in accordance with the highest principle that is in us (i.e. reason), for small though it may be in bulk yet in power and in preciousness it excels everything else . . . Such then for man is life in accordance with pure intellect (since this principle is most truly man) (Aristotle, *Nicomachean Ethics,* 1177b–8d).

Old certainties had gone and though ancient rites were still zealously performed in the conviction that what was traditional should be preserved, many people were at bottom agnostics or even atheists. The observance of established rituals must have meant little to many worshippers.

The expansion into new lands could only accentuate these often contradictory trends. For many reasons the new world of monarchic states with their new city foundations and, equally, the old cities of Greece proper and the Aegean basin now felt the impact of fresh religious attitudes and came to adopt new forms of religious experience. Contact with non-Greek populations who worshipped different gods, the deliberate encouragement of certain cults for reasons of state policy, the adoption either spontaneously or in reply to official hints or pressure of ruler-cult, the consciousness in individuals of new, personal emotional needs amid social isolation, the response to the uncertainties of a world in which swift changes brought frequent striking reversals of fortune (so that Fortune herself was often invoked as a powerful deity) – all these combine to create a confused and kaleidoscopic picture of change hard to get into focus.

It will be convenient in the first instance, therefore, to draw a distinction beween religious developments which occurred on the initiative of those in authority, kings and governments, and those cults and practices which men adopted of their own free will because they seemed to satisfy a genuine need.

II

The new kings who succeeded Alexander were all in a sense usurpers and so looked for religious support to help legitimize their pretentions and reinforce the claims of their new dynasties. It is a feature common to virtually all the new royal houses that they adopted some special protector god, necessarily from among the Olympians, since they still carried the veneration which sprang from a weight of tradition. The Antigonids in Macedonia claimed descent from Heracles, and placed his club as an emblem on their coins. This was clearly intended to link them with the Argeads, the family of Philip and Alexander, for as Polybius indicates 'Philip V throughout the whole of his life was at great pains to prove that he was related by blood to Philip II and Alexander' (v, 10, 10). And, as Livy tells us (in a passage based on Polybius),

the Argives believed that the kings of Macedonia were sprung from them, and in addition many of them were linked by bonds of private hospitality and family friendship with Philip V (xxxii, 22, 11).

This supposed descent, which thus linked the Antigonids too with the city of Argos, was taken seriously and according to Plutarch in the course of the battle of Pydna (168), which brought Antigonid rule in Macedonia to an end,

> the Macedonian king (Perseus), as Polybius tells us, . . . turned rein and rode off to the town in cowardly fashion, pretending that he was going to sacrifice to Heracles (*Aemilius Paulus*, 19).

This interpretation of Perseus' action as an act of cowardice was later turned against him.

The Seleucids found a special protector in Apollo. Seleucus was reputedly Apollo's son and had Apollo's symbol, an anchor, as a birthmark on his thigh (Justinus, xv, 4, 2). That claim was already accepted in 281 at Ilium where an inscription set up in honour of Seleucus, who had liberated the city from Lysimachus, records the granting of many privileges to the new king, including an altar at which the gymnasiarch was to sacrifice annually, the naming of a month *Seleuceius* and the establishment of a quadrennial 'crowned' festival (see p. 147) with musical, athletic and equestrian sections 'as for Apollo, the ancestor of the dynasty' (*OGIS*, 212). The last phrase is partly restored, but the wording seems assured, since it is confirmed by other inscriptions referring to the kinship of various Seleucids with the god.

The Ptolemies were especially devoted to the cult of Dionysus, perhaps as early as Ptolemy I (if a small bronze bust of Dionysus in the Walters Art Gallery at Baltimore does indeed carry Soter's features). His cult was fostered especially by Ptolemy IV, however, and it was probably he who issued a special decree regulating Dionysiac worship.

> By decree of the king. Persons who perform the rites of Dionysus in the interior shall sail down to Alexandria, those

between here and Naucratis within ten days from the day on
which the decree is published and those beyond Naucratis
within twenty days, and shall register themselves before
Aristobulus at the registration-office within three days from
the day they arrive, and shall declare forthwith from what
person they have received the transmission of the sacred rites
for three generations back and shall hand in the sacred book
(sc. on the mysteries of Dionysus) sealed up, inscribing
thereon each his own name *(BGU, 1211 = Select Papyri,
208).*

This decree has been interpreted as a repressive measure, but
others have taken it as evidence for royal patronage of the cult.
The most likely view is that it represents an attempt by the
government to encourage the formal and discourage the informal
celebration of Dionysiac rites. If that is so, it foreshadows a
similar attempt by the Roman government to 'put Dionysus in a
strait-jacket' – the phrase is that of E. R. Dodds, *The Greeks and
the Irrational*, p. 276 – when in 186 it promulgated the famous
senatorial decree on the Bacchanals. The reference in the
Ptolemaic decree to three generations indicates that the
Dionysiac cult had been established for a considerable time in the
Egyptian countryside (where the god was often associated with
Osiris and Sarapis: see p. 121). A famous inscription, copied at
Adulis in the sixth century AD by Cosmas Indicopleustes,
prefaces an account of the achievements of Ptolemy III with a
description of him as sprung on his father's side from Heracles,
the son of Zeus, and on his mother's side from Dionysus, the son
of Zeus (*OGIS*, 54).

The adoption of these patron gods by hellenistic kings
frequently (though not in Macedonia) links up with the
institution of ruler-cult, that is the worship of the dead and later
of the living monarch (and his wife) as gods. Cults to human
beings were not new. The Spartan Lysander, according to Duris
of Samos,

was the first Greek to whom the cities erected altars and made sacrifice as to a god, the first also to whom songs of triumph were sung . . . The Samians too voted that their festival of Hera should be called the Lysandreia (Plutarch, *Lysander*, 18, 3).

This was towards the end of the fifth century and in 357, after Dion had liberated their city, the Syracusans

set out tables and sacrificial meats and mixing-bowls, and as he came to them all pelted him with flowers and addressed him with vows and prayers as if he were a god (Plutarch, *Dion*, 29, 1).

These isolated examples foreshadow the worship accorded to Alexander in his lifetime, which has already been discussed (pp. 41–3).

The first example of such official worship among Alexander's successors was in Egypt, where Ptolemy I set up a cult of Alexander, perhaps as early as 290, and certainly before 285. In 283, on his death, Ptolemy II proclaimed his father a god and, on the death of the latter's widow in 279, set up a joint cult for the two as the Saviour Gods and associated with this cult a festival called the *Ptolemaieia* (see p. 147). Our knowledge of the development of dynastic cult in Egypt depends almost entirely on the possibility of dating documents containing the names and titles of priests of the various members of the royal family who were the objects of cult. From these it appears that a new development took place when Ptolemy II added a cult of himself and his sister and queen Arsinoe to that of Alexander under the title of *theoi adelphoi*, 'the Brother-Sister Gods'. The evidence for this is in an extract from a list of events under various priesthoods from the period round about 270 (*P. Hibeh*, 199).This papyrus contains the entry: 'In that year (sc. the fourteenth of Ptolemy II) . . . the name of the priest of Alexander and those of the Theoi Adelphoi were added to contracts.' Unfortunately we cannot be quite certain whether Ptolemy's accession is here being dated from his father's death in 283/2 or (as was later the case) from the beginning of their joint rule in 285, and so whether the appearance of the new cult is before or after Arsinoe's death in July 270 (i.e. in 272/1 or in 270/69 (or 269/8)); the former seems the more likely.

Henceforth the several Ptolemies added their names (and those of their queens) to the cult in their own lifetime but it was not until the reign of Ptolemy IV Philopator that the Saviour Gods were incorporated in the list. It may be noted that side by side with the growth of this practice of assimilating the living Ptolemies to gods went a decline in their real power and in their independence *vis-à-vis* the native priesthood. But already under Philadelphus the dead Arsinoe was declared a 'temple-sharing deity' (*synnaos theos*) in the temples of all the native gods. Her Greek cult was financed, as we saw (p. 110), by the diversion to it of the sixth-part tax on produce, hitherto a perquisite of the native temples. Indeed, both Arsinoe and Berenice, the daughter of Ptolemy III, who was similarly declared a *synnaos theos* in the temple of Osiris at Canopus by the Egyptian priests, seem to have commanded an unusual spontaneous regard and affection among the Egyptian people, who made their worship something more than a cult imposed from above. Their names, for instance, are found in use by members of Egyptian priestly families.

We cannot fully penetrate the mixture of religious and political motives which led the Ptolemies to make these moves. But they may well have derived encouragement from the attitudes revealed in Greek cities abroad, several of which had already shown themselves eager to thrust honours which came close to divinization on the Ptolemies and on any other kings who might temporarily enjoy their favour or exercise control over them. Thus, according to Pausanias 'the Rhodians gave (Ptolemy I) the name Saviour' (sc. for help against the Antigonid attack of 305) (i, 8, 6), for they had consulted the oracle of Ammon

in order to find out whether they should honour him as a god. With the agreement of the oracle they dedicated to him in the city a square enclosure on each side of which they constructed a portico a stade long; this was the Ptolemaion (Diodorus, xx, 100).

Already in 307 the Athenians had established a cult of Antigonus and Demetrius, now master of the city, under the title of the Saviours (Plutarch, *Demetrius*, 10, 3), so the Rhodian title may have been intended to rival this. In 294 or 291 we hear of further similar honours paid to Demetrius, who now had a separate cult, and according to Duris of Samos a hymn was sung in his honour which included these verses:

O son of the most mighty god Poseidon and of Aphrodite, hail! For other gods are either far away or have not ears, or do not exist, or heed us not at all; but thee we can see in very presence, not in wood and not in stone, but in truth. And so we pray to thee (Athenaeus, vi, 253e).

This hymn, Athenaeus continues, the victors of Marathon sang not only publicly, but also in their homes. 'When the old gods withdraw', comments Dodds, *The Greeks and the Irrational*, p. 242, 'the empty thrones cry out for a successor, and with good management or even without management, almost any perishable bag of bones may be hoisted into the vacant seat.' The hymn to Demetrius is an admission of political and perhaps spiritual helplessness in what had been the leading city of Greece.

Thus ruler-cult found a fertile soil in the Greek cities and the kings themselves were not slow to exploit the advantages which it offered. In the Seleucid realm however its development was slow and unsystematic and for a long time was left to the initiative of the Greek cities within the kingdom. There were moreover many stages on the way to full recognition as a god. Thus the Ilian decree, already mentioned (*OGIS*, 212; see p. 211), which recognized Seleucus I's Apolline ancestry and accorded him a festival, did not actually name him as a god. But the establishment of a sacred enclosure, altar, sacrifices, procession, games, hymn, offering of gold crowns, statues and the use of a dynastic name to designate a tribe or a month in the local calendar – all these leave only a fine line separating the recipient from divine honours.

Antiochus I proclaimed his father a god with the title of Seleucus Nicator but the first Seleucid to institute a *state* cult of himself and all his ancestors was Antiochus III (223–187). The evidence for this lies in a letter of 193/2 written by him to the satrap of Caria, Anaximbrotus, in which he appoints a priestess to his wife's cult:

> King Antiochus to Anaximbrotus, greeting. As we desired to increase still further the honour of our sister-queen Laodice ... we have now decided that, just as there are appointed throughout the kingdom high-priests of our cult, so there shall be established in the same districts high-priestesses of her also, who shall wear golden crowns bearing her image and whose names shall be mentioned in contracts after those of the high-priests of our ancestors and of us (Welles, *R.C.* no. 36; Robert, *Hellenica*, 7 (1949), pp. 17–18).

(Whereas Egypt had its one official royal cult in Alexandria, in the less centralized Seleucid kingdom a different high-priestess was appointed for each separate satrapy.) As regards the figures which made up the cult 'of our ancestors and of us', an inscription from Seleuceia-in-Pieria dating to the reign of Seleucus IV (187–175) lists those included up to then as:

> Seleucus (I) Zeus Nicator and Antiochus (I) Apollo Soter and Antiochus (II) Theos (literally; 'the god') and Seleucus (II) Callinicus and Seleucus (III) Soter and Antiochus (perhaps the son of Antiochus III who predeceased him) and Antiochus (III) the Great (*OGIS*, 245).

Unlike the Seleucids the Attalids were not recognized as gods in their lifetime and we have no evidence for an official dynastic cult in Pergamum but they were given cult recognition in many cities. Especially noteworthy are the honours accorded to

Apollonis, the wife of Attalus I, who received the cult title of Eusebes ('pious') during her lifetime (*OGIS*, 308) and was venerated in many cities. One example is that of Teos, where an inscription gives the details of a festival at which the sacrifice was to be the resonsibility of 'the priest of King Eumenes and the goddess Apollonis Eusebes and the priestess of her and queen Stratonice', and contains the provision for the founding of a temple to Apollonis with the further cult-name of Apobateria (literally 'stepping down': the temple would be erected on the spot where Apollonis came ashore on a visit to Teos) (*OGIS*, 309; better text in L. Robert, *Études anatoliennes* (Paris, 1937), p. 17).

The real significance of ruler-cult is not easy to define. It had a clear political aspect, in as much as cult and divinity, though often accorded spontaneously and in recognition of royal status, in their turn reinforced the power and legitimacy of the king and equally of his dynasty. The existence of dynastic right to the throne was of course one of the main distinctions between a king and a tyrant. Cult also helped relations with the cities since it was thence that the initiative to deification often arose and the incorporation of the king and his wife and ancestors among the city cults did not, to be sure, change the legal relationship between king and city, but did often create ties of goodwill and sentiment. In Egypt the institution was somewhat complicated by the quite independent position of Ptolemy as Pharaoh, and so a divine being, Horus the Falcon-God, eventually after his death to be identified with Osiris and immortal. With the strengthening of the influence of the Egyptian priesthood these concepts must have played an increasing part in men's attitudes towards the royal house.

What the paying of divine honours by the cities meant in terms of religious feeling is another matter. As the hymn sung to Demetrius at Athens makes clear, there was often a background of scepticism towards the traditional gods, which led to their replacement by dynasts wielding real power. But in what sense were such kings regarded as gods? Hardly in the same sense that Zeus was (or had once been) a god. As E. Will observes, to call

Antiochus *Theos*, 'the god', is in some way to qualify his divinity; one would never have spoken of Zeus Theos. And for what sort of god did one approach the traditional gods in prayer?

III

Ruler-cult and the adoption of patron-gods protecting the dynasty both carried obvious political implications. But many new religious developments were a response to changes in individual attitudes and to new social conditions. With the reduced power of the city-states went a decline in men's confidence in their traditional cults and a growing interest in mystery religions and this was encouraged by a falling off in the rationalism that had been characteristic of much fifth-century sophistic thought. These mystery cults involved secret initiation ceremonies and promised individual salvation; examples are the rites of Eleusis or those of the Cabiri on Samothrace. During the hellenistic period they remained basically Greek, and their growing popularity (like that of the Dionysiac cult) represents the accentuation of that other side which had always existed to Greek religion. This trend towards revelation, irrational and emotional, can also be illustrated from Epidaurus, where the cult of Asclepios and the miraculous cures effected among pilgrims who spent a night sleeping in the temple there are attested by many offerings and inscriptions, which reach their peak in the hellenistic age.

For many the decline in confidence in the city-gods meant a growth of scepticism, though this was frequently disguised. The philosophers, for example, were mostly agreed in not rejecting 'the gods' outright. Thus the Stoics under Zeno (335–263) and Chrysippus (280–207) glorified wisdom but Cleanthes (331–232), in a famous hymn, identified the Stoic principle with 'Zeus', and Epicurus (341–270), while arguing that the gods were unconcerned with human affairs, is careful not to reject their existence or to discourage paying due rites to them. These attempts to fit the gods into new philosophical patterns reveal the embarrassment of the philosophers and lead to the taking up of anomalous positions. Determined efforts were made to define the gods in terms acceptable to men who were basically sceptical about their existence. We can trace two trends, which are diametrically opposed. On the one hand, there was the line of thought primarily associated with the name of Euhemerus of Messene (who was writing under Cassander between 311 and 298). Euhemerus wrote a kind of utopia about a visit to an island, Panchaea, in the Indian Ocean where the Olympian Gods, who were originally men and had once reigned there as kings, were now worshipped as gods. Here there was a monument with a golden pillar

> on which the deeds of Uranus and Zeus were inscribed, and after these an account of the deeds of Artemis and Apollo had been added by Hermes (Diodorus, v, 45, 7; cf. vi, 2, 4–10).

Euhemerism did not become really popular until Euhemerus' work had been introduced to the Roman world in a Latin translation by the poet Ennius but his doctrines were known earlier – there is for instance some evidence that Polybius had resort to them in his interpretation of Homer's account of Odysseus' voyage – and they clearly had relevance to ruler-cult.

Alternatively divinity could be depersonalized by the growth of abstractions, a tendency already detectable in the fourth century (see p. 209). The piratical leader Dicaearchus, who plundered the Aegean in the pay of Philip V of Macedonia, so Polybius alleges,

> wherever he anchored his ships, constructed two altars, one of Impiety and the other of Lawlessness, and on these he sacrificed and worshipped those powers as though they were divine (Polybius, xviii, 54,10).

A more orthodox sort of abstract deity was *Tyche* (Fortune), who was widely worshipped in the hellenistic world. *Tyche* plays an important role in the *History* of Polybius· himself, and an ambiguous one, since the historian's practical purpose of offering political instruction to his readers involved the assumption that history followed rational lines, so that by studying the past one could learn to operate effectively in the present, whereas his secondary purpose – to impart moral lessons by giving examples of the vicissitudes that had afflicted men in the past – equally involved the assumption that Fortune played a significant part in men's lives and must be guarded against, or at any rate taken into account. This ambiguity in Polybius' attitude towards *Tyche* corresponds to the ambiguity inherent in the very nature of the concept of Fortune, which can be good or bad, and which, more importantly, wavers between the notion of 'haphazard chance' and 'purposeful and providential action' (which can be the work of either a beneficent or a malevolent power). In the form of a city's *Tyche*, visualized as bearing a mural crown and a cornucopia signifying abundance, men tried to deify fortune as a benevolent goddess but how far men really personalized such an abstraction and whether they had any consistent view about it is a problem almost impossible to answer.

More important to the ordinary man and woman were the oriental cults, especially those of Egypt, which increasingly penetrated the Greek world to fill the gap left by the collapse of belief in the indigenous gods. We have already observed (see p. 121) the great popularity enjoyed in the Greek world by the cult of Sarapis, the new god introduced under Ptolemy I. Equally popular was the worship of Isis, which was already familiar in the fourth century, but became much more widespread in the second. Isis owed something of her importance to her ability to absorb other deities, including those of Olympus. This process of syncretism can be well illustrated from a hymn written in the first century by an Egyptian priest named Isidorus, and inscribed on the temple of Isis at Medinet-Madi in the Fayum.

> The Syrians call you Astarte-Artemis-Nanaia and the tribes of the Lycians Queen Leto, and the Thracians call you indeed the mother of the gods, and the Greeks mighty-enthroned

Hera and Aphrodite and good Hestia, and Rhea and Demeter, but the Egyptians Thiouis, because in your own person alone you are all the other goddesses named by the peoples (*SEG*, viii (1937), 548).

If all goddesses are indeed one goddess and all gods one god, then one is already well along the road to monotheism.

The Egyptian gods were not the only ones to be taken over by the Greeks. Though less popular than Isis and Sarapis, Cybele, the great Anatolian mother-goddess, attended by Attis, the Phrygian god Men, the Assyrian deities Atargatis and Hadad (identified with Aphrodite and Zeus), Melqart (identified with Heracles), Astarte (identified with Aphrodite), Sabazius, Adonis and many others found a home in Greek cities, especially in such cosmopolitan places as Rhodes and Delos, or Demetrias in Thessaly, where an inscribed sacred relief to Atargatis has recently been discovered (V. von Graeve in V. Milojcič and D. Theocharis, *Demetrias*, I (Bonn, 1976) pp. 145–56). In particular cults offering a personal contact with the divinity or the promise of personal survival after death were especially popular. The epithet Soter ('saviour') accorded now to Zeus and other gods as well as to kings who were the object of ruler-cult is an indication of this desire, which often led to the grafting of initiation ceremonies on to eastern cults, which did not previously possess them in that form. This is true of Isis, whose hellenized mysteries provide so striking a climax in book xi of Apuleius' *Metamorphoses*, a work written in the second century AD but relevant to the religious experience of the hellenistic age.

IV

We have so far been considering changes in Greek attitudes towards the traditional gods and new forms of religious experience towards which men were now turning, some with their roots in traditional aspects of Greek religion, others borrowed from Egypt and the east. But no survey of religious ideas in this period can neglect the special history of the Jewish people during the hellenistic age, and in particular the revolt of the Maccabees in the middle of the second century, for in their case a combination of religious and nationalist motives culminated in the violent Hasmonean rising against the Seleucid monarchy and so helped to create the conditions in Palestine which made it fertile soil for the rise of Christianity two hundred years later. We are fortunate in possessing rich and varied sources for these events, some going back to the first half of the second century.

The book of *Daniel* was probably written before 163, since it shows no knowledge of Antiochus IV's death that year nor of the restoration of the temple at Jerusalem by Judas Maccabaeus. It has to be read alongside the commentary of Hieronymus (St. Jerome), especially book xi of this work. There are also *Maccabees* I and II drawing on archives and recent family traditions, the first a strongly Jewish nationalist work written no earlier and probably a little later than 104, and covering the years 175–135, and the second an abridgement of a five-volume Jewish history written in Greek by Jason of Cyrene, covering the years 175–160. Jason wrote in 142, his epitomator around 125. These main sources can be supplemented by the *Letter of Aristeas* to Philocrates, the work of a hellenized Jew of Alexandria, and the less important third and fourth books of the *Maccabees*. Later, in the first century AD, Josephus wrote a comprehensive account of Jewish history, of which book XII recounts the Hasmonean rising.

Whether still living in Palestine or scattered, as many already were, in other lands, the Jews possessed a religion, monotheistic and exclusive, which made it hard for the orthodox to come to terms with the Greeks around them or to acquiesce in the demands of hellenistic kings. Their special beliefs made the Jews an object of dislike to their neighbours and Diodorus, probably following the first-century writer Poseidonius, in his account of the advice given to Antiochus VIII Euergetes to wipe out the Jews completely, when they asked for terms of surrender in 134, retails the anti-semitic slanders which circulated among their enemies.

The Jews alone of all nations avoided dealings with other people and looked on all men as their enemies. They pointed out too that the ancestors of the Jews had been expelled from Egypt as men who were impious and detested by the gods. For by way of purging the country all persons who had white or leprous marks on their bodies had been assembled and driven across the border, as being under a curse; the refugees had occupied the territory round about Jerusalem and having organized the nation of the Jews had made their hatred of mankind into a tradition and on this account had introduced utterly outlandish laws: not to break bread with any other race nor to show them any goodwill at all (Diodorus, xxxiv/xxxv, 1).

These slanders were largely a reaction to the exclusiveness of the orthodox Jews but in the conditions of the hellenistic world many Jews deviated considerably from orthodoxy, especially in the *diaspora*.

A particularly large Jewish population had settled in Egypt, some traditionally established in Alexandria by Alexander himself (Josephus, *Against Apion*, ii, 36–41), others perhaps taken prisoner in the Ptolemaic campaign in Palestine (as Agatharchides related) and others no doubt going there as mercenaries. Still earlier there were Jews at Elephantine in the fourth century. They lived scattered throughout the countryside, and there was a large Jewish community in Alexandria, whose members probably lived among the Greeks until the middle of the second century, but subsequently came together into a ghetto. Strabo, quoted by Josephus (*Antiquities of Judaea*, xiv, 7, 2), informs us that

they have at their head an ethnarch, who administers the community, arbitrates in the courts, concerns himself with contracts and issues decrees, as if he were the head of an independent city.

That this officer already existed in hellenistic times is clear from another passage in Josephus (*Antiquities of Judaea*, xv, 5, 2), which explains that Augustus merely renewed the office. Many Jews in Egypt were considerably hellenized and had abandoned Hebrew for Greek. The *Letter of Aristeas*, probably falsely, attributes to Ptolemy II the initiative for having the Greek translation of the Old Testament which we know as the Septuagint made but the Jews probably arranged this themselves, for a Greek translation was essential to those no longer able to read the original, or unable to read it with ease. Another sign of the hellenization of this community is the book of another hellenized Jew, Aristobulus (known only via later writers), who composed a commentary on the Pentateuch which set out to reconcile the scriptures with pagan Greek writings by supposing that an early Greek translation of the Old Testament had been drawn on by Greek writers from Homer to Aristotle.

For the Jews of Palestine the conquest by Antiochus III in 200 at first brought little change. Here too hellenization had made some headway. The book of *Ecclesiastes* was written about 250 under the full influence of Greek ideas, and the strong counter-current of Jewish orthodoxy can be seen in the *Wisdom* of Jesus ben Sirach (*Ecclesiasticus*), written in Hebrew in 197 and translated into Greek at Alexandria in 132. Fragments of the Hebrew version of this work found at Qumran in 1947 supplement those discovered in the Ezra synagogue at Cairo fifty years earlier and testify to the popularity of this work among orthodox Jews resisting hellenism. It was their vigorous and almost fanatical opposition to all concessions to hellenism and their treatment of all modifications of the traditional rules, laws and tabus of Judaism as a form of apostasy which raised the resistance of the Jews to the Seleucids from the cultural level to that of insurrection.

We cannot here follow the rising of Judas Maccabaeus and his supporters in detail. The conflict arose out of royal attempts to seize the revenues of the Temple under Seleucus IV (which failed through a divine epiphany : 2 Macc., iii, 13–28). Then under Antiochus IV a hellenizer, Jason, became High Priest and promised large contributions to the king

> if he would allow him by his authority to set up a gymnasium
> and ephebic training and inscribe the Antiochenians who
> were in Jerusalem (2 Macc., iv, 9).

The last phrase is ambiguous and has led to much disagreement.
Bickerman, who translates it in the above fashion, takes it to
mean the setting up of a Greek *politeuma*, with gymnasium and
ephebic organization, in Jerusalem, thus creating a second and
parallel government in the city alongside the temple state but
Tscherikover translates the phrase 'to make those in Jerusalem
Antiochenians', which would mean that Jerusalem would
become a Greek city under the name of Antioch. Either version
can be defended and the arguments are not decisive one way or
the other.

From this point the conflict became more acute. Antiochus IV
pressed on with his policy of hellenization, hoping thereby to
unify his kingdom, which had been severely weakened by the
ultimatum of C. Popilius Laenas in 168, which forced his
withdrawal from Egypt (see pp. 238–9), and he plundered the
Temple in his need for cash. The Jews first organized a guerrilla
action under Mattathias and later Judas Maccabaeus, his son,
mobilized full-scale armies and in 164 recovered and purified the
Temple, which had been polluted by Antiochus' provocative
sacrifice of a pig. The war dragged on. Nicanor, a representative
of Demetrius I, perished, and then in 160 Judas himself was
killed. Subsequently the Jewish revolt became entangled with
the dynastic conflicts of the Seleucid kingdom. A series of
campaigns were led by Judas' brothers Jonathan and then
Simon, and eventually in 141 Simon conquered the citadel at
Jerusalem and Demetrius II made a significant concession.

> Now I grant you all the taxes which the kings before me
> remitted and all other payments which they remitted. And I
> have given you the right to mint your own stamped coinage in
> your country (1 Macc., xv, 5–6).

H.W.—H

Minting was a right rarely and usually reluctantly granted.

The Jewish conflict continued but at this point it becomes part of the Roman history of the near east. Within the Jewish communities both of Palestine and of the diaspora – those Jews living in Egypt, Asia Minor and Europe – there was still a gulf between strict orthodoxy and those who embraced some degree of hellenism but the lines were often blurred. Under Roman rule the orthodox Jews of Palestine raised repeated revolts down to the final rising of Bar Kochba at the time of Hadrian. But alongside these intransigent rebels there were other Jews more outward-looking, and it was largely in the context of hellenized Jewry that the rise of Christianity took place. Paul, himself a devout Jew but also a Roman citizen, experienced a call to preach the gospel to the gentiles, which meant in effect the Greek or hellenized communities of Asia Minor and Greece (Galatians, 1, 16) and his first letter to the church in Corinth (1 Cor., 12, 12–26) describes the Christian community in terms similar to those used by the Stoics to characterize the body politic. Later in the second century AD many Christian apologists were to draw extensively on the teachings and language of Greek philosophy and especially on those of the Cynics to present the Christian case. Thus, in the form in which it was eventually to win acceptance as the official religion of the Roman empire, Christianity was essentially the product of a mixed Jewish and hellenistic environment.

I

By the time that the Romans began to make their presence felt in the Greek east, the original elan of the hellenistic kingdoms had already begun to weaken. Despite the achievements of Antiochus III and the impression created by his eastern march into central Asia (see p. 123) the Seleucid monarchy was under pressure from the Parthians in the east and from a series of internal revolts, and in Egypt the power of the Greek ruling caste was gradually being eroded to the advantage of the native priesthood. The importance of these factors as elements in the disintegration of the hellenistic state system is however minimal in view of the decisive effects of the Roman intrusion. This began with the First Illyrian War in 229 and within a few decades subordinated all the hellenistic centres of power to the dictates of the Roman Senate. The character of the Romans and the values and organization of their state set them apart from the Greeks and indeed from all the other peoples of the hellenistic world. Rome was a highly militarized state in which the values of the ruling aristocracy were closely linked to military achievement. Repute, *gloria*, was the reward of *virtus*, manly courage, expressed in service to the *patria* by the holding of high office and the waging of war. Claims to have success recognized by the award of a ceremonial triumphal procession were measured in terms of booty won and enemy slain.

Some of the earliest known Roman inscriptions commemorate the military achievements of Roman consuls.

Lucius Cornelius Scipio Barbatus, Gnaeus' begotten son, a valiant man and wise, whose fine form matched his bravery

most closely, was aedile, consul and censor among you; he
took Taurasia and Cisauna, in Samnium; he subdued all the
land of Lucania and brought away hostages (*CIL* i, 2,
1 = *Remains of Old Latin*, iv, 2).

This verse epitaph on a Scipio who was consul in 298 exemplifies
the values of a warlike and aristocratic society.

The Illyrian wars were not Rome's first contact with the Greek
world. From the sixth century onwards the Latin city had been
subjected to Greek influence through the Greeks in Campania
and also, indirectly, through Etruria, though the Romans seem
always to have had the ability to take what they needed from the
Greeks, often changing its character in the process. The word
triumphus for example was an early borrowing from the Greek
thriambos, a hymn to Dionysus, but the triumph was an
institution peculiarly Roman. There were Greek vases in sixth-
century Rome and by the fifth century the Dioscuri were being
worshipped at nearby Lavinium. The Greeks too were not
without knowledge of Rome. In the fifth century Hellanicus of
Lesbos recorded a version of the founding of Rome by Aeneas
(Dionysius of Halicarnassus, *Roman Antiquities*, i, 72, 2); and a
century later Theopompus, Aristotle, Heracleides Ponticus and
Theophrastus all knew of Rome's existence; indeed Heracleides
asserted falsely that Rome was a Greek city. Nor was this
knowledge surprising, since by the end of the fourth century the
Romans had already expanded into central and southern Italy.
The Samnite Wars (to which Scipio Barbatus' epitaph refers)
brought them up against old-established Greek settlements
around the toe, heel and instep of Italy and from 280 to 275 they
were involved in a war against Pyrrhus of Epirus, a Greek
condottiere of the generation following Alexander and related to
him, who had brought his army to Italy to fight for Tarentum.
The failure of Pyrrhus to stem the Roman advance led to Roman
control of all the southern and central part of the Italian
peninsula and from now onwards the hellenistic world had to
take serious note of the Romans.

In 264 they clashed with Carthage over the control of Messana

on the Sicilian Straits. The sequel was the long First Punic War
(264-241) against the main non-Greek state in the Mediterranean.
It ended with Rome as a naval power and in possession of Sicily.
It suited the Romans not to annex the whole island. Hiero II, the
king of Syracuse, was confirmed as ruler of a large area in the east
of the island and remained a loyal client prince until his death in
215. The western half of the Greek world – Sicily and southern
Italy – was now squarely within the Roman sphere of control and
the Greeks of the eastern Mediterranean were well aware of what
was happening. There were of course regular trading links
between east and west, as the many Rhodian vase handles found
in southern Italy and dating from around 300 indicate. A
'Roman' ship picked up Aratus of Sicyon in Greek waters in 252
(Plutarch, *Aratus*, 12) – perhaps it was really from southern Italy,
for Italians soon learnt to exploit the name of Rome – and a
Roman figures as *proxenos* on an Aetolian list of 263 (*IG*, ix², i, 7a,
l. 51). In particular there appear to have been links between the
Roman west and the Ptolemies. Hiero's taxation system, for
instance, which was later taken over by Rome (our knowledge of
it rests mainly on Cicero's famous orations against Verres, a
corrupt governor of Sicily), exhibits many parallels with the
Revenue Laws of Ptolemy II (see pp. 110–11). The relations
between the two kingdoms were close and although the *Revenue
Laws* lay down a sixth as the proportion of the products of
vineyards and gardens to be paid to the government and Hiero's
system a tithe, there is mention of a tithe in two places in the
Revenue Laws (*P. Rev. Laws*, cols. 24 and 80) and a tithe is also
mentioned on an inscription of Telmessus, dated to 240, when it
was Ptolemaic. It is now known, moreover, that the cities and
rulers which granted *asylia* to the temple of Asclepios in Cos in
242 included Naples and Elea in Italy and Camarina and Phintias
in Sicily (*Abh. Berlin. Akad.* (1952), 1). There can be little doubt
that the approach by the sacred delegates of Cos had the
approbation of Rome, and Cos will have been within the
Ptolemaic sphere of interest at this time.

Roman forces first crossed the Adriatic in 229 in a police action
against the Illyrians.

This is a matter not to be lightly passed over but deserving the serious attention of those who wish to gain a true view of the formation and growth of the Roman dominions (Polybius, ii, 2, 2).

The conflict arose out of Illyrian piracy. The Romans confronted the Illyrian queen Teuta with an ultimatum which was almost bound to lead to war even had the Illyrians not murdered one of the Roman envoys. A successful campaign left Rome with a group of friendly states closely linked to her – Corcyra, Apollonia, Epidamnus, Issa, and the Parthini and the Atintani on the Illyrian mainland (Polybius, ii, 12, 4–8). Thus by 220 and the start of the war with Hannibal the Romans had already made their first modest contact with the Greek world east of the Adriatic and established friendly relations with some of the leading states of Greece proper. In 219, simultaneously with the events in Spain which precipitated the Second Punic War, the Romans sent over a fresh expeditionary force against Demetrius of Pharos, a local Illyrian dynast who had become a friend of Rome in 229, but had since kicked over the traces by sailing south on piratical expeditions in defiance of the treaty made with Teuta. Demetrius was expelled and the Romans took over Pharos and strengthened their grip on Illyria.

II

Polybius chose the year 220 as the starting point for his main narrative of the events which led the Romans from the disasters of the first years of the Hannibalic War to control over 'the whole inhabited world in almost fifty-three years' (see p. 19). We can trace four broad stages in their advance in the east: (a) and (b), the two wars against Philip V of Macedonia (211–05 and 200–197); (c) the war against the Aetolians and Antiochus III of Syria (192–88) and (d) the war against Perseus of Macedonia (172–68). Roman motives in fighting these wars have been and still are extremely controversial; they are not however relevant to our present enquiry, which is directed rather towards tracing the stages of Roman penetration and assessing its effect on the cities and monarchies it encountered.

The First Macedonian War broke out when Philip V, in the hope of securing territory in Illyria, made a treaty with Hannibal, who after three remarkable victories at Trebia, Trasimene and Cannae, had reached an apparently dominant position in his war against Rome in Italy (summer 215). The threat which that war extended to the states east of the Adriatic had not gone unnoticed by intelligent Greeks. Since 220 a war had been in progress between two coalitions centring on the Aetolian League and the Achaean League (with Philip V and the Macedonians) respectively. At a conference called at Naupactus to end this war in 217 Agelaus of Naupactus, an Aetolian, made a striking plea to close the ranks.

> It is evident even to those of us who give but scanty attention to affairs of state that whether the Carthaginians beat the Romans or the Romans the Carthaginians in this war, it is not in the least likely that the victors will be content with the sovereignty of Italy and Sicily, but they are sure to come here and extend their ambitions and their forces beyond the bounds of justice . . . If once you wait for these clouds that loom in the west to settle on Greece, I very much fear lest we may all of us find these truces and wars and games at which we now play so rudely interrupted that we shall be fair to pray to the gods to give us still the power of fighting with each other and making peace when we will, the power in a word of deciding our differences for ourselves (Polybius, v, 104, 3ff.).

It has been argued that Agelaus' speech was made up by Polybius, writing when the implicit 'prophecy' had already become reality but the arguments are on the whole stronger for accepting the genuineness of Agelaus' intervention, for it is rather improbable that Polybius would have chosen one of the hated Aetolians as a mouthpiece for his own views.

Philip's interest in Rome about this time receives interesting confirmation from the letter which he wrote to Larissa two years after the Peace of Naupactus, and in which he quotes the Romans as a precedent for a liberal policy towards recruiting new citizens (see pp. 150–1). Once the war with Aetolia was off his hands he was free to turn his attention to Illyria and the conflict with Rome. The treaty which he made in 215 with Hannibal had limited aims and was mainly designed to secure his position in Illyria, as the following clauses show:

> As soon as the gods have given us victory in the war against the Romans and their allies, if the Romans ask us to come to terms of peace, we (sc. Hannibal and the Carthaginians) will make such a peace as will comprise you too and on the following conditions: that the Romans may never make war upon you, that the Romans shall no longer be masters of Corcyra, Apollonia, Epidamnus, Pharos, Dimale, the Parthini or the Atintani (Polybius, vii, 9, 12–13).

Incidentally, these clauses also show that neither Philip nor Hannibal envisaged that the war would see the extinction of Rome.

Faced by the embarrassment of an additional war in Greece the Romans in 211 made a treaty with the Aetolians, some clauses of which have been preserved in a fragmentary inscription found at Thyrrheum in Acarnania.

> . . against all these . . . the magistrates of the Aetolians shall take such action as he (?) would have done. And if the Romans shall seize any cities of these peoples by force, as far as the Roman people is concerned it shall be permitted to the Aetolian people to possess these cities and their territory; but whatever the Romans seize other than the city and its territory, the Romans shall have this. But if the Romans and the Aetolians take any of these cities together, as far as the Roman people is concerned the Aetolians may keep the cities and their territory; but whatever they take other than the city, both shall possess it jointly. If any of these cities go over to or

join the Romans or the Aetolians, as far as the Romans are concerned the Aetolians shall be allowed to take over these men, cities and lands into their confederation ... autonomous ... for the Romans ... peace (*SVA*, 536).

This compact and the nature of the war which followed it aroused great resentment among the Achaeans and Philip's other allies, for while it showed the Romans to be uninterested in annexing territory, it underlined their zest for loot and plunder, including human plunder. The savagery with which they waged war in Greece (they sacked the Achaean city of Dyme and enslaved its population (Livy, xxxii, 22, 10)) won them much ill-will which it subsequently required a determined propaganda campaign to eradicate.

The First Macedonian War ended in 205 with the Peace of Phoenice, made after the Aetolians had already concluded a separate peace with Philip, but it was not to last. In 200 a Roman commander was again in the Balkan peninsula and this time Philip was attacked within the frontiers of Macedonia. The Second Macedonian War (200–197) was noteworthy for the Roman exploitation of the theme of Greek liberty (for its earlier use by Antigonus I and its subsequent use as a slogan see pp. 51–2, 93). At various crucial points in the war 'freeing the Greeks' was put forward as a prerequisite for any settlement and the Roman victory of 197 was followed by the declaration of Greek freedom, already quoted on p. 98. The reality was different. The war had in fact placed a considerable constraint upon the independence of the leading Greek states, the Aetolian and Achaean Leagues. In addition the dominant position of the Romans was already affecting cities as far away as Asia Minor, who now began to look to the Senate to solve their problems.

This is well illustrated by an inscription of 196 from Lampsacus on the Asian side of the Hellespont, which records a decree honouring a citizen, Hegesias, who had undertaken a dangerous mission which everyone else had declined.

Having been elected and judged worthy by the people he

thought nothing of the dangers involved in being abroad but counting his own affairs of less importance than the advantage of the city, he went abroad into Greece and along with his fellow-envoys met the Roman commander in charge of the fleet, Lucius (sc. L. Quinctius Flamininus, brother of the general) and explained to him at length that the people (sc. of Lampsacus) being kinsmen and friends of the Roman people had sent them to him and that in company with his fellow-envoys he urged and begged him, since the Romans were our kinsmen, to take thought for our city, so that whatever seemed advantageous to its people might be brought about, for it behoved them (sc. the Romans) always to protect the interests of our city owing to our kinship with them and owing to the fact that the people of Massalia, who are friends and allies of the Roman people, are our brothers. And when they had received a suitable answer from him (sc. L. Flamininus) they dispatched this in its entirety to the city; as a result of which the people were in better heart. For in this he (sc. L. Flamininus) made clear that he acknowledged our relationship and kinship with the Romans and promised that if he established friendship or exchanged oaths with any party he would include our city in these. and would maintain our democracy, autonomy and peace and would do whatever might advantage us, and that if anyone tried to injure us he would not allow it, but would prevent it . . . And [Hegesias] having, along with his fellow-envoys met the treasurer in charge of the fleet (sc. the quaestor attached to L. Flamininus) and having persuaded him to be of continuing assistance, received from him too a letter to our people, and knowing this to be advantageous incorporated it in the official dossier . . . (here a line is missing) . . . and [wishing to accomplish everything] concerning which he had the decrees, he sailed to Massalia, a long and dangerous voyage, and there coming before the Six Hundred (sc. the Council in that city) he requested and brought it about [that he received envoys] to join him in his embassy from Massalia to Rome; and judging it useful they asked for and received from the Six Hundred a helpful letter on our behalf to the people of the Galatian Tolistoagii. And having arrived in Rome with his fellow-envoys and those sent from Massalia and having had an interview with the Senate along with them, he heard (sc. the Massaliotes) declaring their goodwill and kind disposition towards us and renewing their existing friendship with us and explaining to them (sc. the Senate) that they are brothers of our people and that their goodwill arises out of their kinship. And he (sc. Hegesias) also made clear about [the situation] and the matters concerning which the people sent this embassy and together with his fellow-envoys he urged them to take thought for the safety of their other friends and kinsmen and to protect our own city because of our kinship and the existing ties of goodwill between us and the letter of introduction which we had from the Massaliotes, which merited a reply advantageous to the people; and upon the envoys urging that they might be included in the treaty which the Romans made with the king (sc. Philip V), the Senate included us in the treaty with the king, as they also write, and concerning all other matters the Senate referred them to the Roman consul, Titus (sc. T. Quinctius Flamininus, in fact proconsul at this time) and the ten . . . And on reaching Corinth with . . . and Apollodorus he met the general and the ten and having spoken to them about the people and having urged them with great zeal to take care on our behalf and to contribute to our preserving our democracy and autonomy (there is an anacoluthon here); concerning which he received a . . . decree and letters to the kings (probably Eumenes of Pergamum and Prusias of Bithynia) (*Syll.*, 591).

The prolixity and repetitiveness of this inscription may reflect the incompetence of those drafting it, but it also gives some idea of the tedious harangues to which Roman commanders, legates and Senate began to be subjected from now on. It also throws light – and it is for this reason that it seemed worthwhile quoting it at length – on the steps which a Greek city in Asia thought it advisable to take in 197/6 on the eve of the Roman peace with

Philip to obtain the goodwill of the Romans. The reason is not far
to seek. Though nowhere mentioned in the surviving part of the
inscription, the danger Lampsacus feared came from Antiochus
III, who at that very time was proceeding against Smyrna and
Lampsacus. Hegesias' embassy, which took him to Greece,
Massalia, Rome and back to Greece to Flamininus and the ten
commissioners (sent to supervise the peace), must have begun in
197. But from Livy we learn that in 196, when Antiochus was
attempting to compel all the cities of Asia Minor to accept his
suzerainty,

> Smyrna and Lampsacus asserted their freedom and there was
> the danger that, if they were conceded what they claimed,
> other cities in Aeolis and Ionia would follow the lead of
> Smyrna, and others on the Hellespont that of Lampsacus
> (xxxiii, 38, 3 ff.).

Already in 197 Lampsacus in her dilemma had turned to Rome.
The Lampsacenes were regarded as akin to the people of Ilium
and they in turn claimed kinship with the Romans because of the
foundation of Rome by Trojan Aeneas. The Massaliotes were
'brothers' of the Lampsacenes since both cities were colonies of
Phocaea. There is no evidence, as some scholars have thought,
that Lampsacus was in danger from the Galatian Tolistoagii.
Hegesias merely used the occasion of his visit to Massalia to
obtain a letter from this great city, which stood in an area
surrounded by Gaulish peoples, and was influential also with the
Gauls of Asia Minor, to smooth relations with the latter, perhaps
with a view to hiring mercenaries (though that is speculation).
This inscription thus illuminates very clearly not only the
manner in which Rome was being drawn into the affairs of Asia,
but also the elaborate network of relationships which the Romans
had to take into account in their new diplomacy.

III

The war with Philip left the Aetolians hostile and disgruntled. They regarded Cynoscephalae as largely their victory, yet the Romans brusquely rejected their claims to several cities in Thessaly which had belonged to Philip. At the same time the advance of ,Antiochus III to the Hellespont was affecting his relations with Rome. The two currents converged and in 192 the Aetolians rashly resolved 'that Antiochus should be summoned to liberate Greece and to arbitrate between the Aetolians and the Romans' (Livy, xxxv, 33, 8). This meant war; and the war as usual ended in a resounding victory for Rome. The Aetolian defeat reinforced Roman influence in Greece proper (though the Romans still made no annexations) and the settlement in Asia banished the Seleucids from all districts west of the Taurus range. But in the liberated areas the much publicized principle of Greek freedom was no longer upheld. The general principles behind the Roman settlement were these:

> All autonomous towns which formerly paid tribute to Antiochus but had now remained faithful to Rome were freed from tribute; all which had paid contributions to Attalus (the king of Pergamum) were to pay the same sum as tribute to Eumenes (his successor); any which had abandoned the Roman alliance and joined Antiochus in the war were to pay to Eumenes whatever tribute Antiochus had imposed on them (Polybius, xxi, 46, 2–3).

These Roman arrangements established the Attalid dynasty as the dominant power in Asia Minor. They included a long list of special dispositions, rewarding Rhodes as well as Pergamum. Henceforth all territorial and political problems in Asia Minor, as well as in Greece, were referred to the Romans, who tended to resolve them not in the spirit of arbitrators (as the Greeks expected) but, somewhat naturally, in the light of Roman self-interest.

Diplomacy now required almost annual embassies to Rome. These were no doubt often exasperating to the Romans, but they also laid a great burden on the Greeks and indeed involved them in learning a whole complicated system of patronage and canvassing support at Rome. A decree of Abdera (166) honouring two ambassadors to Rome illustrates the point.

> Undertaking an embassy to Rome on the people's behalf they endured hardship to body and spirit alike, interviewing and winning over the leading Romans by patience day after day and enlisting our country's patrons to give her help on behalf of our people, and by a juxtaposition of the facts and by daily attendance in their *atria* (viz. the halls of Roman houses where clients attended for the morning salutation) they won over those who looked to and gave their protection to our opponent (sc. Cotys, king of Thrace, who was laying claim to certain territories) (*Syll.*, 656; cf. P. Herrmann, *ZPE*, 7 (1971), 72–7 for new readings).

This inscription gives some idea of the work which might fall to a Greek embassy charged with an important mission to Rome, even before the actual senatorial hearing took place.

IV

During the war with Antiochus Philip had fought as a Roman ally, expecting territorial rewards. From the end of that war down to his death in 179 relations between Rome and Macedonia became increasingly sour as decision after decision in territorial disputes went against the king (see p. 98). His successor Perseus (179–168) was disliked by the Romans from the start – they had backed his younger brother Demetrius for the succession but Philip had executed him for treason – and regarded with suspicion because he tried to recover influence and win goodwill in Greece. In 172 the Senate decided to eliminate him and after a war which perhaps proved harder than they had expected

Perseus was defeated at Pydna in southern Macedonia and dethroned (168); he later died in an Italian prison. The same summer, and immediately following their victory at Pydna, the Senate delivered a diplomatic blow to Antiochus IV of Syria, who had invaded Egypt. He had just crossed a branch of the Nile at Eleusis, when he was met by the Roman envoy, C. Popilius Laenas.

Upon Antiochus greeting him from a distance and then holding out his hand, Popilius handed to the king a copy of the Senate's decree, which he had by him, and told him to read it first; he did not, or so it seems to me, think it proper to make the conventional sign of friendship before he knew whether the intentions of the man he was greeting were friendly or hostile. When the king, after reading it, said he would like to communicate with his Friends about this intelligence, Popilius acted in a manner which was felt to be offensive and exceedingly arrogant. He was carrying a stick cut from a vine (probably as a mark of office) and with this he drew a circle round Antiochus and told him he must remain inside this circle until he gave his decision about the contents of the letter. The king was astonished at this authoritarian procedure but after a few minutes' hesitation said he would do all that the Romans demanded; whereupon Popilius and his suite all grasped him by the hand and greeted him warmly. The contents of the letter were that he was to put an immediate end to his war with Ptolemy (Polybius, xxix, 27, 1–7).

The brusque and abrasive gesture of this Roman noble towards the king of Syria was deliberate and was intended to demonstrate where power now lay. As Polybius makes clear, the year of Pydna put an end to real independence throughout the Greek east and this was especially true in Greece proper where the Achaean League had been punished for its supposed lukewarm loyalty by drastic action as soon as the war was over. One thousand leading politicans from Achaea alone — Polybius

was one of them – were sent to Rome for personal investigation
and kept in Italy for sixteen years; of the numbers similarly
deported from other states we are not informed. Macedonia itself
was divided into four independent republics but after a revolt by
a pretender in 149 it was reduced to a Roman province. In 146 the
Achaeans were confronted with an ultimatum, the acceptance of
which would have torn the League apart. They therefore
resorted to a vain revolt, which was quickly put down. Corinth,
where Roman envoys had been insulted, was razed to the ground
by decree of the Senate.

By now (146) Roman domination was unchallengeable. But, as
this brief sketch has shown, from the time of her first incursion
east of the Adriatic Rome had exercised a disturbing influence on
the whole hellenistic world. Though there is no evidence that the
hellenistic states ever, formally or informally, recognized the
principle of a balance of power, in fact such a balance had existed
because no great state was in a position to destroy any of the other
great states. Cities of course could be and were wiped out (as
Mantinea was at the hands of the Achaeans and Macedonians in
223) but that had always been true and merely reflects the
vulnerability of small states. In fact the greater hellenistic powers
seem not to have envisaged the total destruction of their
adversaries; for example, the treaty between Philip V and
Hannibal (see pp. 231–2) presupposed Roman survival after her
hoped-for defeat, and one reason for Polybius' intense in-
dignation against Philip V and Antiochus III for their alleged
compact to plunder the dominions of the boy-king Ptolemy V
was his exaggerated belief that it was intended 'to divide up the
kingdom and be the destruction of the orphaned child' (Polybius,
xv, 20, 6).

In the third century cities could play off one power against
another but once the Romans arrived on the scene, everyone
looked more and more to them. Within the cities and
confederations – and even to some extent within the kingdoms, if
we consider how the Romans encouraged Demetrius, Philip V's
second son, to aim at the throne – pro-Roman parties grew up,
and the Romans themselves welcomed and exploited the fact. In

the winter of 170/69 C. Popilius and Cn. Octavius were sent down into central and southern Greece from Thessaly by the consul and

> visiting the Peloponnesian cities attempted to convince the inhabitants of the leniency and kindness of the Senate, quoting the recent decrees (sc. which restricted the right of Roman magistrates to impose orders without senatorial instructions); they also indicated in their speeches that they knew who were those in each city who were hanging back more then they should as well as those who were rushing forward to help (Polybius, xxviii, 3, 3–4).

Neutrality was no longer enough and so, as the danger increased, fierce struggles developed between the supporters and opponents of Rome. At Rhodes, for instance,

> there was acute civil discord, Agathagetus, Philophron, Rodophon and Theaedetus resting all their hopes on Rome, while Deinon and Polyaratus relied on Perseus and the Macedonians (Polybius, xxviii, 2, 3).

Rhodes was one of several states where (as Polybius indicates: xxx, 6–9) politicians who had chosen the wrong side discovered that the penalty for their mistake was death – either at the hands of Rome or their own citizens, or else by suicide. In his speech to the Senate, defending Rhodes against the charge of having supported Perseus, Astymedes declares that:

> had the whole people been responsible for our error and estrangement from you, you might possibly with some show of justice maintain that displeasure and refuse forgiveness, but if, as you know well, the authors of this folly were quite few in number and have all been put to death by the state itself, why do you refuse to be reconciled to men who were in no way to blame? (Polybius, xxx, 31, 13–15).

In fact the Rhodians were spared the disaster of a Roman

punitive campaign but by making Delos a free port the Senate reduced Rhodian revenue substantially. Henceforth the power of Rhodes was broken, her ability to police the seas declined and piracy once more flourished in the eastern Mediterranean.

V

The effect of Roman domination on the cities of mainland Greece and the Aegean was to split them into factions and after 168 to deprive them of their main leaders by carrying these off to Italy. The monarchies were also affected, but in a different way. The extent to which Rome interfered in the day-to-day affairs of the kingdoms should not be exaggerated. There was a margin for independent action, and that at some times more than others, but independence always involved risks. We possess an interesting dossier of inscriptions, dating to the years 163–156 from Pessinus in Galatia, which contains several letters from King Attalus II of Pergamum to Attis, the high priest of the temple of Cybele at Pessinus. One of these describes a discussion at Attalus' court which had led him to abandon a military enterprise evidently planned in conjunction with the priest (the inscription is unfortunately obscure on the details of this project).

> King Attalus to priest Attis, greeting. If you are well, it is as I wish; I myself am in good health. When we came to Pergamum and I assembled not only Athenaeus [Attalus' brother] and Sosander [the priest of Dionysus Kathegemon in Pergamum] and Menogenes [an eminent statesman under Eumenes and Attalus], but many others also of my kinsfolk [an honorific expression], and when I laid before them what we discussed at Apamea and told them our decision, there was a very long discussion, and at first all inclined to the same opinion with us, but Chlorus vehemently held forth the Roman power and counselled us in no way to do anything without them. In this at first few concurred, but afterwards, as day after day we kept considering, it appealed

more and more, and to launch an undertaking without them began to seem fraught with great danger; if we were successful, the attempt promised to bring us envy and detraction and baneful suspicion – that which they felt also towards my brother [Eumenes II; see below] – while if we failed we should meet certain destruction. For they would not, it seemed to us, regard our disaster with any sympathy but would rather be delighted to see it, because we had undertaken such projects without them. As things are now, however, if – which God forbid – we were defeated in any matters, having acted entirely with their approval, we should receive help and might recover our losses, with the gods' favour. I decided therefore to send men to Rome on every occasion to make regular reports on cases where we are in doubt, while we ourselves make thorough preparation so that if need be we can defend ourselves (Welles, *R.C.*, no. 61).

This revealing letter – it was probably not engraved on marble until long after it could carry any political implications or do any political damage – shows the dilemma of a hellenistic king contemplating independent action; but it also shows that even after his brother Eumenes had fallen into disfavour at Rome for being reputedly uncertain in his sympathies during the Third Macedonian War (a point mentioned in the letter) and after the humbling of Antiochus IV at Pelusium, it did not automatically occur to Attalus to refer every item of foreign policy to the Senate. Some kings went out of their way to adopt a humble pose when dealing with the Senate. Polybius singles out Prusias II of Bithynia as given to this kind of behaviour and describes events of 167/6:

In the first place when some Roman legates had come to his court (sc. perhaps in 172), he went to meet them with his head shorn, and wearing a white cap and a toga and shoes, exactly the costume worn at Rome by slaves recently manumitted or *liberti* as the Romans call them. 'In me', he said, 'you see your *libertus* who wishes to endear himself and imitate everything Roman'; it would be difficult to find a more humiliating observation . . . On the present occasion, on entering the senate-house (sc. at Rome) he stood in the doorway facing the members and putting both his hands on the ground bowed his head to the ground in adoration of the threshold and the seated senators, with the words, 'Hail, saviour gods!', thus making it impossible for anyone after him to surpass him in unmanliness, effeminacy and servility. And on entering he conducted himself during his interview in a similar manner, doing things that it would be improper even to mention. As he showed himself to be utterly contemptible, for that very reason he received a favourable answer (Polybius, xxx, 18, 3–7).

In contrast to Prusias' warm reception was the treatment accorded the same winter to Eumenes, who, as we have just seen, had fallen out of favour. Embarrassed at his proposal to come to Rome and defend himself the Senate,

affecting to be displeased by visits of kings in general, issued a decree that no king should present himself to them; and next, when they heard that Eumenes had arrived in Italy at Brundisium, they dispatched the quaestor bearing this decree and with orders to tell Eumenes to inform him if he stood in need of any service: if there was nothing he required, he was to order him to leave Italy as soon as possible (Polybius, xxx, 19, 6–8).

These passages illustrate the reduction of the hellenistic kingdoms and their kings to a condition of ineffective and humiliating dependence on the Senate.

VI

Roman domination was also economically disastrous to the Greek east. The succession of wars fought there had been immensely profitable to the Romans. In an analysis of the figures for indemnities imposed and booty carried in the triumphs of Roman generals from Greece alone in the wars down to 167, J. A. O. Larsen in T. Frank's *Economic Survey of Ancient Rome*, Vol. IV, p. 323, calculates that Rome profited from those wars to the extent of nearly 73,250,000 denarii (a Roman pound of silver was worth 84 denarii) and the indemnity imposed on Antiochus (Polybius, xxi, 17, 4–5) together with the booty exhibited in L. Scipio's triumph (Livy, xxxvii, 59, 3–5) would add a further 85,000,000. After 167 the policy of exacting tribute, already practised in Sicily, Corsica and Sardinia, was extended to the Greek world. Livy reports that

> it was decided to divide Macedonia into four regions, each with its own council, and that it should pay to the Roman people half the tribute which it had been wont to pay to the kings (Livy, xlv, 18, 7).

In Illyria likewise

> tax equivalent to half what they had paid to the king was imposed on the people of Scodra, the Dassarenses, the Selepitani and the rest of the Illyrians. Illyria was then divided into three parts (Livy, xlv, 26, 14–15).

This halving of the tribute is not to be interpreted as either an act of generosity or a lack of interest in wealth; it is a fair assumption that the Romans had assessed the size of burden the two exhausted areas could support. Furthermore, the Macedonian silver mines, closed down on the abolition of the monarchy, were according to Cassiodorus reopened in 158. He says that in that year mines were *discovered* in Macedonia, but this has generally been interpreted to refer to their reopening and it has been plausibly suggested that this reopening coincides with the resumption of minting silver coins at Rome in 157 (M. H. Crawford, *Economic History Review* (1977), p. 45).

After 146, according to Pausanias (vii, 16, 9), 'tribute was imposed on Greece'. This can only have been true of those cities

which were involved in the Achaean War but these were now
attached administratively to the province of Macedonia, and had
to pay taxes to Rome. Hence in the second half of the second
century and even more in the first, a regular stream of tribute was
reaching Rome from Greece and Asia Minor. Much of this later
returned to the same area in the form of loans to help the
unfortunate provincial communities to meet the demands of
Roman tax-collectors, as payment for land which increasingly
Romans were now acquiring in the east, and to pay for luxuries
sent by the east to Rome – including slaves. This process was
intensified in the first century, when there were more Roman
provinces, but it was already operating in the second century and
was a factor in the progressive impoverishment of the hellenistic
world in terms of wealth and population which lasted down to the
setting up of the Roman principate. It was exacerbated by the
private greed of Roman officials, members of a class for which, as
Polybius noted (xxxi, 25, 6–7), conspicuous expenditure and
extravagance had become a way of life since the fall of the
Macedonian kingdom. Scipio Aemilianus, he tells us, was wholly
exceptional in his integrity.

> When he became master of Carthage (sc. in 146), which was
> considered the wealthiest city in the world, he took absolutely
> nothing from it to add to his own fortune, either by purchase
> or by any other means of acquisition, and this although he was
> not particularly well off, but only moderately so for a Roman
> (xviii, 35, 9).

Usually, however, Roman governors regarded the spoils of office
as essential to maintain their status and finance their further
careers, all of which added to the burden of the Greek east.

VII

Our discussion of the effects of the impact of Rome on the hellenistic world has already brought us to the other side of the picture – the effect contact with Greece had upon the Romans themselves. The evil side of this relationship we have just seen; the Romans, especially the more old-fashioned, and the Greek Polybius, no doubt echoing his patron, Scipio Aemilianus, accorded it due prominence. But there was another, more positive and, in the long run, more important side. We have not the space here, and it would take us beyond the scope of this study, to look in detail at the manner in which contact with Greece affected all aspects of Roman life from the third century onward. Soldiers returning from eastern campaigns and Greeks coming to Rome as hostages, envoys, detainees, traders, professional men or slaves familiarized the Romans with the Greek language and Greek ways. Doctors and philosophers brought Greek skills and a Greek pattern of education; Romans of the old school like Cato resisted both, but half-heartedly and ineffectively. The plunder of cities such as Syracuse or Corinth brought Greek works of art to Rome and whetted the appetites of Roman nobles for more. Private houses became more luxurious and Rome a more agreeable city to live in, at least for the rich, with amenities comparable to those of the great hellenistic centres.

The third century also saw the beginnings of Roman literature, again under the influence of Greece. Livius Andronicus (*c.* 284–204), the earliest Roman poet, was himself a Greek from Tarentum who taught Latin and Greek and made a verse translation of Homer's *Odyssey*. Q. Ennius (239–169), a larger and more influential figure, came from Calabria, where he was in contact with the Greek philosophical schools of southern Italy; his *Annals* were a great epic of the Roman past. It was primarily the need to present the Roman past (and to defend Roman policy in the present) to the Greek world that conjured up the beginnings of Roman history-writing and its earliest practitioners, Fabius Pictor, Cincius Alimentus and Postumius Aloinus, were Roman statesmen, writing not in Latin but in Greek. Even Cato, whose *Origines* was the first work in Latin prose and initiated Roman history in the native tongue, was more influenced by Greek models than its author's reputed contempt for all things Greek would lead us to expect.

Another aspect of hellenization was the growth of a native theatre. The versatile Ennius wrote plays derived from Sophocles and looking back to the Trojan cycle. Naevius wrote tragedies, historical plays based on Roman subjects, and comedies (as well as an epic on the Punic War). But the most important writers for the Roman stage at this time (or indeed at all) were T. Maccius Plautus (*c*. 254–184) and P. Terentius Afer (*c*. 195–159). We have many plays by both Plautus and Terence and until the recent discovery of some original plays on papyrus we had to depend on them for any notion of the work of the great Athenian comic writer Menander; now it has become easier to appreciate the extent to which both Roman playwrights in different ways exploited and adapted their hellenistic originals to produce something new and Roman. Indeed it was part of the Roman genius not merely to copy but to transform.

The culture of Greece, both the older classical authors and writers of the contemporary hellenistic world, gave the writers of Rome models and the stimulus to create an indigenous Roman literature. It is impossible to imagine Roman masterpieces of the late republic and early empire without the hellenic element; Cicero, Sallust, Horace, Virgil, Catullus and Ovid, all are the products of a tradition going back to Greek origins, but none the less Roman for that. For about three centuries, from the time of Flamininus onwards, most educated Romans were bilingual and open to the full impact of hellenistic culture. Roman philosophy was a part of Greek philosophy, Roman art was developed from Greek forerunners. At a much earlier date the Italian gods and the *numina*, the impersonal forces which dominated the external world of Roman religion, had been personalized and frequently identified with Greek gods with similar characteristics and from the early-second century onwards cult began to be instituted for

Roman generals like Flamininus, thus paving the way for the assumption of divinity by Roman emperors. The Romans fashioned their early history so that it dovetailed into the Trojan cycle and Rome itself, like so many of the ports of the eastern Mediterrenean, welcomed an influx of eastern deities from Syria and Asia Minor. Eventually, with the setting up of the empire, the whole Mediterranean was to coalesce into a single cultural continuum in which many aspects of the hellenistic world lived on, adapted to the provincial organization imposed from Rome. In particular, when the monarchies had gone, the cities continued to be the vital units of civilized life throughout the east and they remained so until the increasing centralization and dead weight of bureaucracy crushed all initiative out of them in the third and fourth centuries AD.

VIII

The hellenistic age left many problems unsolved: what age does not? The relationship between the kings and the cities, first raised under Alexander, remained a matter for perpetual, shifting compromises. Nor did any kingdom overcome the conflict of interest between those who lived in the cities, the members of the ruling groups and those serving in the army and the bureaucracy on the one hand and, on the other, the workers on the land, whether these were free men or serfs. The evil of slavery of course still remained, though it was less important in the vast spaces of Seleucid Asia or in Egypt than it was where the Greek market economy had penetrated. The clash between Greeks and the indigenous peoples, though, as we have seen, it is not a simple story, continued to embarrass all the monarchies except Macedonia (though we cannot trace it equally well in all). In particular the secular poverty of the peasantry was an intractable problem, for which there was no solution in the absence of any substantial improvement in the techniques of production. In this field, as we saw, the only startling progress came in military science. Whether in due course some of these problems might have been solved, we cannot tell. Probably not, for the main achievements of the hellenistic age seem to have occurred in the third century, when the ruling caste was still socially mobile and the new kingdoms still showed flexibility and offered a career open to talent (see pp. 75 ff.). The earlier kings surrounded themselves with men chosen freely from all parts for their ability and adaptability. By the second century the Egyptian record – it is the only one we can read in detail – has substituted a career bureaucracy with a multiplicity of honorific and often meaningless distinctive titles which go with certain posts. Probably then the creative force was already spent when the Romans arrived.

But we are naturally less interested in the hellenistic world for its failures than for its achievements and for the contribution which it made to the cultural history of later times. It was an age of scholarship in which the great research institutes of Alexandria worked over and transmitted the texts of the classical writers. It was an age too in which men's horizons were widened physically by the voyages of such explorers as Pytheas and Megasthenes, and intellectually by the scientific achievements of an Eratosthenes or an Archimedes. If the literature it produced would not be reckoned by many to be among the world's greatest, Theocritus and Callimachus exerted a considerable influence both at Rome and later, and along with Herondas are still read with pleasure. Its architecture and its fine planned cities stand as forerunners of those of the Renaissance and the eighteenth and nineteenth centuries. Its art too, often violent and sometimes sentimental, captures our attention and it has had a powerful influence on the development of taste.

Though the flame of rational enquiry had begun to burn low and we can detect a growth in the attraction of mystery religions and eastern cults, it remained a time singularly free from obscurantism and censorship, one in which men could easily move around and find a home elsewhere if they ran into trouble. Normally, however, they were free to speculate and publish their beliefs and their discoveries. Its main schools of thought, Stoicism, Epicureanism and Cynicism, have all been influential in the history of philosophy and represent patterns of belief to which men still subscribe today and if the cults and religious doctrines of the age have vanished, the cultural continuum of the hellenistic world and its fringes was later to be the cradle of two world religions.

Though it was an era of warfare, for about a century (down to the destruction of Mantinea in 223) hellenistic war was shorn of at least some of its horrors. If the sacking of cities and the enslavement of their inhabitants increased after that date, the Romans must take much of the blame. In the field of political experimentation hellenistic Greece took a new step in developing the concept of federal government, which was to be not without significance for later political theory and affords proof, if proof were needed, of the continuing intellectual vitality and creativity of the Greek people. The kingdoms and the cities too during these three centuries developed a system of diplomatic interchange which was taken over by the Romans and so through the practices of the empire was transmitted to later times. The hellenistic world possessed no universal legal system, but the codes of the various states largely overlapped and tended more and more to approximate to each other, as we can deduce from the increasing use of foreign judges (see pp. 143 ff.). The flexibility of Roman law as it developed through the edicts of the *praetor peregrinus* and the provincial governors and the notion that the resultant *ius gentium* was to be identified with the law of nature postulated by the Stoics would probably have proved barren, had not Roman governors found a degree of legal uniformity already existing in the cities and states which fell within their provinces. Here too, if indirectly, we can trace a legacy from the hellenistic world. So, once again, we return to Rome, the destroyer and at the same time the heir of this fertile age of Greek civilization. For it is through Rome that so much of this legacy has come down to western Europe and its offshoots and, no less potently and even more directly, to the Byzantine and orthodox world of eastern Europe.

Date Chart

	Greece and Macedonia	Egypt and the East
336	Accession of Alexander	
334		Alexander crosses into Asia
		Battle of Granicus
333		Battle of Issus
331		Foundation of Alexandria
		Battle of Gaugamela
330		Death of Darius
326		Battle of Hydaspes
325–4		Alexander returns to Susa
323		Death of Alexander at Babylon
323–2	Lamian War	Perdiccas in power in Asia
320		Perdiccas murdered
		Meeting at Triparadeisus
319	Death of Antipater	
317	Philip III Arrhidaeus murdered	
316	Cassander executes Olympias; foundation of Cassandreia and Thessalonica	
316–5		Death of Eumenes
311		Peace between satraps and Antigonus
310(?)	Alexander IV murdered	
305–4		Demetrius' siege of Rhodes
301		Battle of Ipsus: death of Antigonus

	Greece and Macedonia	Egypt and the East
297	Death of Cassander	
294	Demetrius I king of Macedonia	
288	Lysimachus and Pyrrhus partition Macedonia	
285		Demetrius surrenders to Seleucus
283		Ptolemy I dies; Ptolemy II succeeds
281		Lysimachus killed at Corupedium
280	Ptolemy Ceraunus king of Macedonia Achaean League refounded	Seleucus assassinated Antiochus I sole king in Seleucid realm
279	Gauls invade Macedonia and Greece	
277	Antigonus II defeats Gauls at Lysimacheia; becomes king of Macedonia	
274–1		First Syrian War between Ptolemy II and Antiochus I
274	Pyrrhus invades Macedonia	
272	Pyrrhus' death at Argos	
268–1	Chremonidean War: Antigonus II takes Athens	
263		Eumenes I succeeds Philetaerus at Pergamum
261		Antiochus II succeeds Antiochus I
260–53(?)		Second Syrian War between Antiochus II and Ptolemy II

	Greece and Macedonia	Egypt and the East
251	Aratus frees Sicyon	
249(?)	Alexander of Corinth revolts from Antigonus II	
246	Aetolian reorganization of the Soteria	Ptolemy II dies: Ptolemy III succeeds Antiochus II dies; Seleucus II succeeds
246–1		Third Syrian (Laodicean) War between Ptolemy III and Seleucus II
245	Aratus' first generalship Antigonus II recovers Corinth from widow of Alexander	
244	Agis IV accedes at Sparta	
243	Aratus seizes Corinth	
241	Death of Agis IV	Attalus I succeeds Eumenes I War of Seleucus II against his brother Hierax: Hierax master of Asia Minor
239	Demetrius II succeeds Antigonus II War between Macedonia and the Achaean and Aetolian Leagues begins	(?)Diodotus sets up independent kingdom in Bactria
238–27		War of Attalus I against Hierax and against the Galatians Attalus master of Asia Minor
235	Accession of Cleomenes III at Sparta Megalopolis joins Achaean League	

	Greece and Macedonia	Egypt and the East
229	Demetrius II succeeded by Antigonus III Athens achieves independence War breaks out between Sparta and Achaea	
227	Cleomenes' revolution at Sparta Achaean contact with Macedonia	Carian expedition of Antigonus III
226–5	Spartan successes against Achaea	Death of Seleucus II: accession of Seleucus III: death of Hierax
225–4	Achaeo–Macedonian agreement	
224	Antigonus III in Peloponnese	
224–3	Foundation of Hellenic League	
223		Seleucus III assassinated: succeeded by Antiochus III
223–2		Achaeus recovers Asia Minor
222	Cleomenes defeated at Sellasia	
221	Philip V succeeds Antigonus III	Ptolemy IV succeeds Ptolemy III
220–17	War of the Allies against Aetolia	
220		Antiochus III suppresses the pretender Molon
219–7		Fourth Syrian War between Antiochus III and Ptolemy IV
218–02	(Hannibalic War)	
217	Peace of Naupactus	Battle of Raphia
216–3		Antiochus III defeats the rebel Achaeus

	Greece and Macedonia	Egypt and the East
215	Alliance between Philip V and Hannibal	
212–05/4		Antiochus III's eastern expedition
211	Alliance between Aetolia and Rome initiates First Macedonian War	
207–186		Disaffection in Egypt: upper Egypt under separate kings
206	Aetolia and her allies make a separate peace with Philip V	
205	Peace of Phoenice ends First Macedonian War	Antiochus III returns to Seleuceia
204		Ptolemy V succeeds Ptolemy IV
203–2	Philip V and Antiochus III make a compact against Egypt	
202–200		Fifth Syrian War between Antiochus III and Ptolemy V
200		Battle of Panium: Antiochus seizes Coele-Syria
200–197	Second Macedonian War	
197	Battle of Cynoscephalae	Eumenes II succeeds Attalus I
196	Roman declaration of Greek freedom at the Isthmus	
196–79	Philip V rebuilds the power of Macedonia	
194	Romans evacuate Greece	
192–88	Syrian War between Rome and Antiochus III	
191	Antiochus defeated at Thermopylae	
189	Defeat of the Aetolians	Antiochus defeated at Magnesia

	Greece and Macedonia	*Egypt and the East*
188		Peace of Apamea
187		Seleucus IV succeeds Antiochus III
180		Ptolemy VI succeeds Ptolemy V
179	Perseus succeeds Philip V	
175		Antiochus IV succeeds Seleucus IV
173–64		Maccabean revolt in Judaea
171–68	Third Macedonian War	
170–68		Sixth Syrian War between Antiochus IV and Ptolemy IV, Ptolemy VIII and Cleopatra II (joint rulers)
168	Battle of Pydna: end of Antigonid dynasty in Macedonia Four republics set up in Macedonia	Popillius' ultimatum to Antiochus IV at Pelusium
160		Attalus II succeeds Eumenes II
149–8	Rising of Andriscus in Macedonia; Macedonia becomes a Roman province	
146	Achaean War: sack of Corinth	
139		Attalus III succeeds Attalus II
133		Death of Attalus III; Pergamum becomes a Roman province
132–30		Aristonicus' revolt in Pergamum

Alexander's March

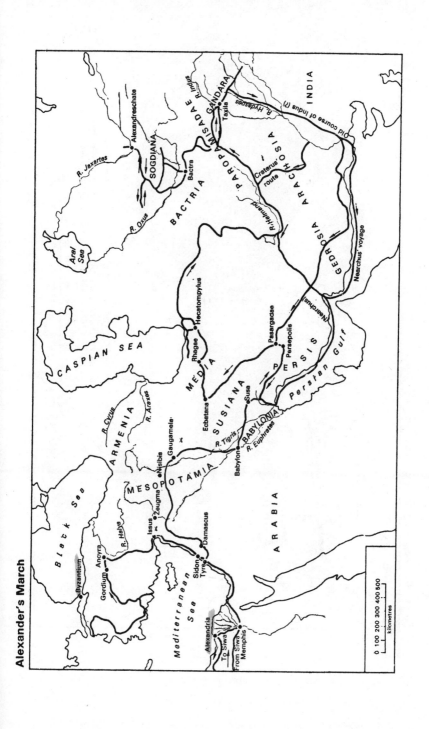

The Hellenistic Kingdoms c. 275

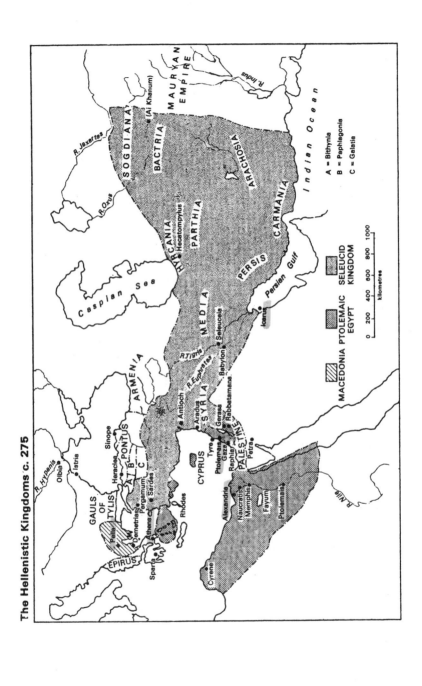

Greece, Macedonia and Crete

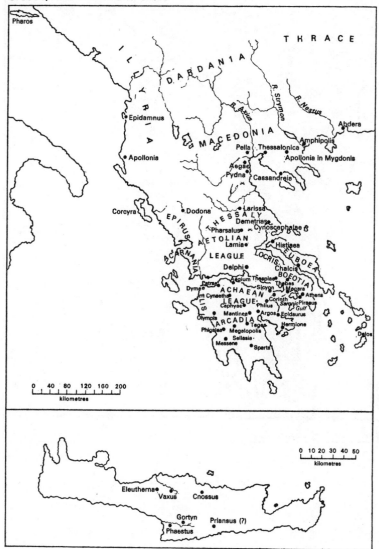

Asia Minor

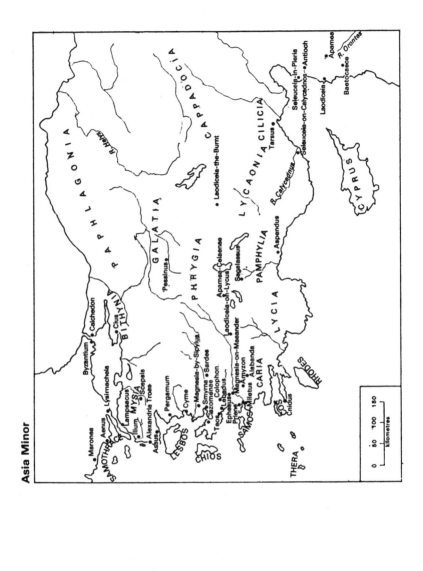

Abbreviations

The following abbreviations have been used in referring to inscriptions and papyri and to one or two other publications:

1 *Inscriptions*

Bulletin épigraphique, by J. and L. Robert, published annually in *Revue des Études Grecques*.

CIL = *Corpus inscriptionum latinarum* (Berlin, 1869–).

Durrbach, *Choix* = F. Durrbach, *Choix d'inscriptions de Délos* (Paris, 1921).

Fouilles de Delphes = G. Colin, E. Bourguet, G. Daux and A. Salas (eds), *Fouilles de Delphes, Vol. III, Inscriptions* (Paris, 1929–).

IG = *Inscriptiones graecae* (Berlin, 1873–).

IG² = *Inscriptiones graecae, editio minor* (Berlin, 1913–). This is really a revised edition of the preceding item.

Insc. Cret. = M. Guarducci (ed.), *Inscriptiones creticae*, 4 vols., (Rome, 1935–50).

Michel, *Recueil* = Ch. Michel, *Recueil d'inscriptions grecques* (Brussels, 1900).

Moretti = L. Moretti, *Iscrizioni storiche ellenistiche, Vol. 1, Attica, Peloponneso, Beozia*; *Vol. II, Grecia centrale e settentrionale* (Florence 1967 and 1976).

OGIS = W. Dittenberger (ed.), *Orientis graeci inscriptiones selectae* (Leipzig, 1903–5).

Remains of Old Latin = E. H. Warmington, *Remains of Old Latin, Vol. IV, Archaic Inscriptions* (London (Loeb edition), 1940). Contains texts and translations.

Robert, *Hellenica* = L. Robert, *Hellenica: Recueil d'épigraphie de numismatique et d'antiquités grecques*, 13 vols. (Paris, 1940–65).

Schwyzer = E. Schwyzer, *Dialectorum graecarum exempla epigraphica potiora* (Leipzig, 1923).

SEG = *Supplementum epigraphicum graecum* (Leiden, 1923–).

SGDI = *Sammlung der griechischen Dialektinschriften* (Göttingen, 1884–1915).

Sherk = R. S. Sherk, *Roman Documents from the Greek East* (Baltimore, 1969). Contains texts and translations.

SVA = H. Bengtson (ed., Vol. II) and H. H. Schmitt (ed., Vol. III), *Staatsverträge des Altertums* (Munich, 1962 and 1969).

Syll. = W. Dittenberger (ed.), *Sylloge inscriptionum graecarum*, 4 vols. (Leipzig, 1915–24).

Tod = M. N. Tod (ed.), *Greek Historical Inscriptions*, 2 vols. (Oxford, Vol. I, 2nd edn, 1946; Vol. II, 1948).

Welles, *R.C.* = C. Bradford Welles, *Royal Correspondence of the Hellenistic Age* (Yale, 1934). The texts are translated and discussed.

2 Papyri

BGU = *Berliner griechische Urkunden (Aegyptische Urkunden aus den Staatlichen Museen zu Berlin)* (Berlin, 1895–).

Corp. ord. Ptol. = M.-T. Lenger, *Corpus des ordonnances des Ptolémées*, Mémoires de l'Académie royale de Bruxelles (Brussels, 1964).

P. Amherst = B. Grenfell and A. S. Hunt (eds.) *Amherst Papyri*, 2 vols., (London, 1900–1).

P. Cair. Zen. = G. C. Edgar, *Zenon Papyri*, 5 vols., *Catalogue général des antiquités égyptiennes du Musée du Caire, 79* (Cairo, 1925–40).

P. Col. Zen. = W. L. Westermann and E. S. Hasenoehrl (eds.), *Zenon Papyri: Business Papers of the 3rd cent. BC, Vol. I*, Columbia Papyri, Greek Series, vol. 3 (New York, 1934).

P. Hal. = Halle Papyri = Graeca Halensis (ed.), *Dikaiomata: Auszüqe aus alexandrinischen Gesetzen und Verordnungen* (Berlin, 1913).

P. Hibeh = B. Grenfell and A. S. Hunt (eds.), *Hibeh Papyri*, Pt. I (London, 1906).

P. Lille = P. Jouguet and others (eds.), *Institut papyrologique de l'université de Lille: Papyrus Grecs* (Paris, 1907–28).

P. Petrie = J. P. Mahaffy and J. G. Smyly (eds.), *The Flinders Petrie Papyri*, 3 parts (Dublin, 1891–1905).

P. Rev. Laws = B. P. Grenfell (ed.), *Revenue Laws of Ptolemy Philadelphus* (Oxford, 1896).

P. S. I. = *Papiri greci e latini* (Pubblicazioni della Società italiana per la ricerca dei papiri greci e latini in Egitto) (Florence, 1912–).

P. Tebt. = *Tebtunis Papyri*, 4 vols. (London-New York, 1902–76).

P. Yale = J. F. Oates, A. E. Samuel and C. B. Welles (eds.), *Yale Papyri in the Beinecke Rare Book and Manuscript Library* (New Haven-Toronto, 1967).

SB = *Sammelbuch griechischer Urkunden aus Aegypten* (Heidelberg, 1931–). Contains both papyri and inscriptions.

Select Papyri = A. S. Hunt and G. C. Edgar (eds.), *Select Papyri*, 2 vols. (London (Loeb edition), 1932–4). Texts and translations.

UPZ = U. Wilcken, *Urkunden der Ptolemäerzeit*, 2 vols. (Berlin, 1922–37).

Wilcken, *Chrestomathie* = L. Mitteis and U. Wilcken, *Grundzüge und Chrestomathie der Papyruskunde* (Leipzig-Berlin, 1912).

3   Other publications

Abh. Berlin. Akad. = *Abhandlungen der Preussischen Akademie der Wissenschaften, Berlin. Phil.-hist. Klasse.*

Bull. inst. franç. arch. or. = *Bulletin de l'Institut Français d'Archéologie Orientale* (Cairo).

CRAI = *Comptes rendus de l'Académie des Inscriptions et Belles-Lettres* (Paris).

TAPA = *Transactions and Proceedings of the American Philological Association.*

ZäS = *Zeitschrift für ägyptische Sprache und Altertumskunde.*

ZPE = *Zeitschrift für Papyrologie und Epigraphik.*

Further Reading and Bibliography

General

The works quoted below are mainly in English but I have added occasional titles in French, German or Italian.

For detailed accounts of the Hellenistic period see:

M. Cary, *A History of the Greek World from 323 to 146 BC*, 2nd edn. with a new bibliography by V. Ehrenberg (London, 1963).
P. Grimal *et al.*, *Hellenism and the Rise of Rome* (London, 1968).
M. Hadas, *Hellenistic Culture: Fusion and Diffusion* (New York, 1959).
W. W. Tarn and G. T. Griffith, *Hellenistic Civilisation*, 3rd edn. (London 1952).
There are some good chapters (and bibliographies of the older works) in *Cambridge Ancient History*, Vols. 6 (2nd edn., 1933), 7 (1928), 8 (1930) and 9 (1932); a completely new edition is in preparation.
The best recent account of the political events is in French:
E. Will, *Histoire politique du monde hellénistique*, 2nd edn., 2 vols. (Nancy, 1979–81)
and there are two other excellent new French histories:
Claire Préaux, *Le Monde hellénistique: La Grèce et l'orient, 323–146 av. J.-C.*, 2 vols. (Paris, 1978). This work contains an up-to-date bibliography on all aspects of the period.
E. Will, C. Mossé and P. Goukowsky, *Le Monde grec et l'orient, Vol. 2, Le ive siècle et l'époque hellénistique* (Paris, 1975), especially pp. 247–678.
The following works are also better mentioned here than under separate chapters:
M. I. Finley, *The Ancient Economy* (London, 1973).
T. Frank (ed.), *Economic Survey of Ancient Rome*, 6 vols. (Baltimore, 1933–40; reprinted New York, 1975). This great work, by various authors, contains material for much of the Greek East, both before and after it fell under Rome.

M. Holleaux, *Études d'épigraphie et d'histoire grecques* (L. Robert, ed.), 6 vols. (Paris 1938–68). This collection of Holleaux's articles contains a vast amount of material relevant to the hellenistic world.

A. H. M. Jones, *The Greek City from Alexander to Justinian* (Oxford, 1940).

A. D. Momigliano, *Alien Wisdom: The Limits of Hellenization* (Cambridge, 1975). This deals brilliantly with the intellectual response of the Greeks to the challenge of other cultures, especially in the Hellenistic period.

L. Robert, *Opera minora selecta*, 5 vols. (Amsterdam, 1969–   ). This is a collection of articles (in French) by the most distinguished living Greek epigraphist.

M. I. Rostovtzeff, *Social and Economic History of the Hellenistic World*, 3 vols. (Oxford, 2nd edn, 1953). A classic study, richly and relevantly illustrated and with a very full bibliography.

1   *Introduction: The Sources*

There is no convenient collection of non-literary sources in translation, but one is being prepared for publication at the Cambridge University Press by M. M. Austin.

Translations of the following more important sources (by various hands and ranging from excellent to indifferent) are available in the Loeb Classical Library: Appian, Arrian, Diodorus, Josephus, Livy, Plutarch's *Lives*, Polybius and Strabo. There are also Penguin translations of selections from Arrian (A. de Selincourt), Livy, *Rome and the Mediterranean* (containing books 31–45: H. Bettenson), Plutarch, *The Age of Alexander* (I. Scott-Kilvert), Polybius, *The Rise of the Roman Empire* (I. Scott-Kilvert).

On Polybius:
F. W. Walbank, *A Historical Commentary on Polybius*, 3 vols. (Oxford 1957–79).
——, *Polybius* (Berkeley, Los Angeles & London, 1972).
On Livy:
J. Briscoe, *A Commentary on Livy Books xxxi–xxxiii* (Oxford, 1973). This commentary is to be continued.
P. G. Walsh, *Livy, his Aims and Methods* (Cambridge, 1961).
On the historians of Alexander:
E. Badian, *Yale Classical Studies*, 24 (1975), 146–70, 'Onesicritus'.

J. R. Hamilton, *Plutarch, Alexander: a Commentary* (Oxford, 1969).

L. Pearson, *The Lost Histories of Alexander the Great* (American Philological Association, 1966).

W. W. Tarn, *Alexander the Great*, 2 vols. (of which the second deals with historical and source problems) (Cambridge, 1950; paperback, 1979).

Most of the contemporary sources survive only in fragments, which are collected in:

F. Jacoby, *Die Fragmente der griechischen Historiker*, 3 parts in 15 volumes (Berlin-Leiden, 1923–58).

See also:

A. J. Sachs and D J. Wiseman, *Iraq*, 16 (1954), 202–12, 'A Babylonian King List of the Hellenistic Period'.

J. D. Ray, *The Archive of Hor* (London, 1976).

For editions of inscriptions and papyri see the list of Abbreviations.

2 Alexander the Great (336–323)

In addition to the works of Tarn and Pearson listed above see:

P. Green, *Alexander of Macedon* (London, 1970), paperback with good bibliography.

J. R. Hamilton, *Alexander the Great* (London, 1973).

R. Lane Fox, *Alexander the Great* (London, 1973).

Several articles on Alexander by different authors were collected by:

G. T. Griffith in *Alexander the Great, The Main Problems* (Cambridge, 1966).

See also:

Greece and Rome, 12 (1965),113–228, a special issue devoted to Alexander, edited by J. V. Muir with the assistance of E. Badian. On pp. 129 ff. G. T. Griffith discusses the population of Macedonia.

Tarn's views have been subjected to searching criticism by E. Badian in a series of articles (mostly listed in the bibliography to P. Green's biography, mentioned above). E. Badian has also published a critical review of work on Alexander published between 1948 and 1967 in *The Classical World*, 65 (1972), 37–83.

3 The Foundation of the Kingdoms (323–301)

The best account is in E. Will, *Histoire politique* (see above under Further Reading, General) or in his forthcoming chapters in the new edition of *Cambridge Ancient History*, Vol.7, i.

See also:

R. M. Errington, *Journal of Hellenic Studies*, 90 (1970), 49–77, 'From Babylon to Triparadeisos, 323–320 BC'. This raises chronological problems typical of the whole period.

H. D. Westlake, *Bulletin of the John Rylands Library*, 37 (1954–5), 309–27, 'Eumenes of Cardia'.

But most recent work on this period is in languages other than English. Two examples are:

P. Briant, *Antigone le Borgne. Les Débuts de sa carrière et les problèmes de l'assemblée macédonienne* (Paris, 1973).

C. Wehrli, *Antigone et Demetrios* (Geneva, 1969).

4 The Hellenistic World: A Homogeneous Whole?

On the Hellenistic state see:

V. Ehrenberg, *The Greek State*, 2nd edn. (London, 1969). The second half of this study deals with the Hellenistic state.

On Ai Khanum and the Far East see:

P. Bernard, *Proceedings of the British Academy*, 53 (1967), 71–95 (with illustrations), 'Ai Khanum on the Oxus'.

L. Robert, *CRAI* (1968), 416 ff., 'Des Delphes à l'Oxus'.

D. Schlumberger, *CRAI* (1964), 126–40, 'Une nouvelle inscription grecque d'Açoka'.

On resistance to Hellenism see, besides Momigliano (listed under Further Reading, General):

S. K. Eddy, *The King is Dead: Studies in the Near-East Resistance to Hellenism* (Lincoln, Nebraska, 1961).

V. Tcherikover, *Hellenistic Civilization and the Jews* (Philadelphia & Jerusalem, 1959).

The role of the Greeks as a ruling class is discussed in an article of outstanding importance:

Chr. Habicht, *Vierteljahrschrift für Soziologie und Wirtschaftsgeschichte*, 45 (1958), 1–16, 'Die herrschende Gesellschaft in den hellenistischen Monarchien'.

On mercenaries see:

G. T. Griffith, *Mercenaries of the Hellenistic World* (Cambridge, 1935).

M. Launey, *Recherches sur les armées hellénistiques*, 2 vols. (Paris, 1949–50).

5   Macedonia and Greece

On Macedonia (in chronological order of kingship):

W. W. Tarn, *Antigonus Gonatas* (Oxford, 1913). Out-of-date in detail but still valuable and very readable.

P. Lévèque, *Pyrrhos* (Paris, 1957).

F. W. Walbank, *Philip V of Macedon* (Cambridge, 1940).

P. Meloni, *Perseo e la fine della monarchia-macedone* (Rome, 1953).

On Greece:

R. M. Errington, *Philopoemen* (Oxford, 1969).

W. S. Ferguson, *Hellenistic Athens* (London, 1911). Still useful.

A. Fuks, *Journal of Hellenic Studies,* 90 (1970), 78–89, 'The Bellum Achaicum and its Social Aspects'.

N. G. L. Hammond, *Epirus* (Oxford 1967).

W. A. Laidlaw, *A History of Delos* (Oxford, 1933).

J. A. O. Larsen, *Representative Government in Greek and Roman History* (Berkeley, Los Angeles, 1955).

——, *Greek Federal States* (Oxford, 1968).

——, 'Roman Greece' in T. Frank, *Economic Survey,* Vol. IV, 259–435.

H. A. Ormerod, *Piracy in the Ancient World* (Liverpool, 1924; reprinted 1979).

F. W. Walbank, *Aratos of Sicyon* (Cambridge, 1934).

See also:

J. Bousquet, *Mélanges hélleniques offerts à Georges Daux* (Paris, 1975), 21 ff.

6   Ptolemaic Egypt

Two general histories are:

H. I. Bell, *Egypt from Alexander the Great to the Arab Conquest* (Oxford, 1948).

E. R. Bevan, *A History of Egypt under the Ptolemaic Dynasty* (London, 1927).

On aspects of administration:

R. S. Bagnall, *The Administration of Ptolemaic Possessions outside Egypt* (Leiden, 1976).

L. Mooren, *The Aulic Titulature in Ptolemaic Egypt: Introduction and Prosopography* (Brussels, 1975). On the growth and significance of court titles.

For a study of Ptolemaic foreign policy see Will, *Histoire Politique* (see above under Further Reading, General), i, 153–208.

On economic organization see (besides Rostovtzeff, quoted above under Further Reading, General):

C. Préaux, *L'Économie royale des Lagides* (Brussels, 1939).

——, *Les Grecs en Égypte d'après les archives de Zénon* (Brussels, 1947).

C. B. Welles, *Journal of Juristic Papyrology*, 3 (1949), 21–47, 'The Ptolemaic Administration of Egypt'.

——, *Bulletin of the American Society of Papyrologists*, 7 (1970), 405–510, 'The Role of the Egyptians under the First Ptolemies'.

On Alexandria:

P. M. Fraser, *Ptolemaic Alexandria*, 3 vols. (Oxford, 1972).

On land problems in the Fayum:

D. J. Crawford, *Kerkeosiris: An Egyptian Village in the Ptolemaic Period* (Cambridge, 1971).

7 The Seleucids and the East

E. R. Bevan, *The House of Seleucus*, 2 vols. (London, 1902).

A. Bouché-Leclercq, *Histoire des Séleucides*, 2 vols. (Paris, 1913–14). These are both rather out of date. The most comprehensive study of the organization of the Seleucid kingdom remains:

E. Bikerman, *Institutions des Séleucides* (Paris, 1938);

but T. R. S. Broughton, 'Roman Asia Minor' in T. Frank, *Economic Survey*, Vol. IV, pp. 499–590, contains a good deal of the evidence in translation for Seleucid Asia Minor, especially in relation to land tenure.

See also:

Actes du colloque 1971 sur l'esclavage (Besançon) (Paris, 1972). B. Bar-Kochva, *The Seleucid Army*, (Cambridge, 1976). This also discusses Seleucid settlements.

W. H. Buckler and D. M. Robinson, *Sardis*, vii, i (Leiden, 1932). The first inscription is relevant to this chapter.

G. M. Cohen, *The Seleucid Colonies: Studies in the Founding, Administration and Organisation* (Wiesbaden, 1978).

A. H. M. Jones, *The Cities of the Eastern Roman Provinces*, 2nd edn. (Oxford, 1971). This detailed study gives information on the cities from their foundation onwards.

H. Kreissig, *Wirtschaft and Gesellschaft im Seleukidenreich* (Berlin, 1978). Gives a Marxist interpretation of problems of land tenure and social structure.

D. Magie, *Roman Rule in Asia Minor*, 2 vols. (Princeton, 1950). This work is indispensable for detailed study of Asia Minor in the Hellenistic period as well as the Roman.

O. Mørkholm, *Antiochus IV of Syria* (Copenhagen, 1966) makes full use of numismatic evidence.

D. Musti, *Studi classici ed orientali*, 15 (1966), 61–197, 'Lo Stato dei Seleucidi. Dinastia, popoli, città da Seleuco I ad Antioco III'.

P. Roussel, *Syria*, 23 (1942/3), 21–32, 'Décret des Péliganes de Laodicée-sur-Mer'.

On Pergamum:

E. V. Hansen, *The Attalids of Pergamon*, 2nd edn. (Ithaca, New York, 1971).

R. B. McShane, *The Foreign Policy of the Attalids* (Urbana, Illinois, 1964).

On Rhodes:

P. M. Fraser and G. E. Bean, *The Rhodian Peraea and Islands* (Oxford, 1954).

On the Far East see the works on Ai Khanum listed under Chapter 4. Also:

M. A. R. Colledge, *The Parthians* (London, 1967).

A. K. Narain, *The Indo-Greeks* (Oxford, 1957).

W. W. Tarn, *The Greeks in Bactria and India*, 3rd edn. (Cambridge, 1966).

8   Inter-City Contacts and Federal States

On federal states see the works listed under Chapter 5.

L. Casson, *Travel in the Ancient World* (London, 1974).

Ph. Gauthier, *Symbola. Les Etrangers et la justice dans les cités grecques* (Nancy, 1972).

W. Gawantka, *Isopoliteia* (Munich, 1975).

R. F. Willetts, *Aristocratic Society in Ancient Crete* (London, 1955), especially pp. 225 ff. on piracy and mercenary service.

9   Social and Economic Trends

See Finley and Rostovtzeff (works quoted under Further Reading, General) and Kreissig (quoted under Chapter 7).

On slavery:

I. Bieżuńska-Malowist, *L'Esclavage dans l'Egypte gréco-romaine. 1. Période ptolémaïque* (Warsaw, 1974).

M. I. Finley, (ed.), *Slavery in Classical Antiquity: Views and Controversies* (Cambridge, 1960). Reprinted essays by various authors.

W. L. Westermann, *The Slave-Systems of Greek and Roman Antiquity* (Philadelphia, 1955).

Other topics:

L. Casson, *TAPA*, 85 (1954), 168–87, 'The Grain Trade of the Hellenistic World'.

M. I. Finley, (ed.), *Problèmes de la terre en Grèce antique* (Paris, 1973). Essays by various scholars, some in English and some on Hellenistic themes.

J. U. Powell, *Collectanea Alexandrina* (Oxford, 1925) contains the fragments of Cercidas.

C. Préaux, *Recueils de la Société Jean-Bodin vii: La Ville*, 2e Partie (Brussels, 1955), pp. 89–135, 'Institutions économiques et sociales des villes hellénistiques principalement en Orient',

On the Spartan revolution:

T. W. Africa, *Phylarchus and the Spartan Revolution* (Berkeley, Los Angeles, 1961).

P. Oliva, *Sparta and her Social Problems* (Amsterdam-Prague, 1971).

B. Shimron, *Late Sparta and the Spartan Revolution, 243–146 BC*, Arethusa Monographs (Buffalo, 1972).

W. W. Tarn, *The Hellenistic Age* (Cambridge 1923), pp. 108–40, 'The Social Question in the Third Century'.

10 Cultural Developments: Philosophy, Science and Technology

General:

H. C. Baldry, *The Unity of Mankind in Greek Thought* (Cambridge, 1965).

A. A. Long, *Hellenistic Philosophy: Stoics, Epicureans, Sceptics* (London, 1974).

H. I. Marrou, *A History of Education in Antiquity* (London, 1956).

On science and technology:

A. G. Drachman, *The Mechanical Technology of Greek and Roman Antiquity* (Copenhagen, 1963). A study of literary sources.

B. Farrington, *Greek Science*, revised edition (Harmondsworth, 1961).

M. I. Finley, *Economic History Review*, 18 (1965), 29–45, 'Technical Innovation and Economic Progress in the Ancient World'.

T. L. Heath, *Aristarchus of Samos*, 2nd edn. (Oxford, 1959).

J. G. Landels, *Engineering in the Ancient World* (London, 1978).

G. E. R. Lloyd, *Greek Science after Aristotle* (London, 1973). An excellent survey with full bibliography on pp. 179–84.

O. Neugebauer, *The Exact Sciences in Antiquity*, 3rd edn. (New York, 1962).

H. W. Pleket, *Acta Historiae Neerlandica*, 2 (1967), 1–25, 'Technology and Society in the Graeco-Roman World'.

G. Sarton, *A History of Science. Vol. II, Hellenistic Science and Culture in the Last Three Centuries BC* (Harvard, 1959).

Military technology and war:

F. E. Adcock *The Greek and Macedonian Art of War* (Berkeley, 1957).

B. Bar-Kochva, see Chapter 7.

Y. Garlan, *War in the Ancient World: A Social History* (London, 1975).

P. Lévêque, 'La Guerre à l'époque hellénistique' in J.-P. Vernant, *Problèmes de la guerre en Grèce ancienne* (Paris, 1968), pp. 261–87.

E. W. Marsden, *Greek and Roman Artillery. Vol. I, Historical Development* (Oxford, 1969). *Vol. II, Technical Treatises* (Oxford, 1971). Vol. II contains texts and translations of the relevant works of Heron, Biton, Philon, Vitruvius and other writers on war-machines.

H. H. Scullard, *The Elephant in the Greek and Roman World* (London, 1974).

W. W. Tarn, *Hellenistic Military and Naval Developments* (Cambridge, 1930).

F. E. Winter, *Greek Fortifications* (London, 1971).

On scientists working in Egypt see Fraser, work quoted under Alexandria in Chapter 6.

On Poseidonius see:

L. Edelstein and I. G. Kidd, *Posidonius Vol. I: The Fragments* (Cambridge, 1972).

11 The Frontiers of the Hellenistic World: Geographical Studies

M. Cary and E. H. Warmington, *The Ancient Explorers* (London, 1929).

P. Pédech, *La Géographie des Grecs* (Paris, 1976).

J. O. Thomson, *History of Ancient Geography* (Cambridge, 1948).

12 Religious Developments

H. I. Bell, *Cults and Creeds in Graeco-Roman Egypt*, 2nd edn. (Liverpool, 1954).

L. Cerfaux and J. Tondriau, *Le Culte des souverains dans la civilisation gréco-romaine* (Paris, 1957).

E. R. Dodds, *The Greeks and the Irrational* (Berkeley, Los Angeles, 1959).

P. M. Fraser, work quoted in Chapter 6 for the cult of Sarapis.

Chr. Habicht, *Gottmenschentum und die griechischen Städte*, 2nd edn. (Munich, 1970).

M. P. Nilsson, *The Dionysiac Mysteries of the Hellenistic and Roman Age* (Lund, 1957).

A. C. Nock, *Conversion. The Old and New in Religion from Alexander the Great to Augustine of Hippo* (Oxford, 1933).

——, *Essays on Religion and the Ancient World*, 2 vols. (Oxford, 1972), reprints the author's essays on this subject.

R. E. Witt, *Isis in the Graeco-Roman World* (London, 1971).

13   The Coming of Rome

For a fuller bibliography on this subject see that in Michael Crawford, *The Roman Republic* in this series. A few books, relevant to the theme of the present volume, are given here:

General:

R. M. Errington, *The Dawn of Empire* (London, 1972).

H. H. Scullard, *History of the Roman World, 753–146 BC*, 4th edn. (London, 1980).

On Roman imperialism:

W. V. Harris, *War and Imperialism in Republican Rome* (Oxford, 1979).

On the Romans in Greece:

J. Briscoe, 'Rome and the Class Struggle in the Greek States, 200–146 BC' in M.I. Finley (ed.), *Studies in Ancient Society* (London, 1972), pp. 53–73.

J. Deininger, *Der politische Widerstand gegen Rom in Griechenland, 217–86 v. Chr.* (Berlin & New York, 1971).

J. A. O. Larsen, 'Roman Greece' in T. Frank, *Economic Survey* (see Further Reading, General). Vol. IV, pp. 261–325, shows the cost of the Roman conquest to the Greek states.

Index of Sources

Numbers in italics are page references in this volume.

General Index